The Great
Television
Race

The Great Television Race

A History of the American Television
Industry 1925–1941
by Joseph H. Udelson

THE UNIVERSITY OF ALABAMA PRESS
UNIVERSITY, ALABAMA

The author is grateful to the following for quotations of selected material:
The *New York Times* © 1925–1941 by The New York Times Company.
Reprinted by permission.
The *Chicago Daily News* © 1931 by The Chicago Sun-Times. Reprinted
by permission.
Donald G. Fink.
David B. Smith.

Library of Congress Cataloging in Publication Data

Udelson, Joseph H., 1943–
  The great television race.

  Bibliography: p.
  Includes index.
  1. Television industry—United States—History.
2. Television broadcasting—United States—History.
I. Title.
HD9696.T463U67   384.55'0973   81-7562
ISBN 0-8173-0082-1   AACR2

This study is dedicated to
the educations of
Dina, Chana, and Devorah

Contents

Preface

Following the Second World War, television burst upon the American scene and soon became the predominant mass medium. Yet in most discussions of the origin of this most pervasive of all communications media in human history, television is treated as though it arose, Athena-like, fully developed, in the postwar period. But as with most appearances of the instantaneous in history, this one, too, is illusory.

Yet if popular impressions of television's origins are misguided, more serious treatments scarcely do better. In these, quaint experiments with cumbersome apparatus in the 1920s somehow automatically give way to more modern sets with tiny screens a decade later; then, after the war, monochromatic television as we have it today spontaneously makes its appearance. Although such accounts do recognize the medium's prewar existence, they, too, sadly ignore the complex realities of the creation of the television industry, settling instead for a teleological reductionism that treats its history as an anecdotal record and a linear evolution of the final product.

But in fact the history of the television industry is a tangled record of the successful creation of a unified system, composed of interconnected engineering, programming, and marketing components, completed in 1941 only after numerous false starts, dead ends, bitter strife and intrigue within the industry, and governmental confusion. The kind of television system that exists today in America can be fully understood only after these complexities of its history are disentangled and dispassionately examined.

The sine qua non for this system was the successful development of the engineering component. Experimentation on the transmission of transient visual images began in the 1870s, but it was only in 1925 that C. Francis Jenkins in the United States and John L. Baird in Great Britain successfully demonstrated workable television techniques. These demonstrations, employing heavy, awkward mechanical devices, served as catalysts for a minor television boom. Across the United States, stations began telecasting on regular schedules announced in the press; a variety of programming was offered, and commercially manufactured receivers were marketed. But by 1933 the engineering limitations of these low-definition transmissions caused the boom to collapse. Motion pictures had accustomed the public to a higher-resolution picture than the mechanical apparatus was then able to provide, thus seriously restricting the programming potential; as a result, the capital desperately needed for research and expansion was invested elsewhere.

However, already during the boom years an alternative electronic technology capable of transmitting high-definition pictures was being developed. Philo T. Farnsworth, a young inventor with only a high-school education, working as an independent, and Dr. Vladimir K. Zworykin, a Russian immigrant heading a research team at the Radio Corporation of America, each developed an all-electronic television method. Farnsworth's image dissector and Zworykin's iconoscope were soon competing in the United States, Britain, and Germany. In America, a patent dispute between the rival methods led to a stalemate for several years, until a mutually beneficial arrangement was concluded between RCA and Farnsworth Television in 1939. That same year RCA began regularly scheduled high-definition telecasts from the Empire State Building, and a nascent television boom seemed again on the horizon.

But as RCA perfected the engineering and programming components of its system and prepared to market it to the public, its rivals in the radio manufacture and broadcast industries protested against the television standards supported by RCA and argued for technically superior alternatives. With the industry thus deeply divided, the Federal Communications Commission tenaciously adhered to its traditional policy of refusing commercial authorization to the new medium until the industry could generally agree on a uniform set of standards. Once again there was a stalemate. And without commercial authorization, the financial limitations on marketing the television system severely restricted further expansion, thus again jeopardizing its future.

In 1940 the FCC, under heavy public pressure, finally resolved the dilemma. At its suggestion, the National Television System Committee was organized by industry representatives to serve as a forum in which a set of standards could be designed that would be acceptable to the majority in the industry. In the spring of 1941 the FCC accepted the committee's recommendations and authorized full commercial service. Our contemporary monochromatic television system was now ready for vigorous marketing and began commercial operation on 1 July 1941. Although the Second World War delayed the promotion of the system, in 1947 the television boom based on it began in earnest.

This study of the television system and its components is necessarily exploratory. Little scholarly work has yet been done on many of the key figures in the history of television, such as Jenkins, Farnsworth, Zworykin, and many of the other significant inventors and entrepreneurs mentioned in the pages of this work. Furthermore, the controversies surrounding the achievements of Farnsworth and Zworykin, RCA and Philco, RCA and CBS, in addition to the pioneering efforts in Boston, Chicago, and Los Angeles, are still intensely disputed among the surviving combatants and their supporters. Thus the forgotten and tangled threads of the history of the television industry between 1925 and 1941 discussed in the following chapters should not only provide a basis for comprehending later developments but also delineate areas inviting future research into television's history.

So many persons have assisted my research on the television industry that it is impossible for the contribution of each to be acknowledged here. However, without the help of several people, this study would not have been possible at all. Among these I would especially like to thank television pioneer Hollis S. Baird and Albert Rose of Exxon Research and Engineering Company for their patient and generous assistance; Elma G. Farnsworth, Harry R. Lubcke, Donald G. Fink, and David B. Smith contributed invaluable help. For their kind assistance I am also grateful to James A. Allen of Ford Aerospace and Communications Corporation, Juda Rozenberg of Tennessee State University, Ed Young of the Federal Communications Commission, and the staff of the Industrial and Social Branch of the National Archives. Many of the illustrations are the result of the patient work of Alex Limor. Most specially I would like to thank my wife, Terry, for the tolerance with which she endured endless dinner-table monologues on television's history and for the diligence with which she read and corrected every draft of this study; without her encouragement the research and writing of this work would never have been accomplished. Of course, any errors are my own.

Nashville, Tennessee

The Great
Television
Race

The Birth of the Television System

Television is not a post–World War II achievement; only its conquest of the mass media is. Well over a century has passed since research on television technology first began. The first successful television demonstrations occurred in both the United States and Britain over fifty years ago. And forty years have gone by since commercial television was authorized by the Federal Communications Commission and stations began broadcasting on current American monochromatic standards. On the eve of the Japanese attack on Pearl Harbor, in December 1941, an integrated television system—its technology, its programming requirements, its financing, and its industry standards—had been fully developed and was ready for public consumption. Only the war delayed its triumph in the mass market.

By 1941 the efforts of amateur inventors, corporate engineers, patent lawyers, advertising executives, manufacturing interests, and government administrators in the United States and Europe had been combined to produce the engineering, entertainment, and marketing component subsystems of the television system.[1] Simultaneously, the excited public consumer eagerly anticipated the possibility of investing in the system. And once the war had ended and the engineers and production lines were released from military service, the potential envisioned before the fighting began was finally realized.

The production of this marvelously successful television system is a history of the complicated interweaving of engineering achievements and rivalries, of corporate ambitions and competitions, and of government regulations, antitrust actions, and patent decisions. In the United States it is the story of notable advances, apparent dead ends, and judicious compromises. And unlike many other technological changes, the steadily developing television system was made highly visible for over a decade to an interested public, despite highly secretive laboratory planning and research.

The history of television until its commercial authorization in 1941 divides practically into four overlapping periods. The first is the primarily technical effort to demonstrate the engineering feasibility of the transmission of transient moving images (that is, television). Such feasibility was first demonstrated independently and almost simultaneously in the United States and Britain in 1925.

By 1928 the practicality of television had been publicized to potential consumers now excited by the prospects of television "just around the corner." The attempt to fulfill these public expectations for the immediate realization of television dominates the second period. Low-definition television (which produced pictures with very fuzzy detail) was introduced on a regularly scheduled basis after 1928 in many areas and was receivable throughout the country on commercially produced sets and kits. Radio manufacturers and networks, newspapers, universities, and newly created television interests became involved in technical research, production requirements, and programming experiments. Many actively recruited public participation, and some organized promotional demonstrations to stimulate popular interest.

But, by the middle 1930s the limitations of low-definition television as an entertainment medium had become apparent, and many early broadcasters withdrew, at least temporarily, from the field. A third period now began when emphasis shifted to expensive high-definition television. This period can be characterized by three major trends: a constriction of television broadcasting available to the public as technical development, a costly enterprise with little immediate financial return, became a prime concern; an intense rivalry among competing research facilities; and an effort to create an integrated television system that would include production of transmitting and receiving equipment, ownership of broadcasting facilities, programming, networking, and promotion, advertising, and sales.

By the end of 1939 high-definition television had been perfected and was being provided to the public in limited areas of the country, where receiving sets were also on the market. A fourth period now began with the struggle to persuade the government to authorize commercial television broadcasting, the signal for expanding the industry by making advertising revenue available as its major source of profits. Interestingly enough, the delay in the commercialization of television resulted primarily from competition within the television industry itself. Finally, after intense negotiations among corporate officials, sufficient agreement was achieved to convince the FCC that the public interest would be served by commercialization. And so on 1 July 1941, the cumulative effect of the contributions of these four periods resulted in the introduction of public commercial television broadcasting in the United States.

ENVIRONMENTAL CONDITIONS AFFECTING TELEVISION'S DEVELOPMENT

High-definition television, as marketed in the United States after the Second World War, comprises first of all an electronic camera that picks up the scene by a scanning process that proceeds at several hundred lines per frame and 30 frames per second. To broadcast this information sequentially, the second component, a transmitter, is required; its frequency can be varied (modulated) over a range or band of about 1 million cycles per second (1 megahertz) for black-and-white pictures and several times that for color. Such bandwidths can be accommodated only at frequencies of the order of hundreds of megahertz, that is, at very high and ultrahigh frequencies (VHF and UHF). However, waves do not propagate beyond the horizon, so the typical television transmitter's range is only about thirty-five miles. Before the same program can be shown by a network of several stations, they must be connected by a system of relays about thirty-five miles apart or by coaxial cable. The third component is a television receiver, in which the transmitted signal is electronically decoded and the picture is reassembled on a cathode-ray tube, while the accompanying sound is reproduced much as in a radio broadcast. Most of the discoveries on which this system is based were made well before the Second World War: radiotelegraphy and the cathode-ray oscilloscope in the 1890s, radio broadcasting and the ultrashort waves in the 1920s, the electronic camera and cheap and reliable cathode-ray tubes in the 1930s. Yet this system was unable to produce a successful mass medium until not only the technical but also the economic and political problems had been solved.

Creation of television as an integrated system combining engineering, programming, and marketing components thus necessarily reflected a broad spectrum of environmental conditions. Primarily these conditions provided the perimeters within which the television system, and its component subsystems, could develop. That television emerged amid, and in large part because of, a favorable socioeconomic environment becomes more evident when three particular factors are considered: that television research was not limited to one laboratory staff or one region of the country but was a national (and international) effort conducted by several, often rival, concerns; that there were competing systems, already existing (for example, AM radio, motion pictures) or at a similar developmental stage (facsimile, FM radio); and that television was provided great publicity for over a decade before its commercialization, as already mentioned.

While the technology and the publicity continued to expand to include broadening societal interests, certain environmental constraints conditioned television's development from the earliest stages of its research. As many of these contingencies, attitudes, and concerns, so essential to an industrial society, no longer retain their centrality in a postindustrial age, a brief delineation of them is necessary for an appreciation of how television was successfully developed.[2] Included in these environmental contingencies are those concerning the prevailing attitudes toward technology and the individual, those deriving from the new radio manufacturing and broadcast industry and its government regulators, and those of television engineering.

Industrial Society

Technology was prestigious and popular in industrial society. Its continued advance promised increased prosperity and control over nature. And technology was also not so complex and specialized as to be beyond the ability of the interested layman to comprehend or even imitate. This was still the era of the amateur, an age abounding in technical journals explaining technological principles and of popular journals, and even newspapers, detailing how to "build your own." And many people were doing just that, especially when the cost was not prohibitive, as in early radio and even television.

In an era of competing nationalism, technological development became a symbol of national prestige, along with steel production and battleships. The Americans were certain that the United States had achieved technological "leadership" and were determined to maintain it in the heated competition with European rivals. Yet this national competition did not imply autarky, and so international cooperation was not precluded. Interest in scientific and technical developments abroad, exchange of information and visits, and the obtaining of foreign patent rights were not uncommon. Because technology's potential was perceived as unlimited, such cooperation was believed to serve mutual interests, an attitude that also existed among domestic competitors, as the histories of radio and television illustrate.

The industrial society was one that eagerly supported the pursuit of self-interest as serving the "engine of progress." Material progress and increased productivity were the results of competition spurred by the pursuit of self-interest; technological innovation was the vehicle to get ahead in this competition. Those who made the advances, proclaimed their successes, and profited from them were admired and their names trusted.

In this age of amateurism and confidence in self-interest, the successful individual inventor was a major public figure. Articles by inventors and interviews with them abounded in popular literature, and inventions were commonly connected with the name of their inventors (for example, Alexanderson radio alternator, Fleming valve, Braun tube). A corporation organized to exploit the promise of a technological innovation often adopted the inventor's name as its own, as in the meat-packing, automobile, telephone, and electric industries. Even when a large corporate entity had no obvious connection with one inventor, individual executives and researchers were often public figures (for instance, David Sarnoff and Vladimir Zworykin of RCA).

The American Radio Industry

As technology's prestige provided the general environmental constraints for the development of television, so the emerging radio industry provided its specific conditions. These would include the radio-manufacturing industry, broadcasting, and governmental regulators. In the United States this industry, in fact, mirrored the general industrial environment as applied to a communications technology. It is therefore not surprising that much of television's early history was interpreted at the time in the light of the previous experience with radio.

Radio was developed in the last decade of the nineteenth century and commercially appeared in the United States with the organization by British Marconi of the Marconi Wireless Telegraph Company of America, in November 1899.[3] The major concern of this early radio activity was point-to-point communications (ship to shore, for example), although some early experimenters did begin as early as 1909 to broadcast regularly scheduled news reports and musical programs.[4] In fact, as early as 1916, David Sarnoff, then manager of American Marconi's station at Sea Gate, New York, sent a memo to the firm's general manager suggesting the "Radio Music Box" (that is, radio as a scheme for home entertainment), although the idea was ignored at the time.[5]

The number of amateur radio enthusiasts continued to grow, and by 1917 the components of a practical radio system had been fully developed. But further progress was blocked because these components could not be legally manufactured together since their patent rights were assigned to rival corporations. These rivals included American Telephone and Telegraph, controlling the De Forest audion; General Electric, controlling the Alexanderson alternator; American Marconi, controlling the Fleming vacuum tube; and Edwin H. Armstrong, controlling his feedback circuit (which was soon to be acquired by the Westinghouse Electric).[6]

In April 1917 President Woodrow Wilson ordered the navy, already deeply committed to radio, to assume control of all radio stations and to suspend patent rights—moves aimed at strengthening American military capabilities. However, in early 1919 private ownership was restored, and the patent conflict remained unresolved. Then in March 1919 the government learned of negotiations between British Marconi and GE to provide British Marconi with exclusive rights to the Alexanderson alternator. In the aftermath of World War I there was great concern about domination of the American communications industry by foreign capital. The undersecretary of the navy, Franklin D. Roosevelt, and Admiral William H. G. Bullard, director of naval communications, proposed to Owen D. Young of GE that a company controlled by Americans be organized to provide ship-to-shore and international radio communications for the United States and that this new company be provided with GE licenses to use the Alexanderson alternator.

Young responded enthusiastically to the proposal and on 17 October 1919 created the Radio Corporation of America to operate the necessary stations and market equipment, while GE would concentrate on manufacturing. RCA's Delaware charter required that at least 80 percent of its stock be owned by Americans and that the government have a representative on its board of directors (Admiral Bullard being the first, appointed by President Wilson). In November 1919 RCA acquired control of American Marconi, and the latter's general manager, Edward J. Nally, became RCA president, while David Sarnoff became its commercial manager; Young became Chairman of the Board of RCA, while retaining also his executive position at GE.

RCA and GE arrived at cross-licensing agreements in 1919. Over the next two years cross-licensing agreements were also arranged between RCA and Westinghouse, AT & T, United Fruit, and the Wireless Speciality Company, the latter group receiving substantial shares of RCA stock and places on its board of directors in exchange for their patent rights. As a result of these agreements, RCA was to operate point-to-point radio communications, though not exclusively, and to market receivers, while GE and Westinghouse had exclusive right to manufacture these receivers, 60 percent for GE and 40 percent for Westinghouse; AT & T retained exclusive right to manufacture, lease, and sell transmitters. The result of these cross-licensing agreements was to break the patent impasse and to facilitate the development of the broadcast industry.[7]

Westinghouse soon realized that the availability of continuous radio service would serve greatly to stimulate receiver sales, and so in October 1920 the company began operating radio station KDKA from the roof of its manufacturing plant in East Pittsburg, Pennsylvania; soon it opened several more stations throughout the country. GE entered the broadcast field in February 1923 with WGY, located at its plant in Schenectady, New York. RCA had already begun broadcasting the previous year with its short-lived WDY in Roselle Park, New York; by 1923 RCA was successfully operating WJZ and WJY in New York City. In August 1922 AT & T began operating WEAF in New York City also, as its entry in the field. And besides the big manufacturers, smaller operations, often run for fun or publicity, appeared all over the country; in 1922 more than six hundred stations went on the air. Sales of transmitting and receiving equipment were booming.[8]

Yet this very success brought further patent conflicts, this time between the "radio group" headed by RCA and the "telephone group" headed by AT & T. The original cross-licensing agreements had not envisioned radio as a public broadcast medium but had only taken account of its previous point-to-point operation. The new condition created three areas of intense conflict. First, when Lee De Forest sold his patent rights to AT & T, amateurs were excluded from the requirement to purchase Western Electric transmitters; they could continue to buy parts to construct their own. However, in the radio boom of 1922 AT & T found that of the six hundred radio stations operating, only thirty-five were using Western Electric equipment, the rest having constructed their transmitters as amateurs. By claiming to be amateurs, station operators, in AT & T's view, were unlawfully avoiding royalty payments. According to this interpretation, all commercial stations were to be subject to patent agreements with AT & T.[9]

A second issue was the introduction of advertising ("toll broadcasting") by AT & T in August 1922, as a means of financing its broadcast activities. In the cross-licensing agreements AT & T had reserved for itself the exclusive right to manufacture, lease, and sell transmitting equipment. It now held that the sale of commercial time without authorization by anyone other than AT & T violated its exclusive right to lease transmitting equipment. If enforced this would effectively have blocked others from sharing in this method of financing broadcast expenses, at least without paying royalties from advertising revenue to AT & T first.

A third issue arose from AT & T's development of networking ("chain broadcasting"), interconnecting radio stations in several cities by means of telephone lines, a practice introduced in 1923. Networking could substantially increase advertising revenue by providing a far greater audience than any single station could promise. RCA and the radio group were to be excluded from competing with AT & T in this lucrative venture, as AT & T refused to lease its interconnecting lines to the competition. Hostility further increased as AT & T disposed of all of its RCA stock and, in 1926, announced plans to manufacture receivers when certain RCA patents expired.[10]

But RCA was already under antitrust investigation, and AT & T was fearful of similar action against itself. Both sides therefore agreed to invoke the arbitration clause of the 1920 cross-licensing agreements. In early 1926 a three-part agreement was signed providing for a redefinition of the patent arrangements in the light of the development of widespread radio broadcasting; for AT & T to receive a monopoly for providing interconnections among stations; and for AT & T to sell WEAF and its network to RCA and withdraw from broadcasting.[11]

Of primary importance, both for the future expansion of radio and for the creation of a television industry, is the fact that by 1926 a systems approach in the communications media was already well established. Manufacture and sale of equipment, control of patent rights, operation of broadcast facilities, programming, networking, and advertising revenue were all part of a unified broadcast design. Amateur activity was also viewed suspiciously because of its involvement in loosening patent domination.

In 1926 RCA initiated moves to become prominent in two areas thus far beyond its influence, networking and manufacturing. In February 1925, as a part of the arbitration negotiations, David Sarnoff had proposed that a new company be formed to operate the stations then owned by RCA, GE, Westinghouse, and AT & T, the stations to be interconnected by AT & T lines and financed through advertising revenue. In September 1926 this proposal was realized with the creation of the National Broadcasting Company, originally owned jointly by RCA, GE, and Westinghouse. By the end of the year NBC was operating two networks: the Red network based on the old WEAF chain of AT & T and the smaller Blue network based on the WJZ chain of RCA.[12]

NBC, however, soon faced competition with the creation, in 1927, of a rival network by Arthur Judson and George A. Coats. This network foundered until William S. Paley acquired a controlling interest in what was soon to be named the Columbia Broadcasting System.[13] The competition between NBC and CBS would later play a significant role in the expansion of television.

Two moves toward diversification in manufacturing by RCA helped to provide further interest in the success of CBS. First, in 1927, rumors that RCA and the Victor Talking Machine Company would shortly merge led to a brief association of the Columbia Phonograph Record Company with the project of Judson and Coats. Although this association was brief, its name remained as a legacy to the new network.[14]

The second development was the involvement of RCA in talking motion pictures through RCA Phonophone and the creation in 1929 of RKO Pictures, which was to use its equipment in order to compete with AT & T's domination of this new industry. In 1929, partly in response, Paramount acquired 49 percent of CBS's stock, although by 1932 Paley and his associates had bought it back, leaving CBS operating as an independent broadcast network, unlike NBC, which was the subsidiary of a major manufacturing organization.[15]

To complete the radio system contemplated by RCA's management, it had to cease being merely a sales agency for others and to enter directly into manufacture. The merger with Victor Talking Machine was a move toward this goal. But the major impetus at RCA in this direction was David Sarnoff's late-1929 proposals for "unification" and "separation." Essentially his plan provided that in exchange for its stock RCA would acquire the right to manufacture radio equipment, phonographs, and talking films, and acquire full ownership of NBC, RCA Phonophone, RCA Victor, and 49 percent of GM Radio Corporation, as well as acquiring from GE and Westinghouse all necessary plants, research facilities, machinery, and real estate.[16]

The government challenged the unification scheme as the creation of a monopoly. To prevent an antitrust action, a compromise was reached in November 1932. Under this arrangement RCA achieved the main objectives of unification and separation: the right to manufacture and market radio apparatus under RCA, GE, Westinghouse, and AT & T patents; and the right to grant licenses and retain 100 percent royalties on them, with GE and Westinghouse obliged to pay royalties to RCA on equipment made and sold by them under patents held by the former radio group. However, the independent manufacturing and sales capabilities of GE and Westinghouse were also assured, in order to prevent an RCA monopoly.[17]

One result of unification was that in the fall of 1929 RCA began to create a single research organization at the manufacturing plant of the Victor Talking Machine Company in Camden, New Jersey, combining engineers from its own Van Cortlandt Park staff in New York City with staff members from GE and Westinghouse.[18] This unification of research personnel from the three manufacturers would have great technological and corporate repercussions on the development of television.

The Federal Government and the Broadcast Industry

This brief survey of major corporate alignments in the formative years of the radio industry suggests that by 1930 the concept of the broadcast industry as a concentric set of engineering and manufacturing, programming and networking, and promotional systems was well understood and already available as a model for the development of a similar design for television. The importance of government action for the direction taken by the communications industry is also clearly evident.

The first attempt by the federal government to provide some regulation for the new radio industry came from President Theodore Roosevelt in June 1904. At that time he organized an executive advisory committee, the Interdepartmental Board of Wireless Telegraphy. The board soon recommended that the navy should provide continental point-to-point radio communications, that the army should supervise its specific radio needs, and that the Department of Commerce and Labor should be granted authority to prevent control of American communications by monopolies and trusts. American Marconi and the National Electric Signaling Company, the major commercial firms of the period, opposed the first and third recommendations.[19]

Even at this early date the pattern of government regulation and its interaction with corporate interests becomes evident. Leadership for government regulation was initiated by the executive, not legislative, branch. The primary goal of such regulation was to protect the security of the nation and to prevent monopolization by a single private interest. Concern for technical and engineering matters was totally absent from the recommendations, being left to private activity. But even this type of trade regulation met resistance from the industry.

In response to international conferences, Congress passed the first American radio legislation, the Wireless Ship Act, in 1910. It provided that all large ocean-going vessels be equipped with a radio apparatus and an operator, the provisions to be administered by the Department of Commerce and Labor. Since the law created a market for more sales, the manufacturers accepted it without protest.[20]

The first comprehensive American radio legislation, the Radio Act of 1912, provided that every radio station secure a license from the secretary of commerce and labor. However the act did not grant authority to the secretary to deny or revoke a license, nor did it set any standards or authorize the secretary to do so. The act, that is, provided for regulatory but not discretionary powers, not even within the narrow limits of technical considerations; these were still considered a private concern best left to the industry itself to determine.[21] The aim of this regulatory power of the secretary was mainly to minimize interference in broadcasting, an area where private regulation had proven ineffectual.

On the eve of the First World War, the navy was pressing for permission to compete with commercial broadcasters. Legislation, in the form of the Alexander bill, was introduced in Congress to provide the necessary authorization, but the bill was strongly opposed by private industry. In any case, the proposal became unnecessary when the navy was given a monopoly over all radio operations in the country during the war. Shortly after the armistice, the Alexander bill was revived as a means of continuing the navy monopoly, but broad opposition to the proposal caused it to die in Congress and radio facilities were restored to their prewar owners.[22] Public broadcasting would therefore be developed by private initiative, the government being limited to regulating the broadcast industry. That the navy acquiesced in this policy is evident from its role in the creation of RCA.

As the manufacturers' cross-licensing agreements failed to meet the changed nature of broadcasting in the radio boom of the early 1920s, so did the Radio Act of 1912. Although Secretary of Commerce Herbert Hoover attempted to provide some system of frequency classification and to assign stations according to these defined priorities, a series of federal court decisions reversed his efforts on the grounds that the Radio Act provided no such authority to the secretary. However, between 1922 and 1925 Hoover had also organized four national radio conferences, attended by all interested sectors of the industry, to discuss the growing chaos in broadcasting and the increasing problem of cochannel interference. Pressure from the secretary and the conferences' participants finally led Congress to pass the Radio Act of 1927.[23]

This act established the Federal Radio Commission (FRC) with broad regulatory powers over licensing and frequency allocation, although it had no authority over advertising and network broadcasting, the primary sources of industry revenue.[24] William H. G. Bullard, a retired admiral who had been director of naval communications and was one of the major participants in the creation of RCA, became the commission's first chairman. The Department of Commerce also retained some regulatory powers over broadcasting, and possible antitrust violations in the industry remained the concern of both executive agencies and the Congress.

As a result of investigations by both the executive and Congress, the

Communications Act of 1934 replaced the FRC with the Federal Communications Commission, which had the same regulatory powers that the
earlier agency had possessed. In addition the FCC assumed the remaining
duties of the secretary of commerce and also the Interstate Commerce Commission's supervision of interstate telegraph and telephone communications.[25]

A major initiative was undertaken in 1938 by the FCC to investigate
network monopolistic tendencies in the broadcast industry (though not in
manufacturing, a realm beyond its jurisdiction). The resulting *Report on
Chain Broadcasting* of 1941 was highly critical of several practices and introduced rules to try to reduce network influence over local stations. Challenged by the networks, the rules were upheld by the Supreme Court in
1943.[26]

This survey of governmental regulations of the broadcast industry points
to several important tendencies that would affect the development of television. Six are most noteworthy here: the government was interested in preventing a complete monopoly of broadcasting and of manufacturing in the
communications industry; this industry would develop under private initiative; the government would provide direction for the industry by setting
standards and by opposing monopoly; government regulation of the
revenue-making side of the industry was insignificant; much regulation was
the result of the interaction of government and industry; and conflict between government regulatory agencies and the industry also was a significant factor in determining the direction of policy. Thus television would not
emerge in a political vacuum any more than in an industrial one: it would
grow within a preexisting environment of regulators, policies, and conflicts.

The values of industrial society, the nature of the radio industry, and its
relationship to federal regulatory policy would have significant effects on the
direction and pace of the development of the television industry. As will be
demonstrated in the following chapters, industrial society generated the
impetus for backyard tinkerers and corporate research teams to compete
with confidence in the race to create a marketable system, while the radio
industry provided the model and much of the initial capital for the new
medium. However, ultimately the success of television depended on authorization of commercial service by the federal government. But before any of
these factors could become operative, a successful television technology first
had to be developed.

Creation of a Successful Television Technology

A third environmental element affecting television's development, besides the broad conditions of the general industrial society and the specifics

of the communications industry, was the narrow technological requirements of its engineering component. A striking fact about television is that its engineering existed conceptually long before technology allowed its practical achievement. This was true for its comprehensive engineering design as well as for its particular details. That is, researchers knew how to make television long before the technology was available to allow them to do so. It is therefore not surprising that by the early 1880s the requirements for a successful television technique were explicitly discussed, although specific concrete devices did not yet exist to realize the concept.

Five elements were required to produce a workable television technique. There had to be a substance sufficiently sensitive to light to be affected rapidly by the scenes to be transmitted. A light source generating enough brightness had to exist to respond to the alterations in the photosensitive material in the transmitting apparatus and to reproduce these changes in the receiving apparatus. A single channel (or circuit), as opposed to some conceptually possible but impractical multichannel system, had to connect transmitter and receiver. This single-channel requirement made simultaneous transmission of the entire scene impossible. Instead, the image would have to be scanned sequentially by the transmitter at a rate rapid enough to take advantage of "persistence of vision," so that the eye would view the received image as if it were a single scene simultaneously displayed. And this sequential scanning of the scene would require exact synchronization of the transmitting and receiving apparatuses.[27]

These constraints were imposed by engineering and human optics. For instance, just as the human eye and printed photographs analyze an image into tiny units in order to achieve acceptable detail, so must television. However, while the eye and the photograph are able to present simultaneously all of the tiny elements of an object thus analyzed, this capability is not feasible in television. In a single American television picture, there are approximately 367,500 such elements, taking into account retracing of the beam, and for simultaneous transmission, each element would require a separate circuit (a number impossible to accommodate practically on the radio band).

The alternative to multichannel transmission is sequential scanning, a process in which each picture element is scanned once in a regular order for the transmission of each complete picture. The signal is then sent serially to the receiver, where it is recomposed in an order synchronized with the transmitter. If the scanning is done rapidly enough, persistence of vision (an inherent property of the human eye) will cause the successive impressions to be interpreted as a single unified image. And if this procedure of scanning, transmitting, and rescanning at the receiver is repeated several times a second, the image will convey the impression of continuous motion to the eye. Two of the more important achievements of nineteenth-century television research were the discovery of these constraints on the transmission of transient visual images and the conception of techniques for operating within them.

A great deal of this early research involved an intermingling of television with facsimile, which is, generally, the transmission of a still picture for permanent usage, such as a wirephoto. It should be noted that while there are similarities, there are also significant differences between the engineering requirements of the two. Both are concerned with the transmission of visual images. But while television's images are transient, must be able to include movement, and must occur within the limits of persistence of vision, none of these requirements applies to facsimile. Therefore, while television and facsimile employ similar techniques, television also presents a set of unique problems.

EARLIEST EXPERIMENTS WITH PICTURE TRANSMISSION

Although proposals for the transmission of images did not attract much attention before 1870, earlier suggestions already embodied major essential technical concepts of television engineering. In 1839 Alexandre Edmond Becquerel presented his findings on the electrochemical effects of light, demonstrating a primitive photocell.[28] This linking of light to electricity was the first step in providing a technical base for television.

A Scottish watchmaker, Alexander Bain, proposed a scheme for the "automatic telegraph" in 1843. The aim of this device was to transmit the letters and words of the original message as a series of stains on chemically treated paper, thereby obviating the necessity of coding and decoding messages. Though not a success, Bain's device included the principles of single-channel transmission, sequential scanning, and synchronization.[29] Frederick Collier Bakewell of London proposed an improved version of Bain's device in 1848, while Abbé Giovanni Caselli's 1855 apparatus of similar design was briefly put into commercial service in France, with the financial backing of Emperor Napoleon III, in the 1860s.[30] Thus by the middle of the nineteenth century facsimile devices had been suggested that embodied basic features of television engineering. But the ideas would be of only theoretical importance until the companion technology was developed.

Impetus for serious television research came from the discovery of the photosensitive property of the chemical element selenium in 1873. This was described in a letter to the *Journal of the Society of Telegraph Engineers* from Willoughby Smith, chief electrician of Telegraph Construction and Maintenance Company, which was working on the Atlantic cable. The property had evidently been discovered by Smith's assistant, Joseph May.[31]

Selenium was found to display a decreased electrical resistance when exposed to light. It would thus serve as the basis for a practical photoconductive cell.

Almost immediately researchers realized that with the use of selenium cells, images, not only stills but even those in motion, might be transmitted, and by the end of the decade several such proposals had been advanced. One of the very first was put forward by a Portuguese professor of physics, Adriano de Paiva, in March 1878. His "electric telescope" consisted of a selenium plate scanned by a metal point, with a movable incandescent lamp at the receiver. But de Paiva could not solve the problem of synchronizing this single-channel facsimile system.[32]

In August of the same year Alexander Graham Bell, in an address before the British Association of Great Britain, proposed that just as musical sounds could be produced by rapidly interrupting a telephone current, so might sound be produced by rapidly interrupting a light beam focused on a bar of selenium. Although Bell and his coworker Sumner Tainter intended their "Photophone" to be limited to the transmission of voice by means of light beams acting on selenium, a widespread public impression was that they intended to transmit images, a view not dispelled when Bell deposited his sealed plans for the device with the Smithsonian Institution in 1880. Bell's contribution to the development of television was not his actual work on the photophone (which was secret) but rather the encouragement other inventors took from what they mistakenly believed the prestigious innovator to be doing.[33]

Also in 1878 a French lawyer, Constantin Senlecq, published a brief description of his proposed "Telectroscope." In 1880 a more detailed plan for the device suggested that the transmitter would consist of a large mosaic of very small selenium cells, each cell connected individually to a form of distributor through which contact could be made with a single wire. The receiver would consist of a similar mosaic constructed as a screen of fine platinum wires. Senlecq introduced the mosaics as a means of sequential scanning, although details of their operation are not clear from his description.[34]

In February 1879 Denis D. Redmond of Dublin published a short discussion of his work in the *English Mechanic*. His plan is important both conceptually and practically. Unlike many others who merely proposed schemes, Redmond actually conducted experiments with his "electric telescope" to transmit "a luminous image by electricity."[35] Constructing a mosaic modeled after the human eye, the device succeeded in transmitting images. Redmond wrote, "By using a number of circuits, each containing selenium and platinum arranged at each end, just as the rods and cones are in the retina, the selenium end being exposed in a camera, I have succeeded in transmitting built-up images of very simple luminous objects."[36]

The conception that the eye should serve as the model for television became central to its eventual realization. Implicit in this plan is the necessity to scan successively the object to be transmitted and to do so at a rate rapid enough to take advantage of persistence of vision. But Redmond's attempt was not a success. He, like Senlecq, had no device for actually scanning the object. Thus he was not able to eliminate the necessity for a multicircuit design in his apparatus. This meant that he did not consider the requirement that the transmitter and receiver must be synchronized. And, finally, he found that selenium had an impractical sluggishness in its responses and therefore probably could not serve as the suitable photosensitive substance for taking advantage of persistence of vision.

Another proposal modeled on the human eye was advanced in 1879 by George R. Carey of Boston. He suggested that an elementary circuit be designed with a selenium cell at the transmitter and a light at the receiver. When no light struck the cell, its resistance would be very high and little current would then flow through the circuit; the receiver's lamp would thus not be energized. The reverse would be the case when light did strike the selenium. Carey suggested constructing mosaics of large numbers of such elementary circuits, which could then be capable of transmitting silhouettes, even in motion.[37] Although workable, Carey's scheme, like Redmond's, was not practical, for selenium was simply too sluggish, and its multichannel design was much too cumbersome for practical use.

Despite such problems, popular enthusiasm for the idea of transmitting visual images continued. In April 1880 John Perry and William E. Ayrton, reacting to the reported activities of Bell, suggested a multicircuit scheme in *Nature*.[38] Their transmitter consisted of a large mosaic surface composed of tiny separate squares of selenium. The object to be transmitted would be very strongly illuminated and focused on the mosaic through a lens. The brightness of the light falling on each selenium square would then generate a current proportionate to the shadings of the image. Each selenium square would be connected by a separate circuit to a corresponding mosaic in the receiver. They suggested two versions of the receiver. The second, reflecting their later thinking, would include a mosaic consisting of squares of silvered soft iron and would be "illuminated by a great beam of light polarized by reflection from glass and received again by an analyzer."[39]

Although the proposals presented here do not exhaust the list of suggestions for transmission of visual images advanced during the first decade after the discovery of the photosensitivity of selenium, they do constitute the most significant ones.[40] Central to the research of this first decade was the attempt to construct devices capable of utilizing this property of selenium. But serious engineering difficulty with these schemes arose from their reliance on multichannel designs. Such designs were chosen, even by those recognizing their limitations, because no practical scanning device, the necessary component for all single-channel techniques, had been suggested. This major achievement occurred during the next decade of research.

Experiments with Mechanical Scanning Devices

The first significant proposal for a television scanning system was made in a letter to the *English Mechanic* in April 1882 by William Lucas.[41] His proposal is important, in part, because if refers specifically to television, not to the "printed representation" (that is, facsimile) of many earlier schemes. As he explains, "Now, in the following apparatus . . . an image in light and shade will be formed upon a screen at the receiving end, an exact counterpart of that at the transmitting end; and, more than this, every exact change in the image in the transmitter will be faithfully depicted upon the screen of the receiver."[42] Here precisely is described television as it has been realized in the twentieth century.

The constraints on television forced Lucas to consider the need for an effective method for scanning. His solution was to employ Nicol and achromatic prisms for his receiver. "Suppose the Nicol's prisms to be so placed with regard to each other that the maximum amount of light passes through the two Nicols, next through the vertical prism, then through the horizontal one, and finally forms a small spot of light upon the screen; and it is evident that, by slightly turning the vertical prism about its axis, the spot of light can be moved in a horizontal direction along the screen, and that by turning the horizontal prism, it can be moved in a vertical direction. Hence, by combining the motion of the two prisms, the spot of light can be brought into any position whatever upon the screen."[43] The intensity of the beam of light would be controlled by rotating the plane of polarization of the light passing through one of the Nicol prisms, this rotation being governed by electromagnets operating on the current emanating from the transmitter. This arrangement would assure synchronization between receiver and transmitter.

Lucas further understood how scanning relies on persistence of vision to create the optical illusion of a complete picture. "If now the selenium cell moves over the whole image, and again reaches its first position within the time of visual impression, the spot of light on the screen will also move over the whole screen within the time of visual impression, so that the impression of the spot will not have faded away until the whole screen has been traversed and the first point has again been reached."[44] Here, then, is described the horizontal and vertical scanning utilized by modern television. However, Lucas had difficulty with the details of his plan and never constructed a successful apparatus.[45]

The proposal that offered an apparently immediate solution to the prob-

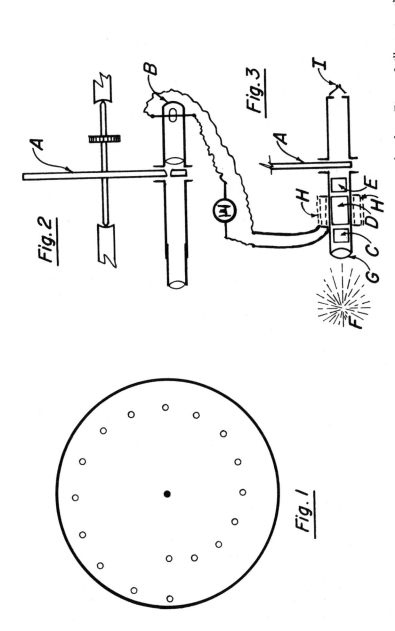

Nipkow's proposed television system. *Figure 1* illustrates the arrangement of the apertures on the disc. *Figure 2* illustrates the transmitter: A shows the placement of the disc; B is a selenium cell. *Figure 3* illustrates the receiver: F is a light source; G, a lens; H, a magnetic coil; C, a polarizing prism; D, a piece of flint glass; E, an analyzing prism; and I, the viewer. (Adapted from Paul Nipkow's 1884 German patent, no. 30,105)

lem of scanning and that was to become a basic component of the first
successful television devices was advanced by a German researcher, Paul
Nipkow. In January 1884 he suggested that a scene might be sequentially
scanned by projecting it through the periphery of a rotating disc punctured
with a number of small apertures arranged in a spiral around it. As the disc
rotated, a different portion of the scene would pass through each aperture
until, with a complete rotation, the entire scene would be sequentially
scanned. Each aperture would thus represent one scanning line.[46] The number of lines per frame helps to determine the quality of the picture, and the
number of frames per second helps to determine the flicker rate. Because
the number of apertures can be varied, the number of lines per frame can be
altered from disc design to disc design. Likewise, because the number of
rotations per second by the disc can be varied, the number of complete
frames viewed each second can be altered from system to system. The need
to arrive at some standardization of these variables would become an important issue in the early years of television broadcasting experimentation.

In operation, Nipkow proposed that the scene to be transmitted be highly
illuminated; it would then be projected through the apertures of the rotating
disc, where the light would strike a selenium cell. The electrical output from
this cell, which would provide the operating current for the light source in
the receiver, would vary proportionately with the intensity of illumination
passing through each aperture.

The resulting signal from the photocell could be transmitted through a
single channel to the receiver. This apparatus would include a high-intensity
light source, the brightness of which would be modulated by the strength of
the current from the transmitter's photocell. This modulated light would
pass through a disc similar to, and synchronized with, that of the transmitter
and thence be projected onto a screen. The sequential scanning of these
light variations by the disc makes possible the accurate reproduction of the
original scene.[47]

Although Nipkow never constructed an apparatus based on this design,
others would, until finally successful demonstrations were given in 1925.
However, even before that time two important variations on the principles
of the Nipkow disc were suggested. In 1889 Jean Lazare Weiller proposed an
apparatus designed to operate in conjunction with telephone wires. For
scanning, however, Weiller proposed, in place of a disc with apertures, a
drum or disc fitted with a number of tangential mirrors around its periphery,
each successive mirror oriented through a small angle so that, as the drum
rotated, the scene was scanned and projected on a selenium cell.[48] The
mirror drum was also employed in early successful television systems.

A second variation was suggested in a 1908 French patent granted to
Rignoux and Fournier. They employed the Nipkow disc but altered the
positions of the light source and photosensitive cell in the transmitter. In

their "flying-spot" method, an intense light source was placed behind the disc and then projected through the apertures of the disc, forming a narrow beam focused on the object to be scanned; as the disc rotated, the beam quickly moved over the object. The light from the beam reflected off the object fell on a photosensitive cell housed outside the scanning mechanism to produce the signal.[49] The advantage of the flying-spot method is that the subject does not have to endure the intense illumination required by the Nipkow proposal. This would make the flying spot an attractive alternative in the early years of television broadcasting.

Although by the final decade of the nineteenth century a practical solution had been found to the problems of scanning and single-channel transmission, attempts made to construct a workable apparatus in the years prior to the First World War failed. Two major obstacles remaining were the absence of a suitable light source for the receiver and the sluggishness of selenium. The *Electrician*, in March 1890, summarized the requirements in an optimistic tone: "It is possible to conceive of some as yet uninvented glow lamp of extraordinary delicacy that may serve the purpose." And "perhaps one day some sort of electro-optical action may be discovered . . . which may place the problem [of the sluggishness of selenium] on a wholly different and simpler basis."[50] Here clearly is an example of concepts awaiting technological realization.

But while television inventors were stalled by these difficulties, researchers in other fields were already developing the necessary technology outlined by the *Electrician*. In 1889 Julius Elster and Hans Geitel, in Germany, discovered that certain electropositive metals, such as sodium, potassium, rubidium, and caesium, display photoelectric activity when illuminated by ordinary light. By 1913 they had constructed a practical photoelectric cell using potassium hydride.[51] Here was the required "electro-optical action." In television research after the First World War, photoconductive cells, like those composed of selenium, were generally abandoned in favor of photoemissive cells, which were capable of providing the photosensitivity required to make the transmission of transient visual images possible.[52]

If the work of Elster and Geitel removed the primary obstacle for the transmitter, D. McFarlan Moore, working for GE, contributed to the development of a successful receiver. About 1917 he produced a negative-glow neon light whose brilliance could be electrically modulated. Working with others over the next few years, Moore further refined his glow-lamp to serve as a light source for television receivers.[53]

Yet at the very time that the various components necessary for the Nipkow method to operate successfully were being developed, a radically different method was being advanced as an alternative. After the First World War, the two methods would become rivals until, by 1941, one had all but been eliminated.

Experiments with Electrical Scanning Devices

This alternative method derived from work begun in 1859, when the effects produced by the discharge of electricity through a vacuum came under investigation. It was observed that in a vacuum tube when a high potential was applied to an electrode (the anode) a discharge of electricity from the cathode at the opposite end of the tube would occur; this discharge was labeled a "cathode ray." An early version of this tube, developed by Sir William Crookes (the Crookes tube), demonstrated that the cathode ray produced fluorescence on the glass wall of the tube, the result of an electrical "storm of projectiles," soon called electrons.

In 1897 Karl Ferdinand Braun, of the University of Strasbourg, developed a cathode-ray tube (the Braun tube) in which an electron gun produced a cathode ray focused on a fluorescent screen by means of deflecting plates electrostatically operated. This tube was further refined in 1905, when Arthur R. B. Wehnelt introduced a hot cathode to the design. This allowed for increased electron emission with a lower potential applied to the anode, resulting in a fluorescent spot of greater brightness.[54]

Braun's cathode-ray tube quickly began to interest some television researchers, who saw it as the solution to the problem of designing a practical receiver. Rather than serving merely as a glow lamp, the cathode-ray tube would combine light source, scanning mechanism, and screen, thereby completely dispensing with the cumbersome mechanical components of the receiver, that is, the Nipkow disc and the motor necessary to rotate it. The new method would thus be more simple and efficient.

The earliest effort to devise a cathode-ray receiver was that of Max Dieckmann in Germany, who applied for a patent for his method in 1906. Dieckmann's receiver employed a cathode-ray tube using deflection modulation and magnetic deflection to achieve scanning in both horizontal and vertical directions. This all-electronic receiver was combined with a mechanical transmitter employing a Nipkow disc. The particular design of Dieckmann's transmitter limited his apparatus to facsimile, although his receiver was not thus limited and could operate as a television device as well.[55] That Dieckmann perceived this is suggested by the direction of his subsequent research, which aimed at creating an all-electronic television system.

In Russia, in 1907, Boris Rosing, a physics professor at the Technological Institute of St. Petersburg, applied for a patent for his "electric eye." Rosing was clearly interested in television and made significant modifications both in the receiver and in the transmitter. The receiver was a Braun cathode-ray tube, modified by the addition of an electron-gun control. This tube was equipped with modulating plates, the electrostatic potential from which caused the stream of electrons projected from the cathode to be deflected away from an aperture; the amount of the stream passing through the aperture was proportional to the potential of the plates and thus to the degree of shading in the scene being transmitted. After passing through the aperture, the electron stream was caused to scan the fluorescent screen at the opposite end of the tube, focused by means of two deflecting coils. This scanning reproduced the televised image. As the sawtooth current operating the coils was derived from the transmitter, synchronization was assured.

Rosing's transmitter eliminated both selenium and the Nipkow disc, although it was not electronic. For the selenium he substituted a photoemissive cell, and in place of the Nipkow disc he introduced two mirror drums. The scene to be transmitted was focused on the plane of the photocell and deflected over it by means of the two drums, one rotating horizontally and one vertically.[56]

By 1908 Rosing began carrying out experiments on actual models and in 1911 succeeded in transmitting his first images. In his notebook he recorded, "On May 9, 1911, a distinct image was seen for the first time, consisting of four luminous bands."[57] However encouraging these first results, they were not satisfactory; problems resulting from the crudeness of his photocell and from his inability to focus properly the electron stream in the cathode-ray tube remained unresolved. Rosing's work was interrupted by the First World War, and in the ensuing revolutionary turbulence in Russia he was arrested and exiled, and then disappeared.[58]

Rosing's experiments attracted widespread interest. For instance, Robert Grimshaw, writing in 1911 in the *Scientific American,* after describing the new technique wrote that "this form of electric telescopy has yielded results such as have been obtained with none of the earlier forms of apparatus, in which mechanical movements are made use of at the receiving station."[59] Although Grimshaw recognized that more improvements were necessary, he expected the solutions to be "near at hand."

Grimshaw also discussed the uses to which television might be put. He suggested that it might be utilized to investigate the depths of the sea and the ocean floor and to explore the crust of the earth by lowering a camera into volcanic craters; it could also be used at lighthouses and military posts. Television, Grimshaw thought, could be employed in industry for the inspection of plants, shops, and other installations from a central desk.[60] Interestingly enough, while the scientific, military, and industrial possibilities of television were clearly envisioned even at this early date, its entertainment value was not perceived at all.

Simultaneously with Rosing's work in Russia and with Dieckmann's in Germany, an Englishman was also turning to the cathode-ray tube as the solution to the problems plaguing television technology. But A. A. Campbell Swinton believed that it could be applied to the transmitter as well as to the receiver, thus developing a completely electronic television system. The first mention of this concept appears in a letter from Campbell Swinton to the editor of *Nature* in June 1908. In it he suggested that "the problem of obtaining distant electric vision can probably be solved by the employment of two beams of kathode rays (one at the transmitting and one at the receiving stations) synchronously deflected by the varying fields of two electromagnets placed at right angles to one another and energized by two alternating electric currents of widely different frequencies, so that the moving extremities of the two beams are caused to sweep synchronously over the whole of the required surfaces within the one-tenth of a second necessary to take advantage of visual persistence."[61]

Here, then, is an extraordinary example of the concept preceding the technology. Ignoring details, Campbell Swinton's 1908 letter describes the television technology employed today.

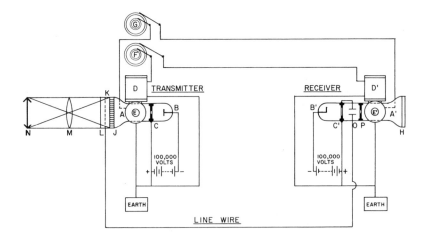

A. A. Campbell Swinton's 1912 proposal for an all-electronic television system. In the transmitter: A is a cathode-ray tube; B, the cathode; C, the anode; D and E are electromagnets placed at right angles to each other; F and G are dynamos; J is a screen composed of small photosensitive metallic cubes scanned by the electron beam emitted by B and deflected by D and E; K is a gas- or vapor-filled receptacle that conducts the electrons discharged by J when it is exposed to light; L is a screen of metallic gauze onto which the lens, M, focuses N, the image to be transmitted. In the receiver, A' is a CRT fitted with a cathode, B', which emits an electron stream through an aperture in the anode, C'; D' and E' are electromagnets analogous to, and synchronized with, D and E in the transmitter; H is a fluorescent screen, which is scanned by the cathode ray; O is a metallic plate connected to L in the transmitter; P is a diaphragm fitted with an aperture arranged to cut off the cathode rays coming from B' to prevent them from reaching the screen, H, unless they are slightly repelled from plate O when they pass through the aperture. (Used with permission of the British Institute of Radiology)

In 1911, in his presidential address to the Röntgen Society, Campbell Swinton returned to the subject of his 1908 letter and told his audience that "among the many scientific problems that await solution, problems which, if satisfactorily solved, would have an enormous effect on the habits of mankind, is that of distant electric vision."[62] To achieve this solution, he now greatly elaborated on this earlier proposal.

The transmitter would consist of a Crookes tube which would discharge a cathode-ray beam through an aperture at one end, the beam being deflected electromagnetically. This electron stream would scan a mosaic composed "of a number of small metallic cubes insulated from one another, but presenting a clean metallic surface to the cathode rays on the one side, and to a suitable gas or vapour . . . on the other. The metallic cubes . . . are made of some metal, such as rubidium, which is strongly active photoelectrically . . . under the influence of light."[63]

The image to be transmitted would be focused by a lens through a gauze screen in the tube onto the mosaic, which would be simultaneously scanned by the cathode ray on the opposite side; the electron stream thus provides the mosaic with a negative charge. Where no light from the projected image falls on the photoemissive cubes, this charge would be dissipated in the tube itself, but from the cubes on which bright light does fall, the negative charge would pass through the ionized gas to the gauze screen, providing the signal to the receiver.

Each cube in the mosaic constitutes one picture element. A single horizontal line could be composed of several hundred such cubes, each cube scanned sequentially so as to provide a separate signal to the receiver. The cathode ray would thus scan horizontally all the picture elements in one line, then move vertically to scan the next line, until the entire mosaic had been covered once. The cathode ray would then return to the top of the mosaic to begin the process again. Campbell Swinton expected that the mosaic could be scanned once every tenth of a second.[64]

His receiver would also consist of a cathode-ray tube, one end of which discharged the electron stream, again electromagnetically deflected, and the other end consisting of a fluorescent screen. The cathode ray of the receiver would scan the screen synchronously with the cathode ray scanning the mosaic of the transmitter and would thus illuminate the fluorescent material just where picture elements in the mosaic were illuminated. The image being televised would then be faithfully reproduced by the receiver.[65]

Campbell Swinton believed his all-electronic proposal had the advantage over the Nipkow-disc scanner of achieving "the required rapidity and accuracy of motion of the parts" that a mechanical system could not so readily accomplish.[66] But the primitive quality of cathode-ray tubes at the time and the difficulty of devising a suitable mosaic delayed the realization of this technique by two decades, and Campbell Swinton's only attempt to actually construct an all-electronic apparatus failed.[67] Nevertheless, when television was granted commercial authorization in the United States in 1941, the television method most widely used employed techniques following, generally, this conceptual design presented in 1911.[68]

Thus, by the outbreak of the First World War, the theoretical principles of television and the conceptualization of alternative mechanical and electronic applications of these principles already existed. Most of the components of the mechanical method had even been developed, while progress was also being made on the elements necessary for the all-electronic method. Even the word *television,* denoting the transmission of transient visual images, had entered the English language.[69] However, the exigencies and disruptions of war halted most television research. But following the armistice, this work was resumed; radio was substituted for wires as the medium for transmission, the necessary components were assembled, and workable television was demonstrated.

Television Successfully Demonstrated

After the Peace of Paris, research on television and facsimile achieved practical results. By 1921 facsimile transmission was demonstrated successfully in the United States.[70] Four years later, television, too, was a success. The man who was responsible for this first practical realization of television technology in America was Charles Francis Jenkins.

Jenkins was born August 22, 1867, near Dayton, Ohio. A tinkerer of broad interests, his first efforts, begun in 1887, dealt with the recording and reproduction of motion on film. This led to the development of his "Phantoscope," first demonstrated in June 1894 and soon to become a widely used motion-picture projector. In 1898 Jenkins constructed an automobile with the engine in front, instead of under the seat, and in 1901 he built Washington, D.C.'s first sightseeing bus. Jenkins introduced one of the first automobile self-starters in 1911, and in 1916 he helped to found the Society of Motion Picture Engineers.[71]

His interest in television coincided with his research in motion-picture technology. In July 1894 Jenkins published an article in the *Electrical Engineer* proposing a method for transmitting pictures electrically. In the September 1913 issue of the *Motion Picture News* he proposed a mechanism for television. However, neither of the apparatuses Jenkins suggested was practical.[72]

Although the war interrupted his efforts, Jenkins's interest in motion pictures again provided the stimulus for his television research. At the Toronto meeting of the Society of Motion Picture Engineers in May 1920, he introduced his prismatic rings as a device to replace the shutter on a film projector.[73]

C. Francis Jenkins with his mechanical television receiver, circa 1930. (Courtesy of the Library of Congress)

Each ring consisted of a disc of thick glass, the outer edge having been ground into the shape of a prism whose section varied gradually around its circumference. When light was directed through the edge of the disc it was refracted according to the angle of the prismatic section at that point; as the disc rotated, the light beam would be caused to move downward. By superimposing a second disc over the first so that their overlapping edges revolved at right angles to each other, a light beam, scanning vertically and horizontally, was produced.[74]

Employing the prismatic rings as scanning devices, Jenkins turned to facsimile and its utilization of radio transmission. On 19 May 1922 he sent his first successful laboratory radiophotos. Then on 3 October 1922 he held a public demonstration with the cooperation of the U.S. Navy and the Post Office Department. Employing a facsimile transmitter equipped with a prismatic-ring scanner at his laboratory at 1519 Connecticut Avenue in Washington, Jenkins sent photographs by telephone wire to navy radio station NOF in Anacostia, from which it was broadcast to a receiver back in Washington at the Post Office Building on Sixteenth Street.[75] On 2 March 1923 a public demonstration of Jenkins's radio photography took place with the transmission of pictures of President Warren G. Harding, Secretary of Commerce Hoover, Governor Giffort Pinchot, and others from station NOF to the Evening Standard Building in Philadelphia.[76] These experiments encouraged the U.S. Navy to employ the Jenkins equipment to broadcast weather maps to ships at sea.[77]

Already in 1922 Jenkins was publicly explaining that if the rate of prismatic-ring facsimile scanning could be increased, television would be possible. Contemplating what prospects such an achievement might create, an author in the November 1922 issue of *Scientific American* wrote that "there is no reason why we should not, with the new [television] service broadcast an entire theatrical or operatic performance, so that instead of going to a movie house for an evening's entertainment, we can turn a switch and see the latest play and hear it spoken at the same time."[78]

The following year, on 14 June 1923, using his prismatic-rings method, Jenkins successfully achieved television transmission in his Washington laboratory. Within two years he had also succeeded in transmitting motion pictures from standard film, thus realizing his 1913 speculations.[79] He was now prepared for a public demonstration.

This demonstration occurred on Saturday, 13 June 1925. The receiving apparatus was set up in the laboratory on Connecticut Avenue. Present in this studio with Jenkins were Secretary Curtis D. Wilbur and Admiral David W. Taylor of the navy, George K. Burgess, head of the Bureau of Standards, and William D. Terrell, chief radio expert of the Department of Commerce. The transmission originated from NOF in Anacostia. Watching a 10-by-12-inch screen, the viewers saw a ten-minute broadcast of a small Dutch windmill in motion, originating from a film produced by Jenkins. Although only in silhouette, Jenkins claimed, "the moving objects shown were as clear as any of the moving pictures of twenty years ago." He further predicted "that the process would be perfected until baseball games and prize fights could be sent long distances and reproduced on a screen by radio."[80]

A slightly different account of this first public television broadcast in the United States describes the screen as 6 by 8 inches and the show as "a Dutch windmill with vanes spinning. The loud speaker says: 'The mill will now slow down.' It slows down. Again: 'The mill will now stop.' It stops. 'The mill will turn backward.' It turns backward."[81]

Writing about the uses of "Radio Vision," as he preferred to call television, Jenkins explained: "In due course, then, folks in California and Maine, and all the way between, will be able to see the inauguration ceremonies of their President, in Washington; the Army and Navy football games at Franklin Field, Philadelphia; and the struggle for supremacy in our national sport, baseball. . . . The new machine will come to the fireside as a fascinating teacher and entertainer . . . with photoplays, the opera, and a direct vision of world activities."[82]

But in 1925 Jenkins could not yet realize these possibilities. His technique allowed for only rather crude results. In the design of this early equipment, in both transmitting and receiving apparatus, Jenkins employed two prismatic rings. In the transmitter a beam of light issuing from a "crater" neon tube, developed by D. MacFarlan Moore, passed through the prismatic sections of the rings, one revolving rapidly for horizontal movement and the second revolving slowly for vertical movement, to scan the film across a photoelectric cell. The receiver, similarly, had a neon glow-lamp, its brilliance determined by the transmitted signal from the photoelectric cell. This light passed through a set of rotating prismatic rings onto a screen in the raised lid of the receiver's cabinet. Synchronous motors were used to harmonize the rings of the transmitter and receiver, although the received image still had to be "framed" manually for each transmission. But this arrangement, transmitted by NOF on 1875 kHz., produced only 48-line silhouettes.[83] Much work remained to be done, and much of the original equipment modified, before picture quality would be adequate to realize Jenkins's description of television's promise.

Meanwhile, in Britain, in early public demonstrations of television there, picture quality was already improving. There John Logie Baird had begun experimenting with television in 1923 and succeeded in transmitting his first laboratory pictures in a Hastings garret sometime in 1924. He then moved to Frith Street, Soho. Finally on 25 March 1925 Baird presented his first public demonstration of television, in a London department store (Selfridge's, Oxford Street), presenting three shows daily for three weeks. Baird employed a double spiral of lenses and a radially slotted Nipkow disc in this demonstration; this arrangement made possible an 8-line frame, each line subdivided into 50 picture elements, thus producing a 400-element picture. These displays resulted in the formation of Television, Limited in June 1925; that well-financed endeavor supplied Baird with the capital needed to continue his research.

Baird's earliest results, like Jenkins's, were with silhouettes ("shadow-graphs"). But by 26 January 1926, when he provided a demonstration in his Soho laboratory for the Royal Institution, he already was transmitting half-tones. Although these images were blurred and faint, observers agreed that they did reproduce details and "such things as the play of expression on the face."[84] Baird's progress continued until, on 30 September 1929, the British Broadcasting Corporation began regular experimental television broadcasts in London, using Baird's equipment to produce a 30-line picture.[85]

Thus fifty years of research culminated in public demonstrations of the feasibility of "distant electric vision" on both sides of the Atlantic. C. Francis Jenkins and John Logie Baird, working independently and with differing techniques, each separately invented television and almost simultaneously displayed it to the public. That these two men could arrive at similar results in almost the same month is not surprising. For successful television was the incremental result of suggestion, experimentation, and development in a variety of scientific and engineering endeavors. Both Jenkins and Baird were familiar with this previous work, and by 1925 all of the necessary components of a workable system were present, allowing each man to proceed to combine these components into his particular design.

The enthusiasm that had sustained research for five decades now found new expression in the rapid establishment of television broadcast stations. Once television had been proven an engineering reality, efforts were undertaken to duplicate radio's recent successes by presenting it to the public across the country. In this process, television's engineering subsystem would be improved, and the programming and promotional subsystems begun, these last two placing new demands on the first. However, these pioneers of television broadcasting would also learn, to their great disappointment and often to their misfortune, that television was still a concept ahead of its technology.

Pioneering Public Telecasting

Within three years of Jenkins's successful television demonstration there were eighteen "visual broadcast" stations licensed by the Federal Radio Commission.[1] These stations were located in every section of the country, and, except in the South, there were soon to be several more. Operating on the shortwave frequencies, signals from many of these stations could be received throughout the nation. A variety of commercially manufactured television-receiver kits and even fully assembled sets were soon on the market for those eager to "look in" to the new medium. And as a television audience began to form, programming became an increasingly central concern, for this audience had to be entertained, if its interest was to be maintained and if its size was to be increased. But it was mainly the novelty of this new technology and its exciting promises for the future that attracted new participants. And attract it did! By 1931 America was in the midst of a minor television boom.

And accompanying the boom were important advances by the industry. Technical possibilities and necessities were investigated and determined. Even something so fundamental as the frequencies appropriate to television transmission were only now established. Programming, with the development of appropriate staging techniques, was explored, as were various promotional ploys aimed at attracting public support and financial assistance for the new medium. At the same time, major manufacturing and broadcasting interests became committed to the advancement of television.

But despite these important achievements, the boom did not last. By 1934, the year of C. Francis Jenkins's death, it was over. Although television was an engineering success, it was a failure both financially and as entertainment, at least this "low-definition mechanical" variety.[2] In the United States television, like radio before it, was expected to produce a profit. This required eventually winning a sufficiently large audience to attract advertising revenue. At first a large capital outlay would be needed to establish television service, and this initial investment could be sustained for a time by a firm with revenues from its other endeavors, such as manufacturing or radio, or even by investors willing to anticipate sizable profits from television itself.

But soon it became apparent that low-definition mechanical television could not meet these expectations.

To attract an audience, television had to approximate the visual standards of motion pictures. Mechanical television during this era could not do this; its images were still crude. The low definition of television's pictures meant that it could not stage the sorts of entertainment necessary to win broad popular support. But without this promise of a sizable audience, investment in television would be very limited. Only a very few firms, able to sustain over a long period of time large expenditures for television without the prospect of immediate financial return, could undertake the extended laboratory research needed to improve television's picture definition.

However, if the technical limitations of mechanical television were not immediately realized, the economic ones certainly were. Therefore, many of these pioneering telecasters expected, reasonably, to sustain their station investment and new research with even limited advertising revenue, which would supplement, and also stimulate, the growth of a new television manufacturing industry. These promoters believed that improvements in picture quality would require, at most, inexpensive adjustments to existing home receivers, such as purchase of a more advanced disc. But the Federal Radio Commission refused to authorize any commercial utilization of television. The FRC decided that commercialization prior to the achievement of acceptable quality would violate its regulatory responsibilities by appearing to encourage public investment in equipment likely to become obsolescent soon. This policy, established in the earliest years of television's history, was maintained also by the later Federal Communications Commission, until, by 1941, acceptable quality had been achieved.[3]

With the combination of low definition, restrictive regulation, and depression finances, the boom years of mechanical television were very short. This pioneering effort to establish television broadcasting collapsed when the demands placed upon the engineering subsystem by the new programming and promotional requirements could not be met by the existing technology. Yet its contributions were significant for the future directions of each of these three component television subsystems. The history of this brief era, particularly in the primary centers of the new industry (New York, Boston, and Chicago), provides essential elements for the accurate understanding of the successfully integrated system finally granted commercial authorization by the FCC in 1941.

EARLY AMERICAN EXPERIMENTAL TELECASTS

The 1925 demonstration by Jenkins did not immediately spark the television boom. In fact, at the outset the accomplishment of this tinkerer and his small staff attracted little sustained public attention. Rather, it was a much-publicized demonstration, in 1927, by the talented research team of American Telephone and Telegraph that excited popular enthusiasm and served as the catalyst for the swift expansion of American telecasting. This contrast—the efforts of the individual inventor and his small laboratory competing with the staff of a large corporate entity—is paradigmatic for the history of television throughout the period.[4]

AT & T's demonstration of 17 April 1927 was complicated and spectacular. It was organized by Dr. Herbert E. Ives and his research team. The transmission was viewed by a distinguished audience of representatives from the communications industry, press, and academics at the Bell Telephone Laboratories in New York City. Here two receiving apparatuses were displayed, the first measuring 2 by 2½ feet, "designed to serve as a visual adjunct to a public address system," and the second 2 by 2½ inches, "suitable for viewing by a single person . . . primarily intended as an adjunct to the telephone."[5] Fifty-aperture, 15-inch Nipkow discs synchronously rotating 18 times a second were employed for both transmission and reception, although the transmitter employed the flying-spot method (called by Ives "beam scanning") rather than the more usual lighting technique. The demonstration consisted of two parts.

The first part, originating in Washington, D.C., involved a brief appearance by Secretary of Commerce Herbert Hoover, followed by AT & T Vice President John J. Carty and others. This transmission was by wire. In the second part, the transmission was broadcast from AT & T's experimental radio station 3XN in Whippany, New Jersey, utilizing three separate frequencies: 1575 kHz. for video, 1450 kHz. for sound, and 185 kHz. for synchronizing pulse. This broadcast consisted of three "acts": an address by Edward L. Nelson, an engineer at Bell Laboratories, a "vaudeville act" featuring "a stage Irishman, with side whiskers and a broken pipe, . . . [who] did a monologue in brogue," and then did a quick change and returned in black face "with a new line of quips in negro dialect"; and, finally, the third act, "a short humorous dialect talk."[6]

There was some fading and ghosting of the received images, which also occasionally appeared in the negative, but in general the audience was impressed. As one of its members reported, "When the television pictures were thrown on a screen two by three [sic], the likeness was excellent. It was as if a photograph had suddenly come to life and began to talk, smile, nod its head and look this way and that," although the images on the large screen were not as impressive.[7] Nevertheless, here were half-tones, not merely silhouettes.

Although AT & T claimed it had intended its television research to complement the telephone as a means of two-way communication, the program broadcast suggested to one observer that "the commercial future of television . . . is thought to be largely in public entertainment—super-news reels flashed before audiences at the moment of occurrence, together with drama and musical shots on the ether waves in sound and picture at the instant they are taking place in the studio."[8] And it was exactly television's promise for instantaneous transmission, in contrast to the motion-picture newsreel and films then common, that excited enthusiasm in early television programming.

Within two years Ives and his Bell Laboratories staff introduced further important innovations: telecasting by ordinary light and color television. The first development came the year following, in August 1928, using equipment similar to that employed in the 1927 demonstration, except for an increased sensitivity of the photocells. In this performance a tennis player on the roof of the Bell Laboratories Building in New York was televised by natural light to a receiver with a 2-by-3-inch screen located on the seventh floor of the building. Although insisting that the new apparatus was experimental, the Bell engineers alluded to the importance of this development for television programming: they "indicated that the new photoelectric cell will permit the transmission of scenes such as prize-fights, tennis matches, baseball and football games."[9] Here might be found television's special forte.

Then on 27 June 1929, Ives and his staff demonstrated a method for color television at Bell's New York laboratory. They used the same basic apparatus as in their previous demonstrations, merely altering the arrangement of photocells in the transmitter and of the glow-lamps in the receiver. For transmitting, Ives employed three photoelectric cells, each provided with a separate color filter—orange-red, yellow-green, and greenish blue. Each photocell required a separate video transmission channel. In the receiver, each signal operated a separate glow-lamp. The light of the beams from the neon lamp with a red filter, the argon lamp with a blue filter, and the argon lamp with a green filter was projected simultaneously through the scanning disc by means of a semitransparent mirror. This produced the composite color picture.[10]

On a tiny screen the audience at this AT & T demonstration, transmitted through wires, witnessed a variety of colorful scenes. An American and a British flag were each displayed, followed by a man picking up a piece of watermelon. The viewers were able to see the color of the watermelon, the red of the man's lips, the colors of his skin and hair. Recognizable also were the colors of a pot of geraniums in bloom and a bouquet of multicolored roses, as were those on a large striped ball and on a woman's dress.[11] Although the demonstration was impressive, technical difficulties, particularly the requirement of multichannel transmission, prevented exploitation of Ives's technique.[12]

Until unification of the radio group's researchers under the aegis of the Radio Corporation of America, General Electric also provided the public with exciting television displays. GE's Ernst F. W. Alexanderson first attracted attention to this firm's work when, in December 1926, he unveiled his television projector employing a large mirror drum.[13] Slightly over a year after the first AT & T television demonstration, Alexanderson staged a show to present his new GE television receiver. The apparatus was about 4 feet high, with a 3-by-3-inch viewing aperture on the upper front panel of its cabinet. A 24-inch scanning disc with 48 holes was employed in both receiver and transmitter. The receiver employed a neon glow-lamp and the tiny images appeared on the screen with a pink tint, a characteristic of the neon tube.

Alexanderson's demonstration was broadcast over two channels: the video on shortwave on 37.8 meters and the sound over GE's standard radio station in Schenectady, New York, WGY, on 755 kHz. An enthralled viewer in Schenectady reported that a "man smokes a cigarette at the transmitter and he is seen several miles away on the receiving 'screen.' Then he comments on the cigarette and his voice is heard as the audience at the receiving set sees his lips move. Then a ukulele player steps before the broadcast apparatus."[14] David Sarnoff hailed the demonstration as epoch making, while GE engineers predicted that within five years such sets "may be in most of the homes that now possess loud-speakers."[15]

Going quickly beyond demonstrating television's feasibility, GE, on 11 September 1928, televised a melodrama, J. Hartley Manner's *The Queen's Messenger*. The video portion was broadcast twice, at 1:30 and at 11:30 P.M., on two frequencies, one shortwave and one on the standard medium-wave band, while the sound, over WGY, was broadcast over shortwave. This particular play was chosen primarily because of its simplicity in staging: it included a cast of only two characters. Nonetheless, even this required three cameras: one for each actor and one for the props, for example, a hand holding a drink. A separate camera for props was necessary because the other cameras were neither mobile nor capable of showing more than one actor's face at a time. Yet even this primitive staging required that consideration be given to studio layout and facial makeup.[16]

However, GE had already overcome part of the problem with its cameras, introducing a new portable version. This camera was employed publicly for the first time also in September 1928, when WGY telecast Governor Al Smith's speech on the steps of the capitol in Albany accepting the Democratic party's presidential nomination, a clear example of television's ability to present news instantaneously.[17]

A final demonstration, before unification, was given by Alexanderson in May 1930. At Proctor's Theatre in Schenectady, he had set up a 6-by-7-foot screen on which to project a telecast from GE's experimental visual station W2XCW, operating on the shortwave frequency channel 2100–2200 kHz.[18] This was part of a general trend at the time to attempt large-screen projec-

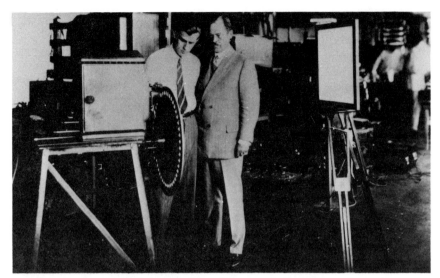

Dr. Ernst F. W. Alexanderson (right) and Ray D. Kell with a mechanical scanning disc, in 1927. (Courtesy of RCA)

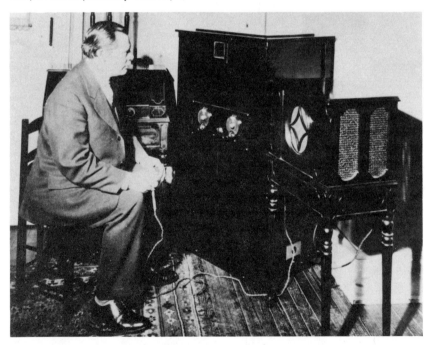

Dr. Ernst F. W. Alexanderson in front of a television receiver at his home in Schenectady, New York, in 1928. He developed the apparatus, whose small screen is at the top. (Courtesy of RCA)

tion for theater use. Although the demonstration created a favorable impression, the general decline of mechanical television shortly thereafter and GE's temporary withdrawal from this field of research meant there would be no immediate consequences for the concept.

Another event that attracted much interest at the time but had no immediate repercussions was John Logie Baird's attempt to enter the U.S. market. On 8 April 1927 Baird claimed that for the past several weeks he had successfully been transmitting television from his London station to a receiver located near New York City. He told reporters that if the experiments proved practical, he would soon market a commercial receiver in America.[19]

On 8 February 1928, Baird staged a transoceanic telecast for the press. The transmission, sent from a 2-kw. station fifteen miles outside London, was received in Hartsdale, New York. The program consisted of the faces of Baird, a reporter, and a Miss Howe being shown, each viewed separately as they turned their heads from side to side.[20] A viewer reported, "The images were crude, imperfect, broken, but they were images none the less. Man's vision had spanned the ocean; transatlantic television was a demonstrated reality."[21]

But not, of course, for long. Baird's accomplishment depended on utilization of shortwave frequencies for television transmission (in this instance, 45 meters). These frequencies would soon be abandoned as not suitable for the increased picture definition that the industry found the public demanded. So neither this attempt, nor later more conventional ventures, provided Baird with the vehicle for a successful entry into the U.S. markets.[22]

Although AT & T, GE and even John L. Baird attracted the headlines at this time, other, less-noticed occurrences in 1928 really signaled the beginning of the television boom. Now began the establishment, often by owners of small radio stations, of telecasting for public reception, instead of for occasional press events. While the press demonstrations aroused general interest in a corporation's anticipated product, public broadcasts, often advocated by those unable to sustain extended financial investment, aimed at attracting immediate popular support. The company with a large research budget displayed its television to industry officials, engineers, and the press; the small broadcaster turned to the public, especially to radio amateurs.

Even at this early date, regular telecast schedules were sometimes attempted. Already in May 1928 GE had introduced scheduled television broadcasts over WGY between 1:30 and 2:00 P.M. every Tuesday, Thursday, and Friday, on the standard medium-wave radio band.[23] However, these telecasts consisted only of the faces of men "talking, laughing or smoking."[24] They were primarily field tests meant for the firm's research engineers. GE's September program demonstrations were thus exceptional in this regard.

The first station to attract attention to its telecasting for the public was WRNY, in New York City, owned by Hugo Gernsback, publisher of *Radio*

News. In early June 1928 the station installed in its Hotel Roosevelt studios a television transmitter designed by Theodore Nakken of Brooklyn. Telecasts would be carried by WRNY on its standard radio channel, 920 kHz., and also by its shortwave sister station, W2XAL, on 9705 kHz. Since it was not yet technically possible to broadcast video and audio simultaneously from one station, performers' images would be telecast just before they sang or spoke.[25]

On 12 August 1928 WRNY conducted its first television tests, between 5:43 and 6:30 P.M. and again after 11:00 P.M. The tests evidently consisted of scanning the faces of an engineer from Pilot Electrical Company and of the station's chief engineer. The regular television broadcast schedule was instituted two days later, for a New York audience Gernback estimated at two thousand.[26] These regular television transmissions occurred each hour for five minutes and consisted of an announcer first describing what would be seen followed by the silhouettes of a live performer, or printed letters, designs, or diagrams. Reception on the shortwave frequency was found to be clearer than that on the lower medium-wave one, an important technical indicator for the future. And of this future, Gernsback predicted that within five years it would be possible to broadcast ball games and boxing matches.[27]

WRNY's telecasts were associated with manufacturing, as were the broadcasts of many of these smaller operations. The station's equipment designer, Theodore Nakken, was involved in the production of commercial television apparatus, apparently in association with Pilot Electrical Company; and Pilot's receiver ("televisor"), with its 2½-inch picture, was recommended by *Radio News*.[28] Although WRNY and Pilot did not long remain active, this pattern continued in New York as well as in Boston and Chicago.

Boston's entry into the television era was at first more tentative. There the *Boston Post* sponsored telecasts over WLEX, in Lexington, Massachusetts, throughout April and May of 1928. By the end of the year W1XAY in Lexington was telecasting on shortwave at 61.5 meters on an irregular schedule, employing a 48-aperture disc. Unlike WRNY, film instead of direct pickup was used here, film being much simpler to scan. But like the New York operation, Boston's television was, at least indirectly, connected with manufacturing. The station's chief engineer, Alfred J. Pote, had formerly been connected with Raytheon Manufacturing Company of Boston, as Delbert E. Replogle, also involved with the station and soon to be prominent in New York telecasting, still was. Raytheon was a producer of the neon tubes so essential to television and was at the time considering the possibility of manufacturing commercial receivers.[29]

In Chicago television transmissions began on 19 June 1928, when radio station WCFL, on its regular medium-wave 620-kHz. frequency, broadcast an image of the head and shoulders of E. N. Nichols, secretary of the Chicago Federation of Labor, the parent organization of this "Voice of

Labor." The equipment employed had been developed by Ulises A. Sanabria, whose inventive designs would dominate Chicago television for several
years, and his associate, M. L. Hayes.[30] Commenting on the quality of these
pictures, one reporter wrote, "It is difficult to describe the exact grade of
their definition, but it can be said that the televised faces are distinctly
recognizable."[31] And Virgil A. Schoenberg, chief engineer at WCFL, explained that while film, not live performers, was telecast, it was not merely
black-and-white silhouette motion pictures, "but the kind used in theatres,"
and that $100,000 had already been invested by WCFL in television
development.[32]

PIONEERING TELEVISION STATIONS

WGY, WRNY, WLEX, and WCFL, although pioneers in the television
boom in 1928, did not long maintain their telecasting activities. In New
York, Boston, and Chicago new stations and new interests soom became
predominant. However, in Washington, D.C., television's inventor,
C. Francis Jenkins, was also inaugurating a regular television service, and
this service remained a significant force throughout most of the boom years.
On 2 July 1928 his broadcast station, W3XK, began a regular schedule of
"radiomovie" transmissions (as Jenkins then preferred to call his silhouette
film telecasting) on 6420 kHz., with a 48-line picture, between 8:00 and 9:00
P.M., on Monday, Wednesday, and Friday evenings. The transmissions
were still limited to silhouettes because Jenkins, and the other stations as
well, had to remain within the very narrow 10-kHz. band allotted for radio
broadcasting while half-tones required at least 100 kHz. Already by this time
Jenkins had abandoned his prismatic rings for a 48-lens, 15-inch Nipkow
scanning disc, rotating 15 times per second. Jenkins frankly explained that
his broadcasts were aimed at encouraging amateur participation, a theme he
would further elaborate on during the following years.[33]

These five stations, while in the 1928 television vanguard, were certainly
not alone. An early list of stations published by the *New York Times* in July
1928, includes seven more stations: W2XBU in Beacon, New York; a Westinghouse station in East Pittsburgh; three RCA stations, W2XBS and W2XBU
in New York City and W2XBW in Bound Brook, New Jersey; W4XA in
White Haven, Tennessee; and W6XC in Los Angeles.[34]

By October three more stations were listed in a *Radio Broadcasting* sur-
vey. These include two new GE outlets in Schenectady and a new Chicago
station associated with the *Chicago Daily News*'s WMAQ.[35] A November
FRC communication adds six others: two new Chicago stations, W9XAG of
Aero Products and WIBO, a standard radio outlet operated by the Nelson
Brothers Bond and Mortgage Company; a new station in Long Island City,
New York, W2XBT; two new Los Angeles operations; and a new GE station

in Oakland, California.[36] In all, twenty-one television licenses had been issued by the end of 1928.

However, many of these early licenses went to radio amateurs interested in television as an exciting extension of their hobby. Typical of these may be the explanation provided to the FRC by one such applicant:

> My desire is to get into the branch in conjunction with regular amateur radio work. My idea was to receive and possibly transmit pictures to other amateur stations, so equipped.
>
> The purpose of which is to create a new hobby as well as to carry on experiments which might develop into future contributions to the Art itself.[37]

Few of these amateurs received licenses; fewer still actually transmitted; and none of these amateur operations lasted very long.

Some of the other licenses never went beyond the planning stage. A Tennessee applicant provides an example of this. A radio outlet there had been granted a television construction permit in July 1928, but when its site was inspected in February 1929, the Atlanta supervisor of radio for the Department of Commerce found that no construction had yet been undertaken. "The owner of the station gave the Inspector the impression that he was merely trying to retain some sort of claim on a channel for television work."[38]

Probably a more accurate estimate of the number of television stations operating at the close of 1928, or soon thereafter, would be fifteen:

Station	Location	Licensee
WRNY	New York City	*Radio News*
W2XAL	New York City	*Radio News*
W2XBS	New York City	RCA
W2XBV	New York City	RCA
WGY	Schenectady	GE
W2XAF	Schenectady	GE
W2XAD	Schenectady	GE
W2XBU	Beacon, New York	Harold E. Smith
W2XBW	Bound Brook, New Jersey	RCA
W2XAV	East Pittsburgh	Westinghouse
W1XAY	Lexington, Massachusetts	J. Smith Dodge
W3XK	Washington, D.C.	Jenkins Laboratories
W9XAA	Chicago	Chicago Federation of Labor
WMAQ	Chicago	*Chicago Daily News*
WIBO	Chicago	Nelson Brothers Bond and Mortgage Company

Of these original fifteen stations, six would remain in operation until the collapse of the boom, and three are claimed as the progenitors of currently operating television stations.[39] However, during the five boom years several more stations would begin broadcasting, at least two of which are still on the air today.

The boom in mechanical telecasting was primarily the creation of communications-equipment manufacturers seeking new markets. Many in these firms also believed that the availability of silent "televisors" would further stimulate radio sales, in order to allow for the reception of the synchronized audio portions of televised programs.[40] Thus large manufacturers, such as AT & T, GE, and Westinghouse, began quite early to promote television actively. They were soon joined by smaller concerns, such as Pilot Manufacturing. Eventually, largely as a result of the reorganization of the radio group, the main impetus for mechanical television came from smaller, more specialized manufacturers, namely, Jenkins Television, Shortwave and Television, and Western Television.

However, even at this time there was a secondary financial interest advocating mechanical television: radio networks sought to develop television as a field for regional and national commercial programming. Thus by 1931 CBS in New York and the Don Lee System in Los Angeles, neither with any manufacturing interest, were actively promoting mechanical television in order to explore the commercial opportunities inherent in its programming potential.

These two interests—equipment manufacturing and commercial programming—continued to characterize those heavily investing in television even after the mechanical technique had been replaced by electronic television. But with the new technique, the network interests had come to predominate. By 1941 the most active promoters of television were radio networks: NBC, CBS, and the Don Lee System. Manufacturing interests—for example, Philco, Farnsworth, GE, and Zenith—were still present, although now following the network lead and generally willing to accept their programming.

RCA, of course, was a unique case throughout this era of television history, for after unification it became a leading manufacturer, and it already operated the largest radio networks in the nation. But RCA was not really an exception to the general pattern of television promotion. During the mechanical era, it eschewed entertaining telecasting entirely and instead concentrated on developing equipment. Only after RCA had a complete engineering system ready for marketing did it concentrate on programming and its commercial utilization. And by 1941 RCA was able to provide both the most advanced equipment and the sophisticated programming necessary for commercial network use. Not surprisingly, David Sarnoff vigorously advocated private financing for the television industry, as opposed to the alternative system adopted in Britain, where telecasting depended on a noncommercial public corporation, which permitted private industry to profit from equipment sales but denied it any income from advertising revenue.[41] DuMont, a new concern entering the television field only in 1938, attempted, with limited success, to emulate the RCA pattern. Thus the promotion of television from its first public demonstration in 1925 to its commercial authorization in 1941 was conducted by those two corporate interests—manufacturing and programming—which expected to gain financially most directly from the success of the new medium.

But in 1928 reception of television transmissions was still quite problematic. For instance, a firm producing radios in the Boston area investigated the possibilities of manufacturing television receivers and was discouraged from doing so upon discovering that WGY's afternoon telecasts on the regular broadcast band did not reach Boston or even Springfield, Massachusetts. In fact, because of problems with synchronization, the firm was unable even to receive the shortwave telecasts of W1XAY in suburban Lexington.[42] However, telecasters and their audience generally remained undaunted, and significant progress was achieved in resolving the problems of frequency range and synchronization. However, these two issues were actually symptomatic of a much greater question facing the nascent industry.

Already in 1928, among the fifteen stations, a serious difficulty arose that was not conclusively resolved until 1941—standardization. There were three separate areas of difficulty in 1928. First, there was the question of frequencies utilized for television. Some stations, like WRNY and WGY, telecasted on the standard medium-wave radio band, while the others operated on a variety of shortwave frequencies from 31 to 61 meters. A second problem was the number of lines per picture transmitted. These varied from 24 for WGY to 60 for W2XAV. And, finally, there was no agreed number of frames per second transmitted, but rather a continuum ranging from WRNY's 7.5 per second to WGY's 21. Since each of these factors constitutes an independent variable (though a part of an integrated system), only if there was standardization of all three could one apparatus receive satisfactorily signals from all stations. Both the FRC and the industry had already begun, in 1928, to work toward this goal.

THE FRC AND TELEVISION

The Federal Radio Commission performed three major tasks during this initial television era. First, it had to determine the appropriate frequencies and bandwidths for visual broadcasting. Second, it had to set procedures and standards for assigning stations to these frequencies. And third, the commission had to regulate the nature of the service made available to the public; that is, the FRC was responsible for deciding whether television was to be exclusively experimental or whether some commercial service would also be permissible. The first task primarily reflected technical considerations, while the other two rested upon the commission's perception of the public interest. However, while the second function determined the fate of individual broadcasters, the third affected the future of the entire industry.

In 1927, the FRC's first year of existence, the determination of broadcast frequencies for television was already an issue. At that time it was decided to allow such broadcasting on the standard medium-wave radio band (that is, 550–1500 kHz.) with a 10-kHz. band spread. Television experimentation was also permitted on shortwave frequencies, 1500–2000 kHz. (part of today's "tropical band").[43] By 1928, with the number of television stations rapidly expanding and technical requirements becoming more evident, significant adjustments of these arrangements were made by the commission.

Summarizing current technical information, the FRC, in its 1928 *Annual Report*, quoted an engineering brief submitted to it by Alfred N. Goldsmith:

> A 5-kilocycle band will permit the television broadcast of a crude image of a head, with comparatively little detail. A 20-kilocycle band will permit the broadcasting of the head and shoulders . . . with more detail. An 80-kilocycle band will permit transmission of the picture of two or three actors in fairly acceptable detail.
>
> The allocation of bands of 100-kilocycles wide for television is strongly advocated, since this is clearly the minimum basis for a true television service of permanent interest to the public.[44]

It was this last criterion—a true television service of *permanent* interest to the public—that was the central determinant of all FRC (and FCC) policy.

Although the commission allowed telecasting to continue on the medium-wave radio spectrum with a 10-kHz. band, it now limited these broadcasts to one hour a day and banned any at all from 6:00 to 11:00 P.M., in order to prevent interference with regular commercial service.[45] By 1929 these broadcasts were further limited to the hours of 1:00 to 6:00 A.M.[46] The last such experiments on this band were concluded by 1931, with the termination of broadcasts on 660 kHz. by Westinghouse's W8XT.[47]

To accommodate television broadcasts utilizing 100-kHz. channels, frequencies above the medium-wave radio allocations were necessary. Consequently, in 1929 five television channels were assigned by the FRC in accordance with the decisions of the North American Radio Conference, held in Ottawa in January 1929. Four channels, 2000–2100, 2100–2200, 2750–2850, and 2850–2950 kHz., were established exclusively for American television, while 2200–2300 kHz. would only be used in the South and Southwest, so no interference to Canadian services could occur.[48]

For two reasons this arrangement quickly became unsatisfactory, and new alternatives had to be sought. First, since these were shortwave frequencies, stations hundreds of miles apart could interfere with each other. Because there were only four active channels (2200–2300 kHz. remained unused), stations often found their broadcasts disturbed by distant stations assigned to the same channel; sharing time on common frequencies by agreeing to vary scheduling (a common feature in radio then) only slightly alleviated the problem.

More serious was the discovery that the 100-kHz. bandwidth was not sufficient for the transmission of images of quality likely to provide "true television service of permanent interest to the public." The FRC reported, "The consensus of engineering opinion indicates that in order to transmit a picture having satisfactory detail the band width required will be many times that now available in this [shortwave] frequency range."[49] But it would not be possible to accommodate such expanded channels within the existing shortwave spectrum without seriously disrupting other services, so in 1931, to provide the needed frequencies for television experimentation, the FRC authorized three additional television allocations on much higher, little-used frequencies: 43,000–46,000, 48,500–50,300, and 60,000–80,000 kHz. No limitations were placed on the bandwidths utilized in these frequencies.[50]

But these very high frequencies (then called ultrahigh frequencies), which were well suited to television's programming needs, presented new difficulties in engineering. Unlike transmission on medium and shortwave spectrums, broadcasts on VHF have very limited range. While medium-wave and shortwave signals are carried both by ground waves (which follow the earth's surface) and by sky waves (which bounce off the ionosphere), VHF is carried effectively only by ground waves. This means that VHF broadcasts can operate only within a straight line between transmitter and receiver, greatly reducing the range of any one station. This range can be still further reduced should tall buildings or mountains also interpose between transmitter and receiver. The technical necessity of adopting VHF frequencies to provide acceptable programming standards thus introduced new concerns over networking and the financially awesome prospect of having to construct vast numbers of television stations throughout the country. A decade would be required to solve this challenge.

To obtain authorization to broadcast on any of the television channels, it was first necessary to apply to the FRC for a construction permit. If this was granted, then upon fulfillment of its conditions an application for an operating license could be made. If granted a license, the licensee was then obliged to file regular reports indicating its hours of operation, the general results of its broadcasting, and what technical studies were being undertaken.[51]

The FRC granted these licenses selectively. Their main concerns in doing so were to determine the experience of the personnel to be involved in the operation of the new station, the existence of a viable plan of research, the financial resources of the applicant, and the public interest to be served by the granting of the particular license. For instance, the 1932 joint application of WJR, the "Goodwill Station," in Pontiac, Michigan, and of the WGAR Broadcasting Company of Cuyahaga Heights Village, Ohio, was granted after the commission determined that the supervisor of the joint project had already engaged in television broadcasting for over a year; that WJR had already invested $15,000 and planned to invest a further $25,000 in equipment; that the venture did propose a significant, detailed research agenda, to make "observations on space effects, including shadows, skip distances, if any, fading, etc. and, so far as the very high frequencies are concerned, the effects of reflection and obstacles in the way of direct line of sight . . . [and] also effects of transmission over water . . . [and] to determine what can be accomplished by reflection on the very high frequencies; to try out the effects of reflectors . . . on the producing of larger field intensities with respect to possible shadows on transmitter picture."[52] The commission also decided that no existing stations would suffer interference, the nearest VHF visual stations being in Milwaukee, Wisconsin, and Camden, New Jersey.

On the other hand, two other applications that same year, from Pittsburgh and Shreveport, were denied. In each instance, the commission determined that the applicants had no previous technical experience in the field (or had no qualified personnel), had no definite program of proposed research, and did not seem to have the necessary financial resources.[53] In arriving at such decisions the FRC was concerned with promoting the technical development of television by limiting broadcasting to stations that provided concrete evidence of their capability to making contributions. The commission explicitly rejected considerations of public entertainment, the lack of a local outlet, and commercial advantages as relevant criteria for deciding upon license applications.

Already in 1928 the FRC had been urged to authorize commercial television service because "of the fact that a large potential audience in the [medium-wave] broadcast band is already at hand."[54] However, since by 1929 the medium waves had been displaced by shortwave television channels, this first argument faded. The primary condition set by the commission for commercialization was acceptable service to the public, and it judged that, despite the increasing activity and interest, this had not been achieved. In 1930 it reported that "the commission did not recognize visual broadcasting as having developed to the point where it has real entertainment value. Therefore all licenses were issued on an experimental basis."[55] Although improvements in picture quality and expansion of services continued, the commission rejected all arguments that television had achieved the capability of providing the public with genuine entertainment. Again in 1932 it reported, "Such [television] programs fall far short of what the public had been led to expect in the way of entertainment."[56]

A 1930 incident in Boston will serve to illustrate the FRC's adamant objection to even a hint of commercialization. There the local experimental television station, W1XAV, had arranged to telecast the visual portion of some of the programming of radio station WNAC. On 7 December 1930, in a press release headlined "First Chain Commercial Broadcast to Go on Air via Television Tonight," W1XAV announced that it would televise the video portion of a CBS program, "The Fox Trappers," sponsored by "America's largest manufacturing furrier." Enthusiastically, the release announced this as "the first definite indication of the commercial future of television syn-chronized with radio. Tonight's broadcast is probably the beginning of a trend which will bring us to the point in a short space of time when there will be a great chain of television broadcasting stations throughout the country in much the same manner as we now have the great national chains of radio broadcasting stations."[57] Although W1XAV received no payment for the advertising rebroadcast from WNAC, the FRC general counsel ruled that even the free rebroadcast of commercials from radio could not be permitted.[58]

In the FRC's view, television broadcasting had to remain strictly ex-perimental, that is, used solely to conduct research. Only after sufficient technical development could entertainment be a proper consideration and commercial promotion a legitimate activity. The government strictly adhered to this policy for over a decade, until 1941, despite strong opposi-tion from many in the industry, especially during these early years, when smaller firms desperately needed additional financial support to maintain their competitive research endeavors. Because it had been the belief in television as the next investors' paradise that helped create the boom, the recognition that commercialization was not imminent and that much more capital would have to be invested in research before profits would be real-ized discouraged many and limited the resources of several of the smaller firms, particularly in the tight financial conditions prevailing during the depression years.

However, despite the FRC's concern that licensed stations actually oper-ate, conduct significant research, and refrain from all commercial broadcast-ing, its monitoring of telecasting suffered from a significant handicap. Its regional supervisors, charged with enforcing its policies, had no television receivers to monitor the activities of the telecasting in their districts.[59] Occa-sional personal visits were the main form of enforcement, besides the quarterly reports submitted to the FRC by the stations.

If the FRC allocated the television frequencies, licensed stations to use them, and regulated broadcast functions on them, parallel activity by repre-sentatives of the industry attempted to determine standards for transmission and reception engineering and equipment. As one of the earliest discussions of standardization explained, "it is self-evident that before television can become a national service, there must be some degree of standardization of these elements among those who desire to operate television transmitting stations and those who propose to manufacture television receiving equipment."[60]

The goal of such standardization was not to be merely a convenience, but rather standards "which provide for a service of high quality, or, as we will refer to it hereafter, a 'commercial' television service."[61] The measure of such commercial television was "the phrase 'genuine entertainment and education value' [which] really determines the degree of picture detail or the number of picture elements."[62] Thus standardization, beyond its immediate practical benefits, was the industry's strategy for responding to the FRC's demands for quality.

FIRST ATTEMPTS TO ESTABLISH STANDARDS

In 1928 the Radio Manufacturers Association (RMA, now the Electronic Industries Association) established a Television Standardization Committee, chaired by Delbert E. Replogle, then with Raytheon Manufacturing Company and soon to be an executive of Jenkins Television Corporation. The Standardization Committee first met on 9 October 1928, in Chicago. It unanimously recommended scanning left to right, scanning top to bottom, scanning 15 frames per second, and scanning 48 lines per frame (but allowing a secondary frame standard of 60 lines).[63]

Although many stations eventually adopted these recommendations, there were several difficulties with them. First, the number of lines per frame suggested could not be adapted to the scanning system developed by Ulises A. Sanabria and promoted by Western Television of Chicago, a major television manufacturer during this period.[64] Similarly, these standards ignored the research being conducted with cathode-ray tubes for television, already a significant laboratory enterprise. Moreover, the standards that were adopted had an obvious and serious flaw, even when consideration is limited to existing systems to which they could be applied. Specifically, they could be accepted unanimously by the RMA only if two mutually exclusive figures for lines per frame were adopted, although this in itself defeated the purpose of standardization.[65] A further difficulty with these first RMA standards was that they did not include any guidance on the issue of synchronization between transmitter and receiver. Was there to be a transmitted synchronizing pulse of some sort, were synchronous motors to be employed, or was synchronization to depend on the local electrical power source?[66]

But finally, the greatest defect of the RMA's proposed standards was the refusal of the FRC to accept the prevailing quality of television transmission as meeting the requirements of a commercial television service. This lack of a governmental imprimatur for these standards served to encourage experimentation beyond these limits, leading to their early obsolescence. This was not only what the FRC had feared but also what it intended, a policy it and its successor would continue to pursue until the industry's engineers agreed that optimum quality had been attained.

By 1932 this outcome had been accepted by the RMA's Television Committee. Still headed by Replogle, it now replaced its set of standards with a set of goals: to achieve greater picture detail, to develop portable television pickup equipment, to develop satisfactory and reliable range in television transmission, to build a receiver simple to operate and retailed at a reasonable price, and to provide "quiet and satisfactorily illuminated picture equipment for the home."[67] Once these goals had been achieved, the drive for standardization would be resumed.

However, the efforts of the RMA to establish standards was not a futile exercise by any means. Two of its standards were permanently adopted: television scanning now is from left to right and from top to bottom. Furthermore, the failure of the original standards did serve to establish a set of realistic goals that eventually produced television's current standards. And finally, the practice whereby standards were to be formulated by the industry, not the government, was continued and provided the basis for the official authorization of television in 1941. Although this deliberate inaction was the decisive action for some, the FRC and the FCC consistently proclaimed their strict adherence to the well-established governmental policy of leaving engineering decisions to private initiative. As an FRC report explained, "the experimental visual broadcasting stations have been given complete freedom in developing the art."[68]

The central issue in all these discussions of standards was the purpose for which the new technology was being developed. Three areas of concern were involved in this question. First, there was a great deal of speculation about the nature of television programming. Second, there was the issue of how this programming was to be financed. And, finally, there was some anxiety over how television would affect other entertainment media, particularly radio and motion pictures.

THE PIONEERS AND THE USES OF TELEVISION

As we have seen, the question of the nature of television's uses had been addressed at least as early as 1911, when it was suggested that television could serve as an important aid to scientific research and industrial management. In 1923 one of the medium's strongest advocates, David Sarnoff, suggested an expanded interpretation of television's potential. At that time he sent a memorandum to the RCA Board of Directors reminiscent of his 1916 prediction about the future of radio. In this memorandum Sarnoff wrote, "I believe television . . . will come to pass in due course" and then went on to suggest that its programming would include the broadcasting of news and motion pictures for viewing in "individual homes or auditoriums."[69]

In a 1926 *Saturday Evening Post* article, Sarnoff further elaborated his conception of the uses of the new medium: "The whole country will join in every national procession. The backwoodsman will be able to follow the play of expression on the face of a leading artist. Mothers will attend child-welfare classes in their own homes. Workers may go to night school in the same way. A scientist can demonstrate his latest discoveries to those of his profession."[70]

In a 1931 speech, Sarnoff's growing expectations for television reflected the practical experience derived from the actual telecasting that had begun during the intervening five years: "The potential audience of television in its ultimate development may reasonably be expected to be limited only by the population of the earth itself."[71] And the effect of such a potential would be to transform human relations: "When television has fulfilled its ultimate destiny, man's sense of physical limitation will be swept away and his boundaries of sight and hearing will be the limits of the earth itself. With this may come a new horizon, a new philosophy, a new sense of freedom, and greatest of all, perhaps, a finer and broader understanding between all the peoples of the world."[72]

Writing in less grandiose terms, Sarnoff's CBS rival, William S. Paley, stressed television's ability to transmit the images of entertainment instantaneously: "Visualize world-series baseball games, football games, automobile and horse races, transmitted *the instant they occur* on supersized, natural color, stereoscopic [theater] screens."[73]

C. Francis Jenkins, as in his original 1925 discussion, also now approached television programming pragmatically, discussing its possibilities in the light of existing radio experience. Once television had solved its technical difficulties, "one may sit in one's home and see inaugural ceremonies, baseball, football, polo games, mardi gras, flower festivals, and baby parades."[74] Then "music and speech at the fireside, sent from distant world parts, will be the daily source of news; the daily instructional class, and the evening entertainment."[75] He went on to suggest optimistically in 1929 "that by the next presidential election in 1932 men and women from Maine to California can, in the comfort of their own homes, watch the face of the President elect as he delivers his inaugural address, witness the Yale and Harvard football game in the Bowl and the final game of the World Series."[76]

In a 1931 book Edgar H. Felix laid out a sweeping panorama of the programming possibilities of television, a "fitting crown to the achievements of this age of electrical development." "The program possibilities of television . . . appear to be limited only by the breadth of human imagination. In the field of news and sports broadcasts, any event sufficient to arouse general public interest is a subject for a television broadcast. . . . In the field of entertainment, the motion picture, the drama, the musical comedy and in every form of spectacle, there is a logical foundation for a television program. In politics and education, the inanimate loudspeaker [that is, radio] will be given new life and new means of holding audiences, with the aid of information portrayed to the eye."[77]

Such prospects excited most commentators, but at least one, Federal Radio Commissioner Harold A. Lafount, was seriously concerned about the possibility of politically and socially disruptive effects arising from the impact of the new medium. In 1931 Lafount warned, "I believe that television is destined to become the greatest force in the world. I think it will have more influence over the lives of individuals than any other single force. . . . It has been wisely said that our government consists of many home units. The effect of radio and television on these units of necessity will affect the nation."[78] However, Lafount's anxiety was shared by few others at the time.

Instead, the major concern about programming was how it was to be financed. A 1928 article in *Radio Broadcasting* warned against following radio's example of introducing advertising techniques into the medium. The author cautioned, "If picture transmission is used to distribute miniature billboards in the home, its growth will be stifled at the outset. The public is not going to buy picture receiving apparatus to have itself exploited by advertisers."[79]

Zenith, the independent Chicago radio manufacturer, evidently agreed, believing advertising revenue could not adequately cover production and programming expenditures. In 1931 the firm began to investigate ways of developing a system of subscription television.[80]

But Edgar Felix's 1931 description of the promotional potential of television is certainly more accurate of expectations and eventual realities: "The advertisers and the users of radio broadcasting as a goodwill advertising medium have eagerly watched the development of television, impatiently awaiting the day when it will give them the opportunity to exhibit their trade-marks and products in the homes of a vast army of potential buyers. . . . The first satisfactory programs will command a position in the limelight, of immense advertising value."[81]

Felix clearly understood that television, unlike radio, would emerge in a commercial environment already structured to mobilize this mass medium for promotional purposes. He observed, "Television will find a complete structure ready to commercialize it." Therefore, "television must go forward suspected if not conspicuously branded as an advertising medium. . . . The prospect that television will be supported by means other than advertising programs appears exceedingly slim."[82]

Here, then, by 1931, is a description of the complete television system. The new engineering technology was to be employed to provide a unique form of home entertainment and education. This attractive medium would be financed via the talents of the already-existing advertising industry to the mutual financial benefit of advertisers and telecasters. This potential was exciting, alluring, and, for some, threatening.

Others besides Commissioner Lafount were beginning to feel uneasy. In fact, rival media were also becoming alarmed. Descriptions of television's potential had also to include reassurances to those interests threatened by this new mode of popular edification and entertainment. As early as 1926, David Sarnoff felt compelled to assure the press that despite television's potential for bringing news into the public's home instantaneously, this function would serve merely to supplement and not supplant the picture sections of newspapers. And he gave similar assurances to the radio industry.[83]

Other industry spokesmen, too, proclaimed their assurances that television would not displace the existing media. In December 1928 Christmas shoppers were promised that television would not make radios obsolete and that they could safely buy them as presents.[84] Alfred N. Goldsmith, vice president of RCA, repeated these assurances the following year.[85] And William Paley insisted that despite television "broadcast for reception directly in millions of homes" the motion-picture industry would continue to thrive.[86] But despite these soothing disclaimers, as television became more visible in the 1930s rival media grew even more anxious and, in some instances, displayed overt hostility.

But despite such understandable misgivings and hostility, the effort to promote and market the new television medium raced forward. Confidence born of the startling successes of the early experiments encouraged entrepreneurs across the country to enter the television market as broadcasters and manufacturers. An optimism in the economy and in technology characteristic of the decade of the Jazz Age, still undampened by the newer realities of depression finances, supported such ventures. For the nascent television industry, the result was a minor boom, lasting from 1928 to 1933. And although the boom collapsed because of the limitations of the mechanical apparatus then employed, valuable advances in engineering and programming techniques were achieved that were eventually employed by the high-definition television industry that was soon to dominate the medium.

3

The First Television Boom

What exactly was television like in the boom years of 1928–33, that it could stimulate so much optimism and enthusiasm, as well as arouse some muted misgivings? Although stations existed across the nation, three separate television centers eventually emerged that characterize the events of this period. New York, Boston, and Chicago each developed a unique television style displaying very different broadcast conditions and manufacturing techniques. But all three had regularly scheduled programming, with firms retailing receiving equipment and promoting the medium as a whole. It was from these three centers that the television boom pervaded the rest of the country, especially as their telecasts on the shortwave channels could be received in large parts of the nation. A discussion of the efforts to promote mechanical television in these three centers, and a few other unique endeavors, will serve to demonstrate both the significant contributions of low-definition television and the fatal flaw that led to its demise.

JENKINS TELEVISION

New York's television activity can only properly be grasped by first looking at the work in Washington of the most prominent television researcher in America then, C. Francis Jenkins.[1] It will be recalled that the Jenkins Laboratories at 1519 Connecticut Avenue had begun regularly scheduled telecasts on 2 July 1928 over W3XK on 6420 and 1605 kHz. Transmission over this station had actually been inaugurated two months earlier, on Saturday morning, 5 May 1928, with an elaborate invitation announcing the "birth of a new industry—Radio Movies—i.e., Pantomine Pictures by Radio for Home Entertainment."[2] Then the following year, on 22 July Jenkins opened a new broadcast facility on Brookville Pike, about ten miles from Washington, and telecast from it nightly, except Sunday, from 8:00 to 9:00 P.M., on 2000–2100 and 2850–2950 kHz., two of the newly authorized television channels. He also briefly experimented at this time with two-way telecasts over W10XU from a small aircraft flying between Washington and Norfolk or

Philadelphia, using battery-powered equipment.[3] All of these original telecasts were silhouette "movie stories," although by 1930 the station was
experimenting with half-tone still pictures, usually of Lee De Forest, Delbert E. Replogle, and Jenkins. These transmissions were of 48-line frames,
15 frames per second; they had now also been extended from 8:00 to 10:00
P.M. Between visual "movie stories," station identification was made on
audio.[4]

The nature and the transmission range of Jenkins's broadcasts can be
inferred from viewers' reception reports. A Goshen, Indiana, viewer reported, "I have received parts of your baseball game, seen Sambo, the Little
Girl Bouncing the Ball, The Fight, and parts of many others." A Philadelphia
man "looked in" to see

> your picture of a man (Red Mike) sawing the bars of a jail, bending the bars and
> escaping. A man playing a violin and dancing and another man playing a
> saxophone. People listening to a Radio and hearing "Jail Break." A preacher
> named Rev. Sapp. In another picture I saw a pitcher, catcher, umpire and a
> man batting.

And from Baltimore a viewer reported tuning in

> on the last part of the film "That's That." It seemed to consist of much love at
> the breakfast table, many embraces, kissing and a good-bye and then the
> husband going back to the job swining [sic] the pick-ace [sic] and stopping to
> limber up his muscles and finally streaking for home and more embraces.[5]

New "radio movies" continued to attract further attention. From Royal
Center, Indiana, a viewer reported:

> The picture of the Little Dutch Girl also comes in good, I notice she sets a
> bucket under the pump, which is a pitcher pump and pumps it full of water,
> then picks it up and takes it to where she is working, she scrubs and cleans
> everything up in find [sic] shape. . . . Then there is the one called the "Big
> Fight" where the 2 fellows come into the ring, shake hands and go to it, when
> the one is knocked out I can see the referee count to ten very clearly. Then
> there is the picture of the Gold Rush this is also a very good picture. . . . The
> the [sic] picture of "Television Song and Vaudeville Skit", this is also a very
> good picture, one can almost tell the words the lady is singing by the move-
> ments of her lips.[6]

But a television critic in Macon, Georgia, who saw the telecast had a
complaint about this last film shown: "The girl singing 'The Television Song'
came in both times you showed her tonight, but I like her better alone than
with the other [male] singer who appears with her in part of the film."[7]
It should be remembered that such silent film performances would not

have seemed peculiar to an audience at this time. After all, sound motion pictures were still a very recent innovation.

Concerning the production of these programs, Jenkins explained that "our organization is complete and self-sufficient. We write our own scenarios; we built and operate our own movie-studio, the only one of its kind in the world; we designed, built and operate our own film developing and printing equipment, and do our own editing and cutting."[8]

By May 1931 the operation had become more elaborate. Telecasts were now from 4:00 to 5:00 and 9:30 to 11:30 P.M. daily, except Sundays and holidays, with 90 percent of these now being half-tones of 60-line frames at 20 frames per second. A radio station, W3XJ on 1604 kHz., had been added so that synchronized sight and sound could be transmitted. A further significant improvement was introduced in the following months when transmission of "radio movies" was supplemented with live transmissions employing flying-spot, direct-pickup disc scanning. Acoustical quality for W3XJ's audio transmissions was also improved by the installation of special drapes and heavy carpet in the studio. Another new feature of the telecast facility was the suspension of the photocells on ropes so that they could be changed from smaller to larger light fields, depending on the size of the subject to be scanned.[9]

These improvements naturally allowed for more sophisticated programming. Now readings, vocal solos, monologues, dialogues, instrumental solos, tap dancing, and chalk talks were transmitted along with the silent "radio movies." Even two or three people singing together could now be telecast simultaneously. However, despite all of these improvements, at times it was necessary for an announcer to explain the image, "thus aiding the eye in completing the picture."[10]

By the end of 1931 W3XK had moved to headquarters on Silver Spring Road, in Wheaton, Maryland. Now that direct-pickup equipment was being employed, new programming requirements had to be considered. In the new facility experiments with makeup were conducted to determine which complexions reproduced best. And for a puppet show of three plays, miniature scenery with a toy train was tested for effect.[11]

But Jenkins did have trouble from one aspect of this programming, which illustrates the dilemma of the small researcher with limited funds. The FRC, in 1930, suggested that he was transmitting commercial messages. Jenkins admitted to promoting the sale of his television equipment but insisted that it was not for profit but for help in financing his work. His explanation well demonstrates the techniques used by these smaller firms:

> We do offer the radio amateur kit parts for the construction of an excellent receiver for our broadcast movie stories. The kit includes (except motor) every essential in the construction of a really excellent receiver, i.e. a superior *neon* lamp specially made for this kit; a lamp holder; a 12-inch scanning disc (die

perforated); a shaft and cast frame mounting therefor; a motor-hub and driving disc therefor; and a synchronizing screw. All these cost the amateur but $7.50 packed and postage paid,—less than the cost to us,—and the pictures of this assembled receiver are good pictures, the equal, the superior of some, of those obtained with any other 12-inch disc receiver at any price.

But we can well afford this loss because by making these receiver parts available at this low cost we enlist the cooperation of the amateurs of the country in helping us improve our methods, our mechanism, and our broadcasts.

The great corporations engaged in television experimentation have distant receiving stations under their own supervision, and maintained at their own expense. I cannot afford these facilities. Hence our solicitation of the cooperation of the amateur. We broadcast on a printed schedule. . . . The amateur knows where and when to look for us.[12]

Of course, Jenkins was not allowed to continue this solicitation, and the FRC launched an investigation to ascertain whether any other stations were engaged in similar practices.

Jenkins's description of his receiver kit, in addition to the W3XK quarterly reports, clearly demonstrates his abandonment of the prismatic rings in favor of the Nipkow disc. But he found that such receivers suffered from a serious physical limitation: a 2-by-2-inch picture required a disc 36 inches in diameter, while a 4-by-4-inch picture would require a disc 6 feet in diameter.[13] Jenkins therefore manufactured two types of receiving equipment: an inexpensive model employing a Nipkow lens disc and a more sophisticated apparatus using a new device, the drum scanner.[14] This Jenkins innovation was also alternated with the lens disc in his film-transmission apparatus as well.[15]

The drum was a hollow cylinder 7 inches in diameter and 3 inches in length, with a hub that extended from within the hollow cylinder outside to a small motor. Forty-eight (and later 60) apertures, arranged in 4 helical turns, were punctured into the peripheral wall of the drum. Inside the drum hub was a 4-target neon lamp; between the lamp and the drum's periphery were tiny quartz rods, each ending at one of the apertures. Light would travel through these rods to one of the neon targets, located under each of the 4 sets of apertures. Such a drum scanner, making 4 revolutions for each complete picture, produced a 2-inch square picture that was then magnified to about 6 inches. According to Jenkins, "In daily use it has been found that five or six people, the whole family, can very conveniently enjoy the story told in the moving pictures." By increasing the size of the drum, a picture magnified to 10 square inches was possible.[16]

At first the original image was reflected by a mirror onto the magnifying lens, but later the motor and drum were mounted vertically in the receiver's cabinet, so that the image could be viewed directly through the magnifying lens. Still a further modification would replace the quartz rods with a selector shutter with carved slots to mask all but the 12 apertures appropriate to each revolution of the drum. The television receiver was definitely improving in quality and seemed to promise a bright future.[17]

But in December 1931 Jenkins Television Corporation of New York announced it was transferring its portable station, W2XAP, to Washington, where it was to be operated by Jenkins Laboratories in conjunction with commercial sound station WMAL. This arrangement seems to have lasted only until March 1932 and reflected the declining fortunes of Jenkins's Washington operation.[18]

Although the New York operation was only slightly affected, the Washington laboratory's faltering was clearly a result of Jenkins's own deteriorating health. And on 6 June 1934, after a long illness, C. Francis Jenkins, the American inventor of television, died. With his death the research facility in Washington ceased completely to operate.

But the Jenkins Laboratories had long before become primarily a research arm of an ambitious corporate enterprise organized in the greater New York City area. The engineering technology, receiver designs, and programming experiments developed in Washington were to be promoted commercially by this aggressive new firm in the nation's largest market.

Jenkins Television Corporation was founded in December 1928, with a reported $10 million investment by New York bankers. The new concern was to function, originally, as a holding company, manufacturer, and distributor of the inventions of the Jenkins Laboratories in Washington. It was expected that the new operation would derive its profits from the sale of television transmitters and receivers, motion-picture prismatic rings, the transmission of facsimile and television, and the advertising revenue earned from these transmissions. James W. Garside, president of De Forest Radio Company, was the firm's first president, and A. J. Drexel Biddle, Jr., its first chairman of the board. In October of the following year, De Forest Radio acquired a majority interest in Jenkins Television, although the two firms remained separate.[19]

The new operation was originally located at 346 Claremont Avenue, in Jersey City. Here Jenkins Television established its manufacturing plant, and it was also from this plant that the company first transmitted from its new television station, W2XCR, broadcasting "radio movies" in halftones of 48-line frames, 15 frames a second.[20] The firm soon began retailing both Jenkins brand television receiver kits as well as complete sets. After reception on these early Jenkins disc sets, one observer wrote, "The pictures so far reproduced with apparatus which is available for home use are small—in the neighborhood of 1 × 1 and 1½ inches—and often are not any too clear. . . . Pictures can be received, and it will not be long before they will be bigger and better and will approach perfection."[21]

By 1931 the receivers had achieved some elegance, while still retaining a relatively moderate price. A "Jenkins Universal Television Receiver" in a mantle-type cabinet sold for $69.50, although $13.45 for tubes had to be added to this price; other models sold for $100 and $135, while the "Jenkins Radiovisor" kit was $42.50 plus $5.00 for the magnifying lens.[22]

The firm also marketed transmission equipment. A 1932 advertisement proudly announced, "Television broadcasting enters the era of genuine entertainment with the introduction of the Jenkins Television Camera. This direct pick-up method replaces the familiar flying spot with its many inherent limitations."[23]

Besides advertising, the firm engaged in a variety of promotional strategies. For instance, in 1929 they sponsored a "Jenkins Prize Essay Contest," the winner—in this case a New York City College student—receiving a Jenkins television receiver, personally awarded by Lee De Forest.[24]

But the primary means of stimulating public enthusiasm for television was in broadcasting. At the early demonstrations, television "specials" were staged to attract public attention. For instance, in August 1930 receivers were installed in various outdoor locations in the New York area to enable the public to watch a program featuring Ethel Barrymore, her daughter, Lee De Forest, Benny Rubin (a popular vaudeville and movie personality), the New York commissioner of health, a cartoonist, some humorists, and a group of dancers.[25]

However the main strategy employed for arousing public support was the introduction of regularly scheduled telecasting. By the fall of 1930 W2XCR was on the air weekdays from 8:00 to 9:00 P.M., with the synchronized audio portion sent over the De Forest radio station in Passaic. According to a government report, many of these early programs were repetitions of a single format. The filmed program opened with "The Television Song," first performed by a young woman singing a verse; she then faded out to be replaced by a young man in evening clothes singing the next verse; then the two soloists were joined by a chorus for the finale. The radio inspector viewing the telecast reported that the faces of the singers were "seen with excellent definition considering the limitations of forty-eight line scanning." The heads moved about and the motion of the lips was in "perfect synchronization" with the sound of their voices. Besides this opening number, there was usually a "vaudeville sketch," in this instance consisting of two male singers, one playing an accordion accompaniment to their song; in the middle of this song they "lapse into a humorous dialogue which is very amusing." During station identification the announcer, who was seen and heard by direct pickup, mentioned Jenkins television sets and kits, although not mentioning any prices. Following was a film of Lee De Forest speaking on the possibilities of television followed by Delbert E. Replogle, vice-president of Jenkins Television, explaining how the sound and film pictures were being transmitted.[26]

In April 1931 Jenkins Television ambitiously augmented its telecasting

format. W2XCR, transmitting on the 2000–2100-kHz. channel, was transferred to a new $65,000 studio at 655 Fifth Avenue in New York. It now
transmitted 60-line pictures at 20 frames per second, with a 5000-watt output. The telecast schedule was expanded on weekdays to 3:00 to 5:00 and
6:00 to 8:00 P.M., and on Sundays from 6:00 to 8:00 P.M.; the sound portion
was carried by commercial radio station WGBS, 780 kHz. Each program was
to consist of film for the first hour and live entertainment for the second.

The new facilities were lavish and sophisticated. In a booth to the side of
the studio was the flying-spot "televisor," its scanning beam reflected into
two banks of photocells. Attached to the studio was the control room for
monitoring the video images, maintaining synchronization, and regulating
the sound signal. On a lower floor was a film machine for the transmission of
standard motion pictures and the transmitter for broadcasting the pictures
through the aerial on the building's roof. A reception room beside the studio
allowed visitors to watch telecasts on monitors.

For the April 27 opening, special arrangements had been made. Television and sound receivers were set up in the Aeolian Hall at Fifth Avenue and
Fifty-fourth Street for a public demonstration. The inaugural telecast included a long star-studded list of performers, including Lionell Atwill and
Gertrude Lawrence.[27]

This grand opening seemed to signal the dawning of a new and prosperous
television era. The *New York Times* reported, "Radio retailers are expecting
a rich harvest to grow from the seeds of television now being planted. . . .
The dealers realize, however, that the reaping may not begin in earnest for a
year or more."[28]

At first this optimism appeared well founded. Replogle reported to the
FRC that the early months of transmission were concerned with determining the potential of the flying-spot method of televising. "We tried long shots
and close-ups of dancers and every conceivable type that we could bring
before the televisor. In this way we have secured considerable information
as to what is good for televising and what is not." To determine reception
conditions, monitors were set up in department stores in New York; of
course this also attracted the public's attention. The station was also receiving reception reports from Boston, Philadelphia, Baltimore, St. Louis, New
Orleans, and from Canada. And when it was found that the flying spot was
not well adapted to studio telecasting, new camera techniques were introduced, along with improved video signal amplifier equipment.[29]

Even when WGBS was purchased from the General Broadcasting System,
in October 1931, by a firm controlled by William Randolph Hearst, Replogle, for Jenkins Television, was optimistic. He reported to the FRC that
his firm expected more space to be made available to them and that this
would further improve their programming.[30]

But by the new year, W2XCR was in serious trouble. A radio supervisor

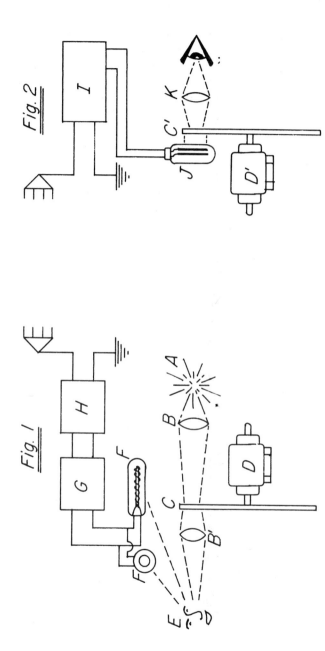

Line diagram of a complete mechanical television system employing the flying-spot technique. *Figure 1* represents the transmitter: A is the source of the scanning light; B and B′ are focusing lenses; C is the disc; D is the synchronous motor; E is the image scanned by the beam of light emitted from A; F is the photocells that produce the visual signal from the light reflected off E during the scanning; G is the amplifier for the photoelectric current; H is the radio transmitter. *Figure 2* represents the receiver; the signal enters at I, the radio receiver, where it affects J, the neon glow tube, whose output passes through the receiver's disc, C′, driven by the synchronous motor, D′; the picture is viewed through lens K. (Adapted from Edwin B. Kurtz, *Pioneering in Educational Television*, University of Iowa Press. Used with permission)

reported in January 1932 that the station had abandoned film telecasts, as it did not have the funds to purchase new motion pictures.[31] Then in February the joint president of Jenkins Television and De Forest Radio, Leslie S. Gordon, requested the stockholders of the two corporations to allow the Jenkins assets to be sold to De Forest and the corporation to be liquidated. Gordon explained that the "commercial development of television has been slower and more costly than originally contemplated."[32] The consolidation was effected in March.[33] But by June, the De Forest Radio Company itself went into receivership, and in March 1933 RCA paid $500,000 for the company's assets, including Jenkins and De Forest television patent rights.[34] RCA, no longer interested in mechanical television, abandoned the Jenkins television operation.

The collapse of Jenkins Television was the result of a combination of several interrelated factors: limited revenues from equipment sales because of public dissatisfaction with television programming; lack of entertaining programming because of a relatively small budget and crude picture quality; the absence of supplementary revenue from advertising, a result of FRC policy; and the constricted depression financial conditions, which reduced the availability of speculative capital. But the engineering knowledge, programming experience, and promotional techniques developed by Jenkins Television would be utilized in succeeding years by more successful ventures.

CBS IN NEW YORK

However, besides W2XCR, there were three other competing New York television stations offering at least some entertainment to the public, including outlets operated by the two national radio networks. The Columbia Broadcasting System, then only three years old, applied for its first television license, in August 1930, in New York through its subsidiary, the Atlantic Broadcasting Corporation, operator of radio station WABC.[35] As the *New York Times* explained, "Realizing that television will be put on a commercial basis in the future, the Columbia Broadcasting System is seeking an entry into the experimental field so as to be prepared for competition when radio is supplemented by visual broadcasting."[36] The new station was located on the twenty-third floor of the CBS Building, 485 Madison Avenue, and operated on the 2750–2850 kHz. channel with a 500-watt RCA transmitter.[37] CBS, not then involved in manufacturing or extensive laboratory research, was motivated by the commercial prospects of the new medium and intended to concentrate on program development.

On 21 July 1931 CBS's new visual facility, W2XAB, sending a 60-line picture at 20 frames per second, was officially inaugurated by Major James J. Walker, who lifted the curtain on the station's bank of photoelectric cells, and then introduced Miss Television, Natalie Towers, to the viewing audience. The sound portion of the broadcast went out over CBS's shortwave radio outlet W2XE on 6120 kHz.[38]

The station broadcast a forty-nine-hour regular weekly schedule, from 2:00 to 6:00 and 8:00 to 11:00 P.M. Typical of CBS's extensive and varied programming is the day's selection for Monday, 2 November 1931:

2:00–6:00	Experimental Sight Programs
8:00–8:30	At-Home Party: Alvin E. Hauser and others
8:30–8:45	Television Mystics: Richard Kenny
8:45–9:00	Doris Sharp, television crooner
9:00–9:30	Columbia Television Education Feature: piano lessons
9:30–9:45	Julya Mahony, soprano
9:45–10:00	Whitman Bennett: The Art of Bookbinding
10:00–10:15	Kay Faye
10:15–10:30	Roger Kinne, baritone
10:30–10:45	Kathryn Parsons, The Girl O'Yesterday
10:45–11:00	The Singing Vagabond: Artellis Dickson

The following Saturday, from 2:00 to 5:30 P.M., W2XAB telecast a football game, employing portable transmitting equipment.[39]

CBS used no film in its broadcasts; its direct-pickup programs consisted primarily of piano and bridge lessons, dancing, boxing, cartoons, and fashion shows, besides test transmissions. A reviewing supervisor of radio estimated that 75 percent of its programming had entertainment value.[40] By the summer of 1932 baseball scores, a "Television Beauty Review," and a mystery series, "The Television Ghost—Murder Stories as told by the ghost of the murdered. Close up projection with weird effects" had all been added to the schedule.[41]

Related to the development of television programming was experimentation with studio requirements. Tests were conducted at W2XAB on the proper hues for facial makeup, the best types of color backdrops, studio lighting, reflectors, and the effects of color filters for eliminating excessive light thrown on the subjects being televised. Field tests were conducted to locate the direction and distance at which fading and double images occurred and to determine the causes of interference. Monitors were also distributed for public demonstrations, where station representatives explained television techniques and solicited the public's comments on what sort of programs they expected.[42]

However, concern over programming also led CBS to a significant engineering innovation. Station officials found that the necessity of having two receivers, one for the video and one for the sound transmission, discouraged many potential viewers. So on 21 July 1932 a new technique was introduced whereby both sight and sound could be transmitted simultaneously on one channel, the sound portion on a carrier wave 45 kHz. above or below the video carrier.[43]

But by 1933 it was evident to CBS officials that the era of commercial television was not about to begin and that W2XAB's programming was more expensive than the investment was worth. The station was therefore disbanded. However, although CBS television retreated from public broadcasting, the network did not abandon the new medium. In July 1932 it was granted a license for a low-power VHF station, W2XAX. In May 1939, when CBS was again pursuing an aggressive public television project, W2XAX's call letters were changed to the more familiar W2XAB. This station is now WCBS-TV.[44] As early as 1929 William S. Paley had felt that the new medium offered great potential to the communications industry, and the network never ceased to be involved with it.

NBC IN NEW YORK

With David Sarnoff also a staunch supporter of video broadcasting, RCA established station W2XBS at its Van Corlandt Park research facility in New York in April 1928. By 1929 it was broadcasting a 60-frame picture, 20 frames per second, regularly from 7:00 to 9:00 P.M. daily on the 2000–2100-kHz. channel. Alfred N. Goldsmith, vice-president of RCA, stressed that these telecasts were only experimental, although he believed that they "will in due course evolve into a service to the public on a commercial basis similar to that of sound broadcasting."[45] In July 1930, as part of the radio-group unification scheme, and also because of Sarnoff's growing conviction that television's future lay with the cathode-ray tube and not the disc, W2XBS was transferred to NBC.[46] RCA now established its primary research facilities in Camden, New Jersey, where it operated W3XAD (and W3XAK in Bound Brook, New Jersey). First on shortwave and later on VHF, this station carried no public programming but served as an intrinsic component of the laboratory facility, much as had been the case with the earlier work by GE in Schenectady.

W2XBS continued its regularly scheduled transmissions from 214 West Forty-second Street. At the end of 1931 it operated on a weekday schedule from 2:00 to 5:00 and from 7:00 to 10:00 P.M., transmitting live subjects, photographs, revolving statues, and various printed signs. Although these telecasts were not intended as entertainment, they did attract "numerous reports of reception . . . from the Southern, Middle Western and New England states and a steadily increasing number of observers in the vicinity of Manhattan."[47]

In 1931 NBC introduced two modifications to its New York television operation. First, it requested that its newly acquired Chicago station, W9XR, be allowed to switch from the 2750–2850-kHz. channel to 2100–2200 kHz., so that its broadcasts could be coordinated with those of W2XBS, now also transmitting on this channel.[48] However, NBC soon abandoned this

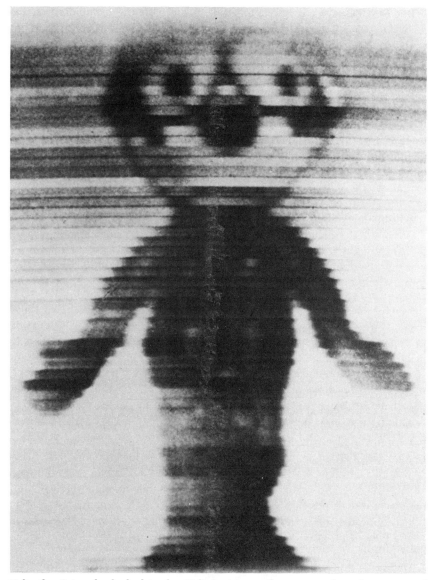

Felix the Cat as he looked in the 60-line pictures that appeared on the screens of television receivers during a 1928 telecast by RCA-NBC. (Courtesy of RCA)

networking project entirely as a result of the second development of that year.

In July NBC announced a most portentous decision. Its television studios were to be installed in the Empire State Building. The network's president, Merlin H. Aylesworth, predicted that "after about a year of intensive experimental tests under actual working conditions television would be developed for public use."[49] These first RCA-NBC field tests were conducted in late 1931 and early 1932. Separate video and audio transmitters operated on the 40- to 80-MHz. channels, transmitting a 120-line picture at 24 frames per second. Since a 120-aperture disc would have been too cumbersome, a 60-aperture disc was driven at twice the normal speed. Another unique feature of these transmissions was that the scanning disc, in addition to picture apertures, also had apertures for transmitting vertical and horizontal synchronizing pulses as part of the video signal.[50]

Although these field tests had no entertainment value, amateurs with 60-aperture discs did "look in." They very soon devised a technique for merging the double 60-line pictures received from the 120-line transmission into a single image by the use of a mirror.[51]

But these 1931–32 tests from the Empire State Building were the last that RCA-NBC transmitted from New York employing exclusively mechanical devices. Already in these tests, cathode-ray-tube receivers were being employed. And in the next series of tests, in 1933, electronic apparatuses were used for both transmission and reception. Once perfected, electronic television would be able to meet the requirements set by the government for commercialization. But Aylesworth, typical of so many, had been too optimistic. The perfection of the new technology would take several more years.

But all along RCA-NBC had taken a completely different approach to its television broadcasting than had all other such ventures. Having the need neither to solicit amateur participation nor to press for immediate commercialization, no effort was undertaken to develop entertaining programming. RCA-NBC had the resources to be methodical and patient. Hence their approach was to develop one system at a time: only after high-definition television had been achieved could programming be properly considered and only after programming had been sufficiently investigated could television be actively promoted.

However, this policy did not mean that the public was ignored. RCA and NBC officials spoke often and enthusiastically about the potential of television, and as early as 16 January 1930 a public demonstration of a W2XBS telecast was arranged at Proctor's Fifty-eighth Street Theatre. The strategy was to maintain enough of television's visibility to stimulate public interest without then discouraging this interest by confronting viewers with an unsatisfactory product.

HOGAN IN NEW YORK

New York's fourth station was the smallest and least ambitious of all the area's ventures; yet despite this, it outlasted both the Jenkins and the CBS efforts, because, like NBC, its owner turned to a new technology. This station was operated by John V. L. Hogan, a founder of the Institute of Radio Engineers and a researcher in radio and facsimile. W2XR was licensed to Hogan's Radio Pictures, Incorporated, in March 1929, in New York City, but Hogan moved it to a mercantile and manufacturing district in Long Island City to avoid causing radio interference to residential listeners.[52] By 1930 Hogan was transmitting silhouettes on a regular schedule and offered to mail literature on television to viewers.[53] By 1932 W2XR was using standard 35-mm films of figures, still pictures, rotating figures, various size letters, and silhouette cartoons to send a 60-line picture at 20 frames per second. A government inspector estimated that half of the station's transmissions could be considered entertainment.[54]

Hogan added sound to his video broadcasts in the form of light classical music. In 1934 W2XR was devoted exclusively to sound broadcasting, while the video outlet, now used purely for research, received the call letters W2XDR. Hogan's Radio Pictures, now involved in research on the cathode-ray tube, continued to maintain its television license until the end of 1940, while his W2XR became commercial radio station WQXR in 1936 and was later sold to the *New York Times*.[55]

BOSTON'S SHORTWAVE AND TELEVISION CORPORATION

Closely related to television developments in New York, and in fact combining portions of the disparate histories of Jenkins Television and Radio Pictures, were the experiences of the television pioneers in the second of the nation's video centers, Boston. In New York there were four competing operations, two with national connections; in Boston there was only one, albeit very enterprising, local endeavor. Like Jenkins Television, its attempt to create a viable broadcasting and manufacturing enterprise based on mechanical techniques collapsed, but on the other hand, like Radio Pictures, it survived into the era of public electronic telecasting.

Although experimental telecasts were first made in the Boston area in 1928, the city's television history really begins with the organization of the Shortwave and Television Corporation and its application for a television construction permit in September 1929.[56] The request was authorized by the FRC, and W1XAV went on the air in January 1930. These first telecasts went out with a 48-line picture at 20 frames per second on the 2100–2200-

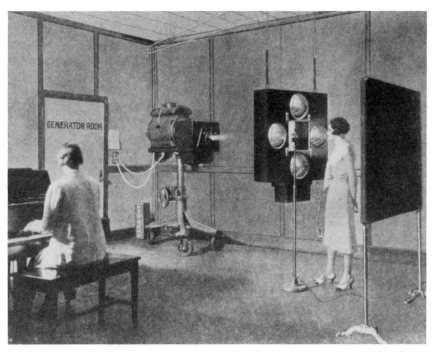

Studio of Boston's visual station W1XAV and sound station W1XAU. Note the photocells suspended from the ceiling in this flying-spot scanning arrangement. (From "The Romance of Short Waves and Television," 1931)

kHz. channel, using a 50-watt transmitter. In December the station switched to the 2850–2950-kHz. channel, and in March 1931 a 60-line picture was being telecast with power increased to 1000 watts.

At first W1XAV's video was synchronized with sound from commercial radio station WEEI, and later with WNAC. And finally, Shortwave and Television Corporation began operating its own audio facility, W1XAU, on 1604 kHz., just above the standard medium-wave band.[57] In October 1931 they began transmitting with a second television station, W1XG on the VHF bands with a 30-watt transmitter.[58] By this time a regular daily schedule, including both direct pickup and silent films with musical accompaniment, was being telecast from 2:00 to 4:00 and 7:30 to 10:30 P.M.[59]

Describing the station's programming plans, Hollis S. Baird, Shortwave and Television's chief engineer, explained that the first step was

> the projection of talking-picture films which will bring to the home entertainment based on sight and sound. . . .

In addition, . . . news flashes need no longer be sent out audibly, for a news event recorded by sight and sound can be put on the air the day it happens, in the evening, when everyone will be at home to enjoy it. Then comes the more involved question of studio productions, direct pickup entertainment.[60]

In addition to engaging in the typical promotional ploys, Shortwave and Television Corporation was unusual in actively encouraging visitors to come to the studio and even to participate in the telecasts. This policy was explicitly included in W1XAV's hourly audio station-identification announcement:

This is the Boston Television Station W1XAV.

We hope you are enjoying the pictures, ladies and gentlemen, which are being shown from our studios at 70 Brookline Avenue, Boston, Mass.

Write and tell us how well you are receiving us. Write and ask for Television information. We will be glad to forward it to you. Come and visit us here at our studios and learn about television transmission. You can be televised or you can watch your friends while they are televised. We repeat the address of our studio, 70 Brookline Avenue, Boston, Mass., just above Kenmore Square.

The Boston Television Station W1XAV now continues with the picture. Look in.[61]

To assist the public to "look in," Shortwave and Television manufactured a series of commercial receiver sets and kits of a unique design. The firm wanted to be able to market their equipment for reception of stations in both the Boston and greater New York area. However, because a uniform power system for the region did not then exist, the use of a synchronous motor to achieve synchronization between the transmitter and receiver was essential. And to further increase the clarity and stability of the picture, these sets followed a unique design developed by Chief Engineer Hollis S. Baird.[62]

[Its] scanning apparatus consists of a band or belt of thin metal in which apertures are punched. The band is placed upon a drum that is rotated by means of an electric motor. The theory of the belt rotating horizontally is to remove the curvature from the scanning lines and provide a scanning area that has right angles.[63]

To retail its receivers, Shortwave and Television made them available in S. S. Kresge Green Front 25¢ to $1 Stores on the Eastern Seaboard. A complete receiver kit, including glow lamp, lens, and cabinet, sold for from $75 to $80, and fully assembled models for $100 to $110.[64]

But not everyone greeted W1XAV's telecasts with joy; some Bostonians, in fact, were quite annoyed by the station. As was the case with many of these pioneering efforts, their telecasts at times inadvertently interfered with some medium-wave radio reception. Angry letters to the FRC ensued, such as this typical example:

Why the Commission allows this purely experimental station to operate and disrupt the whole [radio] broadcast band during the hours they do is beyond me. This is another way of saying that if television today could televise something more than a hatchet-face individual who swings around in a chair I should have one of their receivers here in my home. Its present impracticality seems to justify their being kept off the air till midnight.[65]

Another complaint illustrates the frustrations of the radio listener:

This afternoon they interfered with the Marine Band so that it was almost impossible to get it at all. I finally shut it off, the interference was so annoying; and on the Music Appreciation hour, this morning it was the same way.
[I] would like to know if my pleasure has got to be cut off by this nuisance.[66]

The FRC was not always particularly sympathetic to such remonstrances. For example, after investigating the latter complaint, a radio inspector reported that its author was "an elderly woman living at an Old Ladies Home" whose radio was "susceptible to interference of this kind," being a receiver not of "modern design . . . ; in most cases the complaints of interference are received from persons using what might be termed as obsolete receiving equipment."[67] However, in cases where W1XAV was notified of interference complaints it did send technicians to install a wave trap to try to eliminate the problem, though not always very successfully.[68]

By 1934, with the evident decline of shortwave telecasting, W1XAV was discontinued, and General Television Corporation (as the reorganized corporate entity was now called) concentrated on its VHF station, W1XG, which now transmitted at 500 watts. Hollis S. Baird and his associates also constructed their own electronic transmitting equipment for the station, abandoning their original mechanical apparatus.[69] And therefore, unlike most of the smaller firms, Boston's pioneering television effort, now converted to cathode-ray-tube VHF transmissions, survived into the era of commercial television.[70]

TELECASTING IN THE MIDDLE WEST

If most of the television ventures along the Eastern Seaboard were generally similar in design and operation, the major midwestern telecasters employed a distinct technology and represented unique broadcasting efforts. Not surprisingly, Chicago served as the center for middle western telecasting during these boom years, as the city was already the most important source of radio broadcasting in the nation after New York. In fact, by the end of 1931, with the opening of elaborate studios in the Merchandise Mart, two hundred NBC radio shows originated from Chicago, where the network owned two audio stations. CBS also owned a Chicago radio outlet.[71] How-

ever, the networks were not responsible for Chicago's prominence in telecasting. This was the result of a combination of three factors: a unique
mechanical television technique, the involvement of newspapers in telecasting, and the experimentation of universities with television.

The Chicago Federation of Labor pioneered Chicago telecasting in 1928,
over its standard radio station WCFL. Transmission was soon transferred to
the federation's shortwave outlet, W9XAA, located at Navy Pier, on the
2750–2850-kHz. channel; these telecasts were to be transmitted over equipment similar to that used in the East.[72] Yet by 1931 this station was still not
doing any television broadcasting (although it was active as the "Shortwave
Voice of Labor"), and its engineer reported to the FRC that it did not intend
to begin telecasting until television had first been "perfected" in the
laboratory.[73] In fact, the Chicago supervisor of radio reported in March 1931
that "no such [television] transmitter is now maintained by the
Federation."[74] Before television was "perfected" mechanical television on
shortwave had become obsolete.

Chicago's centrality derived from a scanning system developed by Ulises
A. Sanabria and manufactured by an ambitious firm, Western Television
Corporation. In 1929 Sanabria, a twenty-two-year-old inventor, designed a
scanning disc having 45 apertures arranged around its periphery in three
spirals. Thus instead of scanning each line successively, as the disc rotated,
the first spiral scanned lines 1, 4, 7, 10, 13, and so on; the second, 2, 5, 8, 11,
14, and so on; and the third 3, 6, 9, 12, 15, and so on. In the receiver, these
three crude images ("fields") were superimposed to make up a complete
frame, and 15 of these composite frames were transmitted each second. Such
"interlacing" of scanning lines increases the definition of the image and
reduces flicker without necessitating an addition in frequency bandwidth.[75]
Rights to Sanabria's scanning method were assigned to Western Television
Corporation of Chicago.

This firm was an aggressive promoter and manufacturer of television
equipment. Besides providing scanning equipment for Chicago's two main
stations, and also for the station at the State University of Iowa and for
Canada's first station, operated by *La Presse* in Montreal, Western Television explored a broad range of possible uses for television. Often these
possibilities were announced by means of interest-generating public
demonstrations.[76] For instance, in January 1931, together with the *Chicago
Daily News*, the firm invited six hundred Chicago-area school principals to
visit a television studio "as a first step in keeping in touch with the scientific
development that may become a factor in modern education methods."[77]

The same month, Western Television staged a demonstration of another of
the possible uses of television, this one in business. According to one reporter, "television once more showed its practicability yesterday when it was
used for the transmission of stock reports. . . . Prominent members of the

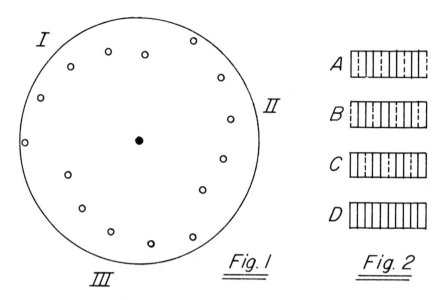

Sanabria's unique scanning disc and interlaced scanning. *Figure 1* illustrates Sanabria's scanning disc with its 3 sets of 5-aperture spirals (unlike his actual system, where the sets consisted of 15 apertures each). *Figure 2* illustrates how this produced an interlaced image in the receiver: the dotted line in A represents that portion of the image scanned by the set of apertures I on the disc; B and C represent the results of the scanning of spirals II and III respectively; D represents the composite image received after one complete revolution of the disc. (Adapted from Sanabria's 1931 U.S. patent, no. 1,805,848)

Hollis S. Baird (left) and Ulises A. Sanabria. (From "The Romance of Short Waves and Television," 1931)

stock exchanges and others high up in the financial world were witnesses to the demonstration and saw the reproduction of the ticker tape on a large screen, as well as upon the screen of a machine made for installation on an office desk."[78]

The "large screen" mentioned in this article was still a further example of Western Television's promotional schemes in the Chicago area. And Sanabria took his version of 6-foot-screen television east to Boston and to the Radio-Electrical World's Fair at New York's Madison Square Garden, gaining national publicity for it.[79]

But as with similar firms in New York and Boston, it was regularly scheduled telecasting that was the primary means employed to promote television. Western Television Corporation operated one of Chicago's two television stations broadcasting regularly scheduled programming. Its station, W9XAO, transmitted the video signal only, while the audio portion went out over standard commercial radio station WIBO, owned by Nelson Brothers Bond and Mortgage Company, the original 1929 licensee of the television station as well.

Western Television began telecasting over W9XAO on the 2000–2100-kHz. channel in 1930 and by 1931 was transmitting on a regular weekday schedule, averaging about three hours of entertainment each day. Besides these regular broadcasts, the station was also utilized for various experimental transmissions. W9XAO's regular programming included silent cartoons, boxing, dancing, musical variety, and live interviews (including with Tom Mix and "Jean Harlow, blond"). And through the autumn of 1931, several Saturday-afternoon football games were telecast.[80]

These transmissions elicited enthusiastic reception reports from Chicago viewers and also from several midwestern states; good reception was reported from as far as 450 miles away. Typical of these reports is this one from an early television reviewer: "We again received your station W9XAO later in the evening for a while you were broadcasting full length pictures of two men who were sparring and wrestling, also saw the good looking girl later in the program."[81]

In January 1931 the station, together with WIBO, telecast a musical comedy, "Their Television Honeymoon," which had "been prepared especially for adaption to television facilities and studio techniques." This required that there be three separate scanners, two for closeups and one for long shots and full lengths. Separate photoelectric cell banks also were necessary for closeup and full-length shots, as were a variety of camera lenses.[82] After several more such performances, new studios and equipment were installed in W9XAO's 6312 Broadway headquarters. "Such equipment is to facilitate the most ambitious programs attempted over television," as a station representative announced.[83]

But despite such ambition and optimism, Western Television Corporation and its station W9XAO did not survive. In addition to the usual forces weakening the smaller television enterprises of the era, there was an added difficulty for this one. In 1931 the FRC had ordered WIBO (along with WPCC, the station sharing its 560-kHz. frequency) to close down so that a Gary, Indiana, outlet could be assigned instead to its frequency. WIBO appealed to the federal courts, but on 8 May 1933 the U.S. Supreme Court upheld the commission's authority, and WIBO terminated its broadcasts.[84] Without this separate audio outlet or the capital to develop its own, W9XAO could no longer provide any semblance of interesting programming, and it disappeared too.

But W9XAO was not Chicago's leading television station at the time. That station was W9XAP, owned originally by the *Chicago Daily News*, and later by NBC. The newspaper, then owner of clear-channel radio station WMAQ, adopted the Sanabria equipment manufactured by Western Television for its station. The stated purpose of this facility was to make Chicago "the television centre of the United States." To accomplish this, the station's "television experts, taking a page from the experience of the sound broadcaster, apparently realize that the program is the main thing." And from the new "talking" motion pictures, the staff understood that good programming means a wide variety of talent arranged in smooth production.[85]

W9XAP began telecasting on the 2100–2200-kHz. channel on 27 August 1930, from studios on the twenty-fourth and twenty-fifth floors of the Daily News Building at 400 West Madison Street, using a 1000-watt transmitter located on the roof. The audio was broadcast over WMAQ. For the first show the announcer was Bill Hay, later famous as the "Amos 'n Andy" announcer, while Ken Murray came over from the Palace Theatre to perform, as did Ransom Miles Sherman, a member of radio's "Three Doctors" comedy team.[86]

On 7 January 1930, five days before W9XAO staged its first televised drama, "The Maker of Dreams," starring Irene Walker, the *Daily News* proudly announced: "The broadcast is to usher in a new era in television. It represents the first attempt to show anything of its kind in the midwest, and what has been done previously of a similar nature in the east, was done in an experimental way and for theatrical purposes. The program tonight is for the benefit of the owners of television receivers."[87]

However, beyond whatever entertainment value there was in this production, a great deal was learned about staging techniques for such "talking movies of the air." Central to the station's considerations was the realization that television drama presents a different set of demands on the director, crew, and actors than do motion pictures. The newspaper's radio reporter, in a feature article, explained that when motion pictures are made, the shots are registered upon the film and placed in proper sequence in the editing department. Not so with television. The continuity must run through as arranged, necessitating instantaneous changes from long to short shots. And besides the need to adapt to this, there were other technical matters that had to be resolved. These included television acting requirements, materials and colors for the actors' costumes, television makeup (in this case specially designed by Max Factor) and television directing.[88]

As the station's technical department gained confidence, even more complicated productions were televised. For instance, in April 1931 the Goodman Theatre players staged Louis Parker's *The Minuet* for its viewing audience.[89] W9XAP even offered its facilities to the Democratic party if it would hold its 1932 national convention in the city. Station manager William Hedges noted that with a planned increase in transmitter power to 2500 watts a five-hundred-mile reception range could be anticipated, and Western Television officials explained that their equipment could now televise three or four persons grouped together.[90]

But besides such "specials," W9XAP televised a rather unimaginative schedule of regular programs consisting primarily of silent cartoons drawn before the station's scanner or portions of WMAQ's local radio fare. However, these programs were telecast intermittently from about noon until approximately 9:00 P.M., allowing the audience more opportunities to "look in" than most other stations. This programming was further arranged to avoid schedule conflicts with W9XAO.

Typical of Chicago's television fare, then, is this program listing from the Wednesday, 22 April 1931, radio page of the *Daily News:*[91]

TONIGHT:

6:30–6:45	W9XAP	Hal Totten sports news with WMAQ
6:45–7:15	W9XAP	Cartoons by John Mattis
7:30–8:00	W9XAO	Mike and Angelo in cartoons
8:00–8:30	W9XAP	Cartoons by John Mattis
8:30–9:30	W9XAO	Silent variety

TOMORROW AFTERNOON:

12:00–12:30	W9XAP	Cartoons by John Mattis
12:33–12:45	W9XAP	S. W. Lincoln reads flashes of the day. Also by WMAQ
1:00–1:15	W9XAO	Synchronized show with WIBO
1:30–2:15	W9XAP	Cartoons by John Mattis
3:00–3:30	W9XAP	Cartoons by John Mattis
4:00–4:30	W9XAP	Cartoons by John Mattis
5:00–5:45	W9XAP	Cartoons by John Mattis
5:45–6:00	W9XAP	Model Airplane Club. Also by WMAQ

Reception of these programs was relatively widespread. Reports to W9XAP in early 1932 show viewers in seventeen states other than Illinois wrote in, from as far away as Richmond, Virginia; Kloten, North Dakota; and

Los Angeles, California. However, some viewers complained of interference from New York stations.[92]

The cooperation between W9XAP and W9XAO went beyond scheduling and equipment. A photograph in *Television News* well illustrates the close relationship of the *Daily News* to Western Television. In it a Miss Speed Freeman, shown at the controls of a Western Television receiver, is identified as an artist for both stations, and Western Television's research engineer and general broadcast engineer are each shown at the controls of the newspaper's W9XAP.[93] Unlike New York, Chicago's mechanical television was a cooperative venture: Western Television developed the technology and the *Daily News*, the programming.

But the future of W9XAP was altered in November 1931, when it was included in the *Daily News*'s sale of 50-percent ownership in the previously CBS-affiliated WMAQ to NBC.[94] Although not particularly interested in a policy of low-definition program development, the network did continue to operate its Chicago television station until 31 March 1933, when RCA-NBC completely committed themselves to electronic television and to a totally different strategy for the development of the television system.[95]

In fact, W9XAP was NBC's second Chicago-area television outlet. In February 1931 it acquired radio station WENR from the Great Lakes Broadcasting Company, a part of the faltering Insull interests.[96] Along with the audio facility had come W9XR visual station. It had originally been licensed in August 1929, on the 2850–2950-kHz. channel to transmit with 5000 watts, using a standard 24-aperture Nipkow disc at 15 frames per second.[97] And this station definitely did transmit, as there were complaints from viewers that its transmissions interfered with those of Jenkins's Washington station.[98]

After acquiring this television station, NBC was evidently undecided about what use to make of it. As we have seen, in March 1931 NBC requested that W9XR be reassigned to the 2100–2200-kHz. channel so its broadcasts could be coordinated with those of W2XBS (although Chicago's W9XAP already occupied this channel). Then in April 1931 RCA wrote the FRC to withdraw its request for renewal of W9XR, whose license then expired on 1 May 1931.[99] As previously mentioned, by this time RCA and NBC had decided to abandon their New York shortwave television broadcasts. And since W9XR had no regular schedule and could not be received on the Sanabria-designed equipment employed by the other Chicago stations, there was no need to continue operating this obsolescent facility.

Television in Milwaukee

If Chicago's television's outlets had ceased operating by 1934, four other middle western mechanical low-definition stations continued telecasting until almost the end of the decade, longer than any other similar stations in the entire country. One of these was in Milwaukee. Here, as in Chicago, a newspaper, the *Milwaukee Journal*, which already operated commercial radio station WTMJ, entered the television market.

The Journal Company received its license in 1930 for W9XD and contracted with John V. L. Hogan to construct their VHF station to operate on the 43–46-, 48.5–50.3-, and 60–80-MHz. channels. Although the newspaper's officials disagreed with their Chicago counterparts and insisted that television was still only in the experimental stages, especially in the very high frequency ranges used by their station, they decided nevertheless to enter the field because they "realized that if Wisconsin was to have its share of television, stations outside these [metropolitan] areas must do their part in pioneering." They considered experimenting with VHF television the most promising new area in which to invest.[100]

W9XD began operating in September 1931—"from one and one-half hours before sunset to one and one-half hours after sunset"—until April 1938, when new FCC rules on experimental television licenses caused the Journal Company to cease its transmissions.[101] However, as will be discussed in Chapter 6, the Journal Company did not abandon television, but that same year helped precipitate the struggle between the industry and the FCC for authorization of commercial electronic television.

Educational Television in the Mechanical Era

The remaining three middle western stations were all operated by universities.[102] Most ambitious of these at the time was America's first educational television station, W9XK, operated by the State University of Iowa. Its Department of Electrical Engineering had become interested in television as early as 1928, when the FRC issued it experimental license W9XAZ, but efforts to fulfill the operating obligations were not met by the university and nothing came of this initial attempt.[103] However, the department continued its efforts until, in 1931, word of its interest reached Clement F. Wade, a graduate of the university's College of Law and then president of Western Television Corporation. He offered to provide the necessary scanning equipment if the school would furnish funds for the transmitter.[104]

With this incentive the university again applied for a construction permit, which the FRC issued in January 1932. Edwin B. Kurtz, chairman of the electrical engineering department, and Department staff members James L. Potter and Carl Menzer, assisted by William N. Parker, a Western Television engineer, and Ulises A. Sanabria, constructed the 100-watt transmitter and designed the studio facilities.[105] On 25 January 1933 W9XK televised its first program on the 2000–2100-kHz. channel, the audio going out over the university's radio outlet, WSUI. The video studio was located on the first

floor of the Electrical Engineering Building, with the aerial on the roof.
Adjoining the studio, behind a glass partition, was the control room containing the scanner, the photocells, amplifier, and monitor panel.[106]

Transmitting the standard Sanabria design of a 45-line picture, 15 frames
per second, W9XK (with WSUI audio) regularly transmitted for fifteen minutes twice weekly, on Monday and Wednesday, at 7:30 P.M. Each program
consisted of three parts: first an instrumental or vocal number; then a short
illustrated talk, either on a subject of general interest or as an installment in
some ongoing series of course materials; and, finally, a recitation, dialogue,
or skit performed by members of the speech department. This format design
was meant to contain sufficient educational and entertainment value to make
the program attractive to viewers.[107]

The educational programming was quite varied during the six years the
station operated. It included such series as "Elementary Art Lessons," "Boy
Scout Series," "Girl Scout Series," "Home Planning," "Personal Shorthand," "Iowa Wild Life," "Spring Birds," and "Portrait Sketching." Each
series was taught by members of the university faculty. One such instructor's
description of her television experience provides an interesting insight into
studio conditions with a flying-spot scanner:

> One or two ten-watt lamps provide alleged illumination. . . . The announcer
> makes his little speech, and you are ushered before a small hole in the wall,
> through which a light plays over your face, and around which a row of photoelectric cells stare at you. . . . Your paper is barely legible in the pale, gray
> light. . . .
>
> All this searching publicity is most unnerving, and as the ten minutes near
> their close, the announcer begins frantically signalling from the adjacent
> obscurity that there are just twenty-seven seconds left.[108]

Besides development of an educational television format, W9XK also provided means for technical studies by members of the electrical engineering
department. Studies were made of television modulation systems, a sinusoidal light flux generator, color combinations for televised subjects, sweep
circuits, types of television receivers, and signal-reception conditions.
Beyond these studies, the station also allowed electrical engineering students to gain practical experience in television technology.[109]

But by 1936 it was evident that television's future lay with the electronic
method. So the university obtained a second television license, for VHF
station W9XUI. Notwithstanding, the mechanical station continued to operate for three more years, televising its final program on 29 June 1939.[110]

A second institution to enter telecasting with assistance from a commercial
interest was Purdue University. In 1929 the Grigsby-Grunow Company of
Chicago, manufacturer of Majestic radios, approached Purdue's electrical
engineering department offering to establish a joint venture for developing a

cathode-ray receiving tube. Agreement was reached in May 1929 that the university would provide the staff, laboratories, and equipment for the research, while Grigsby-Grunow would provide the money for them to conduct this work effectively. Purdue obtained an operating television license for W9XG in September 1931, on the 2750–2850-kHz. channel with 500 watts transmission power. The facility for it was constructed on the north side of the campus near the Ross-Ade Stadium, in a 16-by-20-foot building, with a 78-foot aerial next to it. By December the station was broadcasting, and in March 1932 it adopted a regular twenty-one-hour weekly schedule of motion-picture film, primarily newsreels. There were, additionally, several large public demonstrations.[111]

Although professors Roscoe H. George and Howard J. Heim, the station's coordinators, concentrated on developing an electronic receiver, W9XG operated a low-definition mechanical transmitting system. It employed a 30-inch, 60-aperture disc rotating 24 times per second in the film-pickup apparatus. Besides the .015-inch-diameter picture apertures around the disc's periphery, there were 59 more .010-inch-wide slots and a sixtieth ¾ inch wide that produced the synchronizing pulse transmitted as part of the video signal.[112]

After 1932 Grigsby-Grunow was unable to provide further financial support for the project. It languished until, in 1934, an agreement was reached with RCA; the commercial concern provided funds to Purdue to continue its television research by purchasing the rights to all of its pending patents and other inventions relating to television, while allowing the university to continue the free use of them.[113] In 1939 W9XG was closed down for conversion to VHF electronic transmission, but the outbreak of the Second World War interrupted this effort.[114]

The third educational institution to operate a television facility was Kansas State College of Agriculture and Applied Science in Manhattan. It received its license for W9XAK in November 1932, for the 2100–2200-kHz. channel, transmitting a 60-line picture. This outlet continued telecasting until 1939. The college's electrical engineering department then applied for a VHF electronic station, but withdrew its application after the outbreak of war.[115]

The unusual longevity of these three university-operated mechanical outlets was at least partly the result of deliberate FCC policy. In 1936 the commission eliminated the shortwave television channels but made an exception for these three stations, which were allowed to operate only on the 2000–2100-kHz. band. While the government regulators recognized that commercial television's future lay within the higher frequencies, they feared that VHF's very limited range would restrict high-definition television to major urban centers. It was believed that because of the high cost of constructing the large number of television outlets required to serve areas of smaller population density, and because owners of such stations could expect much less return from advertising revenue for their initial investment, much of the country would be left without any television service at all. Therefore the FCC decided to allow low-definition shortwave television research to be continued by these three schools as a potential means for providing at least some sort of television service to "secondary or rural-service areas."[116] But by 1939 a practical means had been developed to provide high-definition television nationally, and so in that year the last remaining low-definition stations finally ceased their operations.

PIONEERING TELEVISION IN THE FAR WEST

West of Kansas there were only two television stations that operated for any significant duration, both in California. One, W6XAH, was licensed to the Pioneer Mercantile Company of Bakersfield. Located at 307½ Humbolt Street, the station was granted its construction permit in September 1931 and began test transmissions on the 2000–2100-kHz. channel the following year. Built by Ralph D. Lemert and Frank Schamblin of Pioneer Merchantile, W6XAH was of unusual design. The builders altered a standard Jenkins transmitter scanner by adding a new disc of 32 apertures, rotated 60 times per second; 3 rotations were required to produce each of the final 96-line frames, with 20 such frames per second. The increase in picture lines was accomplished without the necessity of adding additional frequency bandwidth to the assigned 100 kHz. (normally able to accommodate only a 60-line frame) by using a new single sideband suppressed carried technique. A variant of this method, vestigial sideband transmission, is the standard employed in current American television broadcasting. However, W6XAH ceased operating after 1935 because of the general decline of mechanical television's prospects, the reassignment of the shortwave television channels to other services, and the lack of local interest in the project.[117]

In the Los Angeles area, Don Lee, who owned several California radio outlets and headed a regional broadcast network, began operating W6XS near Gardena in 1931, on the 2100–2200-kHz. channel. In the spring of 1932 the station was moved to the Don Lee Broadcasting System headquarters at Seventh and Bixel, in Los Angeles, where in December this video facility, operating in synchronization with radio station KHJ, initiated a regular telecasting schedule from 6:00 to 7:00 P.M.

Using a 1000-watt transmitter, an 80-line picture, 20 frames per second, was telecast. The programming consisted of filmed action and closeups of motion-picture stars. However, in December 1931 the Don Lee System had also put into operation a VHF station, W6XAO. By 1935 shortwave station W6XS had been deleted, and the Don Lee System was concentrating its efforts on improving its VHF electronic facility.[118]

COLLAPSE OF THE LOW-DEFINITION MECHANICAL
TELEVISION BOOM

By the end of 1933 America's first television boom had collapsed. But the abandonment of low-definition television was due neither to engineering nor financial forces exclusively. In fact, in both of the areas this method had distinct advantages over the electronic alternative. Mechanical television did successfully transmit recognizable transient visual images. And it was able to accomplish this with transmitting and receiving equipment that was relatively inexpensive. Furthermore, its broadcast range, on shortwave, was quite extensive. All of this means that the entire country would be provided with television at rather low cost to both broadcasters and consumers. On the other hand, cathode-ray tube equipment was considerably more costly, and its utilization of very high frequencies drastically limited each station's broadcast range, necessitating heavy capital outlay for large numbers of stations across the country and for interconnecting facilities among these stations.

Nor can the cause of the collapse be assigned to an absence of firms willing to invest heavily in television. RCA actually increased its financial commitment to television after it abandoned the mechanical method, as did Britain's BBC after it withdrew its low-definition service in 1935.

The mechanical method failed primarily because of the demands of television programming. At the time of the boom it was incapable of transmitting programs with sufficient entertainment value to attract the large public investment in receivers needed to draw the advertising revenue that was necessary to provide the television industry with a profitable return on its initial investment.[119] Only high-definition television could accomplish this. But this electronic method required, in turn, a much heavier investment in research and in equipment; further, since it was feasible only on VHF, it required costly investment in the large number of stations needed to reach the primary commercial markets of the country. These escalating financial factors necessarily limited the development and exploitation of electronic television to fewer and larger (or at least better-capitalized) concerns than did the earlier method.

However, although electronic television was thus a significantly altered technology, it did not evolve separately from the mechanical method. It was the latter that set the engineering and programming perimeters within which any successful television system must operate. Furthermore, it contributed theoretical knowledge and new devices to the technical resources available for later television transmitting. Similarly, it provided a rich source of studio design and programming concepts extensively drawn upon by the later endeavor. In many ways, electronic television did not develop simply parallel to the mechanical method, but often climbed upon its shoulders.

This climb upwards, on the other hand, was into a greatly changed systems environment, and this meant that cathode-ray tube television could not merely be a more sophisticated version of its predecessor. Rather, as with all systems, so with television: any alteration in one component effects modifications in the whole. In this case, the exigencies of programming necessitated adoption of new engineering techniques, and this required a transformation of the industry's financing. These changes not only reduced the number of firms engaging in television development, but, with the financial stakes now raised so much higher, also greatly intensified the competition among them. In the decade of the 1930s television's technology finally did catch up to, and coincide with, the long-held conceptions of the nature of the new medium. By 1939 a second boom seemed in the offing.

Electronic Television Systems Compete

If the mechanical television boom had been a false start, the real race had already begun. In the very year that AT & T was impressing the public with its Nipkow-disc telecast from Washington to New York, a young inventor in a San Francisco laboratory was successfully transmitting his first all-electronic images. By 1931 RCA had committed its research facilities to the newer method. And in 1933 they were able to test a complete electronic engineering system. These 1933 tests served to intensify an already frenzied struggle among rival corporations to perfect the technology to the point where it would finally satisfy the demands of the federal government and thus permit commercialization of the medium. In 1939 many in the industry were convinced that they had succeeded.

The years following the collapse of mechanical telecasting contrast sharply with those immediately preceding them. If the boom was the time of the small firm and the amateur, the years that followed were primarily dominated by three corporations and their professional researchers. Nor were there any longer regularly scheduled telecasts for the public. These did not resume until the very last years of the decade, when the engineers were convinced that their system could now be used to test programming possibilities and to attract potential advertisers, for it was during this decade that industry executives came to realize that, unlike radio, television could not be improved incrementally once it had been publicly introduced. Rather, from the start the system would have to be free of significant technological obsolescence. And this realization meant that before advertisers could be solicited to consider purchasing air time, attractive programming had to be created, and this task could not be successfully undertaken until a satisfactory high-definition technology had been perfected. Even after 1935, when efforts began on the programming and promotional systems, it was the engineering competition that continued to dominate the industry.

Yet behind the technological competition was a greater rivalry. The three principals—RCA, Philco, and Farnsworth—each represented an entirely different level of industrial organization. RCA was one of the original radio-group giants; Philco was the leading independent radio manufacturer; and

Farnsworth was the lone inventor. In this three-way struggle RCA sought to extend over television the patent monopoly it already possessed; Philco and Farnsworth each tried to check RCA with alternative technologies of their own. Only in 1939 was the contest between RCA and Farnsworth, a rivalry that had spread to Britain and Germany, finally settled, while RCA and Philco continued their bitter struggle until 1941.[1] Out of this clash of corporate and engineering conflicts emerged the television system marketed to the American consumer.

PROGRESS IN ELECTRONIC TELEVISION

As already discussed in the first chapter, by the eve of the First World War, several researchers had become convinced that the cathode-ray tube (CRT) was the most promising means of removing the obstacles preventing the achievement of successful television transmission and reception. Max Dieckmann in Germany and Boris Rosing in Russia both experimented with CRT receiving apparatus during the first decade of the century, while in Britain, A. A. Campbell Swinton proposed employing a CRT in the transmitter as well as the receiver, thereby eliminating all mechanical devices from television.

An important design, similar to those of Dieckmann and Rosing, was introduced in the United States in 1917 by a British researcher living in New York and working for AT & T. In a patent application filed that year, Alexander M. Nicholson described a transmitter employing an oscillating mirror that scanned the scene to be sent and produced both a video and a synchronizing pulse for the signal. This signal was then transmitted on a 50–100-kHz. bandwidth to a CRT receiver. In this receiver a beam of electrons was to be focused on a fluorescent screen, scanning it in synchronization with the transmitter's scanning. By means of a transformer, the composite video-synchronizing signal would be impressed on a detector to distinguish its two sets of information. One provided the picture information to the control grid of the electron beam, another the synchronization pulses necessary to control the movements of this beam. Scanning was accomplished by means of horizontal and vertical deflector plates operated electrostatically (although he also allowed for electromagnetic deflection). Nicholson estimated that 18–20 frames per second could be so transmitted, thus allowing persistence of vision to eliminate flicker in the picture.[2]

VLADIMIR K. ZWORYKIN AND A SUCCESSFUL ELECTRONIC TECHNOLOGY

Nicholson's patent provided the basis for much later American work on CRT receivers, but it still relied on an optical transmitting method. The first

Dr. Vladimir K. Zworykin. (Courtesy of RCA)

important American attempt at a completely electronic system was proposed by Vladimir K. Zworykin, a Russian immigrant who had been a student of Rosing's in St. Petersburg. Arriving in the United States in 1919, Zworykin was hired by Westinghouse, but when his desire to develop a CRT television transmitter was thwarted by the firm's indifference, he left for a position in Kansas City. However, in February 1923 he returned to Westinghouse, where he made arrangements to continue his research in television.[3]

Zworykin recognized that the designing of a CRT transmitter was then the central problem; Dieckmann and Rosing had already proved a CRT receiver possible. In December 1923 Zworykin filed a patent application for a completely electronic television system. The object of the design was to eliminate all mechanical devices from television engineering and, in so doing, also to introduce the concept of "signal storage—i.e., the utilization for the picture signal of charges accumulated photoelectrically by a picture element throughout a picture period."[4] It was this storage principle that would give the Zworykin pickup tube its great sensitivity, allowing it eventually "to provide a system for broadcasting . . . moving pictures, scenes from plays, or similar entertainment."[5]

The design was a variant of that originally suggested by Campbell Swinton. The scene to be televised was focused by a lens through a fine wire collector grid onto a mosaic formed of insulated globules of photosensitive potassium hydride. This mosaic was really the lens side of a composite plate, consisting of the mosaic, a thin film of aluminum oxide that served as the insulator, and a final layer of aluminum foil facing the cathode. As the cathode ray scanned the aluminum foil, its high intensity caused it to pass through the plate to the mosaic, where each particular globule (that is, picture element) would emit electrons corresponding to the intensity of light focused by the lens on it. This current passed to the collector grid creating the signal. The mosaic was scanned 32 times a second, but each picture would then be transmitted twice, for an actual frame rate of 16 per second. When not being scanned by the beam, each globule would be restoring its charge, an obvious advantage for increasing the mosaic's potential sensitivity.[6]

However when Zworykin demonstrated his pickup tube to Westinghouse officials in late 1923, the results were disappointing. A cross was successfully transmitted, but the definition was so poor and the contrast so slight that it was evident that much more work would be necessary before an all-electronic system would be feasible. Primarily, Zworykin would have to discover a more satisfactory target component and also develop a vacuum cathode-ray tube (instead of using the less appropriate argon-filled ones, then the only type available).[7] Once again it was a case of the concept existing before the technology allowed its realization. Nonetheless, Zworykin did establish that a CRT could serve as a transmitter, just as Dieckmann

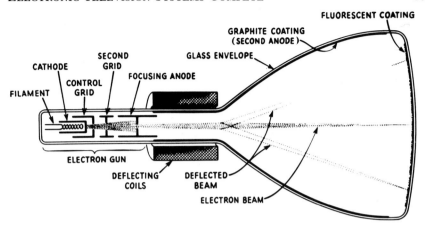

The RCA kinescope picture tube. The electrons emerging from the cathode are accelerated and focused into a narrow threadlike beam deflected across the fluorescent screen of the tube, reproducing the image originating with the transmitting apparatus. (Courtesy of RCA)

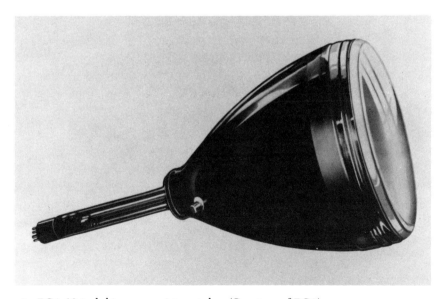

An RCA 12-inch kinescope picture tube. (Courtesy of RCA)

and Rosing had demonstrated its use as a receiver. And his basic design, submitted in 1923, was that used in the first commercial television cameras in the 1940s.

Although Zworykin filed his patent in 1923, it would not be issued for fifteen years. During this interval, a number of patent-interference suits were initiated against it. The first of these cases was brought primarily by Harold J. McCreary in 1927. McCreary had submitted a patent application for an all-electronic color television system in 1924. It was not until 1932 that Zworykin was finally awarded priority for his patent over the claims of McCreary.[8] But by then he had become involved in a patent-interference suit brought by Frederick J. Reynolds of AT & T for his electronic television design issued in 1930. This suit was followed by another by Henry J. Round of RCA. This last case was not settled in Zworykin's favor until 1938, when his patent was finally issued.[9] However, by that time Zworykin and his employer, RCA, had already lost a patent-interference case to the rival all-electronic system that provided the central element in the television engineers' scramble to produce a commercial product. Nonetheless, this array of litigation, a selection from the actual work being done, suggests that research on the possibility of using CRT pickup tubes was relatively active, although eventually only two rival techniques were successfully developed.

Zworykin was not deterred by these difficulties, for in 1928 he did receive a patent for an all-electronic television system that would serve as the legal basis for his further endeavors.[10] Although continuing his research on the pickup tube, Zworykin paused to complete work on a CRT receiver tube. This he first publicly disclosed at the November 1929 convention of the Institute of Radio Engineers.[11] Naming his CRT receiver the kinescope (from the Greek words *kinein*, "to move," and *skopein*, "to watch"), Zworykin summarized the advantages of the electronic apparatus over the existing mechanical alternatives as "the absence of moving mechanical parts, quietness of operation, simplicity of synchronization even on a single carrier channel, ample amount of light; the persistence of fluorescence of the screen which aids persistence of vision of the eye and permits reduction of a number of pictures per second without noticeable flickering. This in turn allows a greater number of lines and consequently better details of the picture without increasing the width of the frequency band."[12]

This first kinescope was a specially designed evacuated CRT with a 7-inch diameter; it was capable of producing a 5-inch picture. The tube's electron beam was focused electrostatically onto the fluorescent screen, its scanning controlled by deflecting plates and coils that were operated either electrostatically or electromagnetically. The composite video signal received by the kinescope included the picture information and the horizontal and framing synchronization pulses; a filter separated the horizontal frequency from the signal in order to operate the deflecting coils, while the picture and framing frequencies were applied directly to the control grid of the electron beam. The result was the production of a green-tinted picture (instead of the pink picture common in mechanical receivers) that could be viewed by several persons even in a moderately light room.[13]

Zworykin had achieved his success, in part, by convincing RCA's David Sarnoff of the desirability of creating an all-electronic system. Sarnoff had already been very favorably impressed by Zworykin's work at Westinghouse and at a meeting of the two men in early 1929, he was completely won over to the advantages of the new method and offered his full support.[14] This commitment was stated explicitly in RCA's *Annual Report* of 1930:

> Television must develop to the stage where broadcasting stations will be able to broadcast regularly visual objects in the studio, or scenes occurring at other places through remote control; where reception devices shall be developed that will make these objects and scenes clearly discernible in millions of homes; where such devices can be built upon a principle that will eliminate rotary scanning discs, delicate hand controls and other movable parts; and where research has made possible the utilization of wave lengths for sight transmission that would not interfere with the use of the already overcrowded channels in space.[15]

This program not only articulates RCA's commitment to the CRT method, but outlines its entire research program as pursued over the coming decade.

RCA AND ELECTRONIC TELEVISION

It was at this time that Zworykin was transferred to RCA's research staff in Camden as part of Sarnoff's unification plan; here he became director of the Electronic Research Laboratory.[16] To demonstrate the feasibility of an all-electronic method, Zworykin set out to develop a workable version of the one missing component: an effective pickup tube. Previously Zworykin had been forced to rely on nonelectronic transmitting devices. In the 1929 demonstration of the kinescope, an optical method employing a vibrating mirror had been used to transmit the filmed scenes to the CRT receiver.[17] Even in the 1931–32 field tests from the Empire State Building, a modified Nipkow disc was still employed in the transmitter, although, of course, the receivers were kinescopes.

Actually Zworykin had again begun experimenting with a CRT pickup tube in 1928 while still at Westinghouse, but the results indicated that much more work would yet be required to design a tube with the necessary sensitivity, so he first completed his development of the receiver.[18] However, once this difficulty was resolved, he returned to the problem of the transmitter tube and finally successfully demonstrated his design in 1931.[19]

The first detailed public discussion of the iconoscope (from the Greek words *eikon*, "image," and *skopein*, "to watch") was given by Zworykin in a presentation to the Franklin Institute in October 1933.[20]

This new tube introduced several significant improvements over the original 1923 design, although retaining the basic concept of a mosaic capable of storing charges. The 1933 version of the tube consisted of two principal parts enclosed in an evacuated CRT. First there was the photosensitive mosaic composed of miniature photocells of silver and cesium deposited as insulated globules on a sheet of mica. Each globule thus represented one picture element in the process of sequential scanning. When a scene was focused through the camera lens onto this mosaic it functioned analogously to the retina of the human eye. That is, it transformed the energy from the light into electrical charges and stored these charges until they could be transformed into the electrical impulses that constituted the picture signal. The electrical charge of each globule varied with the intensity of light focused on it: those which were brightly lit became positively charged, and those receiving less light were less positively charged, and those without illumination received no charge.

To transform these charges into electrical impulses constituting the video signal, the mosaic was scanned by the electron beam, the second major part of the tube. Unlike the 1923 design, the iconoscope resembled an elongated head, containing the mosaic and signal plate, and a long narrow neck, containing the electron gun of the scanning beam. This beam was focused by an electrostatic field (rather than the argon-gas focusing in the 1923 design) and deflected horizontally and vertically across the mosaic electromagnetically. This deflection was linear, from left to right, top to bottom, and was accomplished by employing sawtooth impulses caused to pass through the deflecting coils. The electron gun was situated opposite the mosaic and at a 30-degree angle to its face.

As the scanning beam passed each miniature photocell on the mosaic, the globule would discharge a current proportional to the positive charge it had acquired from the light focused on it. This discharge created the electrical impulse affecting the potential of the signal plate placed behind the mosaic, thus creating the video signal. Since the beam traversed the mosaic sequentially, the entire process could be reproduced in the receiver by reversing the process, provided the transmitter and receiver were properly synchronized.

To achieve this synchronization utilizing only the video carrier, the impulses of the deflecting generators controlling the scanning beam were united with the picture signal in transmission. The synchronizing pulse would not interfere with the video information, for it was inserted when no picture was being sent. This was possible because the scanning beams of both the iconoscope and the kinescope had to be shut off when, after scan-

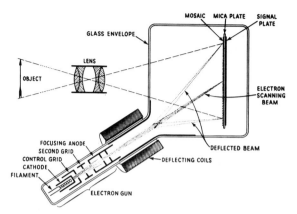

The RCA iconoscope camera tube. The image of an object is focused through the lens onto the photosensitive mosaic, where it is scanned by an electron beam emitted by the electron gun. As this beam, focused by means of an electrostatic field, is electromagnetically deflected over the globules of the mosaic, they discharge, causing a current to flow from the signal plate and producing the visual signal. (Courtesy of RCA)

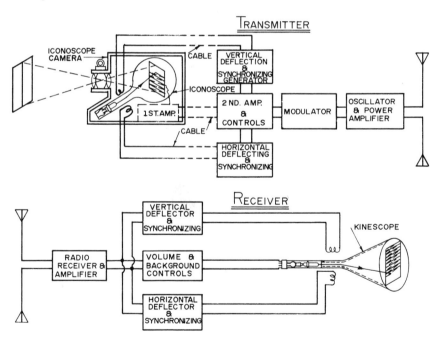

RCA's complete electronic television system. (© 1933 IRE, now IEEE. Reprinted, with permission, from Vladimir K. Zworykin, "Description of an Experimental Television System and the Kinescope," *Proceedings of the IRE* 21, no. 12, December 1933)

ning a line from left to right, the beam returned to the left to begin scanning the next line, and also when, after scanning an entire frame from top to bottom, the beam returned to the top to begin scanning the next frame. It was during the return phases that the synchronizing information would be added to the video signal without causing any disturbance to the picture information. At the time of Zworykin's presentation, the mosaic was being scanned 24 times a second.[21]

Zworykin claimed, in 1933, that iconoscopes capable of transmitting 500-line pictures had already been made, although pictures with much lower definition were being transmitted in RCA's field tests. Nonetheless, "with the advent of an instrument of these capabilities, new prospects are open for high grade television transmission."[22] To determine exactly the range of the iconoscope's capabilities, RCA undertook a second series of field tests in 1933.

The iconoscope was used only in Camden for these tests, where a 240-line sequentially scanned frame was employed. It was found that the increase of detail when compared with the 120-line pictures of the 1931–32 field tests greatly expanded the scope of material that could be used satisfactorily for programming.[23] However, "[e]xperience with this system indicated that even with 240 lines, for critical observers and for much of the program

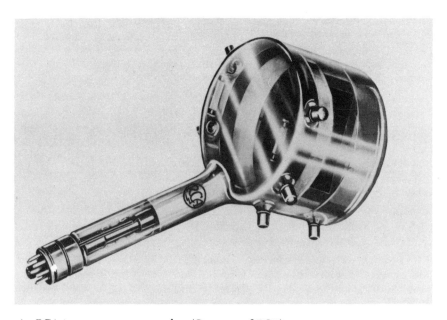

An RCA iconoscope camera tube. (Courtesy of RCA)

material, more image detail was desired."[24] On the other hand, it was also very important for the iconoscope's program potential that its sensitivity and its relative compactness allowed it to be used for both studio direct pickup and for outdoor remotes.[25] But some difficulties were also discovered; besides the need for greater definition, the angle at which the electron beam struck the mosaic created a disturbing keystone-shaped pattern to the picture, instead of producing the desired rectangle.[26] Here was a serious design problem that would have to be overcome. Later tests would disclose even greater problems.

The kinescopes used in these tests were mounted vertically in their cabinets, and the picture was viewed in a mirror mounted in the adjustable lid of the receiver. While they operated satisfactorily, it was found that automobile and airplane ignition systems coming within 100 feet of the receiver's antenna caused serious interference.[27] This, of course, was the sort of difficulty one could expect when broadcasting on VHF.

In a series of field tests conducted in Camden in 1934, significant improvements were added to RCA's electronic technology. In order to reduce further the flicker in the images displayed by the receiver and also to be able to increase the number of lines per frame without having to increase the frequency bandwidth, interlaced scanning was introduced.[28] In the system

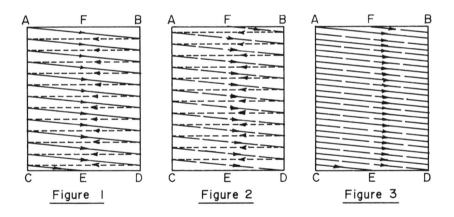

Figure 1   Figure 2   Figure 3

Electronic interlaced scanning. *Figure 1* illustrates the first scanning field of a complete frame. The solid lines indicate the path the electron beam follows when on, while the dotted lines indicate the return path of the beam when off. When the beam reaches point E it shuts off and receives a vertical impulse to move to F, while maintaining its horizontal scanning motion as well. *Figure 2* illustrates the second scanning field of a complete frame. *Figure 3* illustrates the whole frame, the solid lines representing the first field and the broken lines, the second field. Together, through persistence of vision, the two fields produce the optical impression of one complete picture.

then employed by RCA, beginning with the first line, every other line of the transmitter's mosaic and the receiver's fluorescent screen was scanned until the final odd-numbered half-line was completed; after this the beam was blanked out and, while continuing its horizontal scanning motion, it returned to the top to begin scanning the even lines of the same frame. Thus in the 1934 tests, with the 343-line *frame* used, the *field* of 171.5 odd lines was scanned first and then the field of 171.5 even lines. Sixty fields were scanned per second, making an interlaced scanning rate of 30 frames per second, an optimal rate for minimizing flicker.[29] The results of these tests were therefore extremely encouraging: an effective means had been developed for eliminating flicker, which further allowed for an increase in picture definition. This, of course, would broaden the scope of the material available for programming.

RCA'S MILLION-DOLLAR PLAN FOR TELEVISION

The successful testing of the iconoscope, the kinescope, and interlaced scanning led the RCA management to commit itself and its resources, publicly, to the development of a complete television system. In May 1935 David Sarnoff announced that RCA intended to invest $1 million to achieve this goal. These funds would be used to install a new television transmitter in the Empire State Building and to test reception from this station in the New York area with sets operated by the firm's engineering personnel. Furthermore, a television studio would be constructed in the NBC facilities at Radio City.[30] Although this announcement formed a watershed in RCA's television program, Sarnoff still cautioned, "This does not mean that regular television service is at hand."[31] More field tests to determine the transmitter's effectiveness, the quality of picture, and the use of the iconoscope for indoor and outdoor pickup would be necessary. Nevertheless, this was a significant step toward the completion of the system.

That this was a deliberate step undertaken as part of a long-range plan is clear not only from the pacing of the field tests themselves but even more so from the stated objectives of the RCA management. For this firm, television consisted clearly of an integrated system. For instance, in 1933 RCA explained that television development must occur in a number of stages. First, there must be the laboratory research on all engineering problems involved. This must be followed by field tests of the technology in order to experiment with television techniques of studio and remote pickups and reception. After these, new sets of difficulties will have to be met. "These problems relate principally to the cost of erecting and operating the necessary television transmission stations, their interconnection for a wide-range service, the price at which television receiving sets can be successfully manufactured and sold to the public, and the production of suitable programs."[32] Here, then, is a deliberately designed plan for an engineering and manufacturing subsystem, a programming and networking subsystem, and a promotional subsystem—the three essential components of a television system.

In 1934 this systems approach was made even more explicit. As a precondition, "the commercial application of such a [television] service could be achieved only through a system of high-definition television which would make the images of objects transmitted clearly recognizable to observers."[33] This could be accomplished only step by step, "through the processes of research, laboratory development, field demonstration and then to regular service," while also solving the technical and financial problems attendant on providing such a service on a national scale for a country the size of the United States.[34]

In making his announcement of RCA's undertaking, Sarnoff stated his firm's plan explicitly. "Television requires the creation of a system, not merely the commercial development of apparatus. This system must be built in progressive and evolutionary stages."[35] To achieve this, RCA would build a television station in a major metropolitan center (namely, New York), manufacture a limited number of receivers for test purposes, and develop an experimental program service. Still to be solved was the problem of networking.[36]

Clearly, then, by 1935 RCA was ready to move to the stage of field demonstrations (not mere field tests), and within four more years, with the networking problem resolved and much practical experience gained, it would initiate the next step. Following this action, only one final step would be necessary: government authorization of commercial television service. However, unlike the previous stages, this action could not be initiated unilaterally by RCA.[37]

Sarnoff's announcement of RCA's new undertaking in 1935 was greeted enthusiastically. In an article headlined, "Million-Dollar Plan Brightens Television Outlook," the *New York Times*, bemoaning the "five year delay in television," felt that television, now much improved, would at last have the necessary funds for its development, although noting prophetically that "the million is looked upon as a 'drop in the bucket' in relation to what will eventually be spent to put television in the home as a real show."[38]

Business Week and *Popular Mechanics*, representing two other constituencies interested in television, both echoed the *Times*'s enthusiasm, as well as its awareness of further costs involved in providing a national television service.[39] Interestingly enough, both of these publications interpreted RCA's announcement in the light of the fact that Britain and Germany had each recently announced plans to inaugurate regular public television service. Clearly the United States was not going to fall behind its European rivals in this technological competition. That more than competition among the three nations was actually involved in these 1935 developments will become evident from material discussed later.

But not every one was pleased by Sarnoff's announcement. Particularly unhappy was Edwin Armstrong. Armstrong, a veteran radio researcher, had developed a means of eliminating bothersome static and noise from radio transmission by successfully employing frequency modulation (FM) broadcasting. After receiving the patents for his method in late 1933, Armstrong was granted permission by RCA to install an experimental FM radio transmitter in the Empire State Building. But he had used the facility for only about a year when, in April 1935, just before Sarnoff's policy statement on television, RCA asked Armstrong to remove his equipment. [40]

Although not inherently antipathetic, television and FM radio, at this stage in their development, became rivals. No doubt some tension was likely to emerge from the fact that both television and FM radio operated on VHF and therefore would naturally be vying for frequency allocations, and also from the fact that both were making demands on limited research funds, but these factors alone did not cause the rivalry. Rather, it arose from Armstrong's intention to offer FM as a technically superior replacement for AM radio. Naturally, RCA, with its heavy investment in AM broadcasting, could not be expected to be enthusiastic over such a threatening innovation. This was all the more true since television was still believed to represent no serious danger to established broadcast interests. It is therefore hardly surprising that RCA chose to support strongly television's development while ignoring, or even hindering, that of FM radio. However, Armstrong was not so easily deterred, as we shall see in a later chapter. [41]

A second rivalry involving competing technologies external to television engineering itself was going on simultaneously with the competition between television and FM radio. This second contest focused on the methods being developed to facilitate networking. Here the problem to be surmounted was that not only is the transmission range of VHF television quite limited, but because of the great amount of video information being relayed, television stations, unlike radio, cannot be linked by ordinary telephone lines.

To solve this difficulty, AT & T had developed the coaxial cable for television interconnections. In 1935 Bell announced it would spend $580,000 to install an experimental cable between New York and Philadelphia in order to provide a field test for its technology. [42] This was done in 1936, and in November 1937 this coaxial cable was successfully demonstrated as it was used to send a motion picture approximating the quality of high-definition television between the two cities. [43] Here, then, was a practical, albeit expensive, means to solve the conundrum of interconnecting television stations, thereby making networking feasible. [44]

However, RCA had developed a rival method to accomplish the same task. As early as 1933, tests had been conducted to link television stations by means of a series of relay stations. In the 1933 field tests, transmissions had been relayed on VHF between the Empire State Building and the Camden laboratories utilizing a relay station at Arney's Mount, a few miles east of Mt. Holly, New Jersey.[45] And by 1936 RCA had developed equipment capable of handling two-way transmissions between New York and Philadelphia using automatic relay stations located at Arney's Mount and New Brunswick, New Jersey.[46]

Whatever the outcome of the latest rivalry between RCA and AT & T, it was evident by 1936 that the difficulties of networking could be overcome, and this assurance provided increased encouragement for completing Sarnoff's plan for the development of a total television system. This meant the inauguration of the field demonstrations promised in 1935. These were now undertaken, using the new transmitter in the Empire State Building; a 343-line frame with interlaced scanning, 30 frames per second, was sent out on 49.75 MHz. (audio on 52 MHz.), with a 4-MHz. bandwidth.[47]

By January 1937 the picture definition had been increased to 441 lines with discernible results: "more distinct pictures, lines across the pictures disappear, great detail is visible, so that at a sports event even a baseball or football might be televised."[48] As a consequence, NBC predicted that public television might be possible by the autumn of 1938.[49]

The transmitter, installed on the eighty-fifth floor of the Empire State Building, included both video and audio equipment. It was connected to the Radio City studio by telephone line for sound, and for video by both coaxial cable and a UHF receiver operating at 177 MHz.

The NBC television facility in Radio City included a studio with three cameras for live transmissions, a projection room for film broadcasts, monitoring equipment, a central synchronizing generator, and video line amplification and terminal apparatus, which fed both the coaxial cable and the UHF relay transmitter.

For reception, sets with 5½-by-7½-inch screens were being used in the homes of RCA personnel. The kinescope in each set was still mounted vertically, with its screen protected by a sheet of shatterproof glass. The green-tinted picture appeared in a mirror on the inside of the cabinet's lid. There were ten control knobs.[50]

In December 1937 RCA provided the NBC staff at the New York facility with its first mobile television unit.[51] This unit consisted of two "tele-mobiles," one containing the equipment for two cameras and the other housing the 300-watt relay transmitter, sending on 159 MHz. Experiments conducted in the spring of 1938 convinced officials at RCA-NBC that the "mobile units have definitely proved their usefulness in providing entertaining television programs."[52]

While the engineering system was being tested and improved, RCA and

NBC were also rapidly working on developing the other two component systems. The first RCA field demonstration concerned with displaying high-definition television's program possibilities was staged on 7 July 1936, for representatives of the firm's licensees. The audience viewed the show in semidarkness on sets with 5-by-7-inch screens displaying the green hues of their pictures. The program opened with David Sarnoff presenting a review of television's progress, followed by Otto Schairer, vice-president of RCA, explaining that while there were no plans for manufacturing receivers commercially in 1936, three designs for such sets were being tested. These business discussions were followed by a performance of the twenty-member Water City Ensemble dance group, a film featuring the streamliner train the *Mercury*, and a fashion show with Bonwit Teller models. An actor, Henry Hull, then delivered a monologue from *Tobacco Road*; Graham McNamee and Ed Wynn put on a comedy skit; and the program concluded with a film on army maneuvers.[53]

Two months later RCA demonstrated the political possibilities of high-definition television when sequences of presidential candidates Franklin D. Roosevelt and Alf Landon filmed during campaigning were telecast. One viewer, impressed by the quality of the 343-line pictures, commented "that there can be no doubt after seeing Mr. Roosevelt and Mr. Landon on the screen that political campaigning by television will be practical in the not-distant future."[54]

On the afternoon of 6 November 1936, RCA telecast what it announced as "New York's first performance of a complete program planned for entertainment value" (evidently wishing to ignore all the demonstrations of the earlier mechanical era). Viewed on a 7½-by-12-inch screen, the demonstration opened with a welcoming speech by Sarnoff, followed by a newsreel, "Four More Years," about Roosevelt's reelection; film on several other short subjects was also shown; then came a performance by radio singer Hildegarde, and the show closed with a filmed tour of the television transmitter at the Empire State Building and the studios in Radio City.[55]

These demonstrations combining live performances and film material reflected a general programming attitude. Oscar B. Hanson of NBC explained: "Networking and field pick-ups by relay are a very essential part of a television system because the life-blood of television is spontaneity. The use of film alone as a program medium would never meet with public acceptance."[56] The lessons learned by the pioneer mechanical television broadcasters had not been forgotten. And it became clear that Hanson was not engaging in idle speculation: in July 1937, NBC announced plans to establish telecasting facilities at Madison Square Garden in order to be able to feature prize fights, skating, and other such events staged there.[57]

In November a demonstration was staged for the American Radio Relay League. It included the performance of a play based on a Sherlock Holmes story, combining studio acting and scenic shots for special effects, the first full-length drama staged for television in the Radio City facilities. Besides the play, a dancer and two singers performed. But attracting greatest attention was a newsreel which featured highlights from recent Yale-Harvard and Fordham–St. Mary's football games. One spectator, finding it "surprisingly easy" to follow the action, remarked that "the day may not be far distant when football fans will be able to enjoy watching their alma mater in a driving downpour from the comfort of a steam-heated apartment."[58]

By 1938 RCA officials, commenting on their telecasting plans, explained that this would be more a "demonstration year" than one of field tests.[59] Programs for the year included dramatic productions, a Broadway show, vaudeville, comic opera, news events, the telecasting of two full-length motion pictures, fashion shows, presentation of the year's new automobiles, educational talks, and, using the mobile unit, coverage of a figure-skating show and dramatic coverage of a fire at Ward's Island.[60]

Summarizing the experiences of program development during the years 1936–38, David Sarnoff wrote:

> Television will finally bring to people in their homes . . . a complete means of instantaneous participation in the sights and sounds of the entire outer world. . . . With the advent of television, the combined emotional results of both seeing and hearing an event or performance at the instant of its occurrence become new forces to be reckoned with. . . .
>
> In television it will be natural to emphasize types of program material where the addition of visibility will enhance the emotional effect—such as drama, news, or sporting events.[61]

Displaying remarkable prescience, he continued:

> Political addresses will be more effective when the candidate is both seen and heard. . . . Showmanship in presenting political appeal will be more effective than mere skill in talking . . . while good appearance may become of increasing importance. . . .
>
> The widespread public participation in events such as those which occurred during the European war crisis in the summer of 1938, and the intensity of the mass emotions aroused thereby, have given us a glimpse of the possibilities of this phase of radio. It may readily be imaged what will be the results when television adds to the effect of reality by projecting the vision as well as the hearing of the audience to the scene of action.[62]

And summing up, Sarnoff predicted that "television will be a vital element in the lives of those [American] people. It may become their principal source of entertainment, education and news."[63]

The American public, having been told that television was "just around the corner" for a decade, did, indeed, seem eager. In January 1937 *Radio*

News, agitated by the inauguration of regular public telecasting in Britain the previous year, confidently asserted, "Our American public certainly wants television!"[64] And an opinion poll conducted two years later indicated that approximately four million American families were eager to purchase television sets.[65] In fact, this impatience even gave rise to a conspiracy theory explaining the continuing delay: "It has been reported . . . that the larger radio manufacturers have consistently put the brakes on the introduction of television until they felt the financial status of the general public was such that it would be profitable."[66]

But the viewers of RCA's demonstration telecasts, while reflecting the widespread enthusiasm, also recognized that real problems remained. Commenting on the November 1936 show, one viewer noted that television could still not be considered ready until the difficulty of manufacturing affordable receivers had been solved. A second commentator noted that questions of lighting, makeup, air conditioning in the studio, limitations on the sphere of televised action, plus the need for suitable scripts and trained talent had still to be resolved.[67] That criticism was echoed the following year by Orrin E. Dunlap in the *New York Times*, where he complained that "no real showmanship has been in evidence in any of the year's demonstrations."[68] Dunlap also found that after watching the "ethereal 'flicker' " for about ten minutes, his attention began to wander, a result of the fact that, unlike radio, television required total concentration.[69] This was, in fact, a common response among many other viewers.

Finally, Dunlap also noted that television would have to be introduced without upsetting the radio and motion-picture industries.[70] This, as we have seen, was an early concern of those involved in other media. It is therefore not surprising that in making his 1935 announcement concerning RCA's investment in television, Sarnoff emphasized that "while television promised to supplement the present service of broadcasting by adding sight to sound, it will not supplant or diminish the importance and usefulness of broadcasting by sound."[71] He repeated this view in testimony before the FCC during the summer of 1936.[72] Similar remarks were addressed to the motion-picture industry, although many in this industry, and in radio, remained skeptical of such assurances.[73]

But the major reason industry spokesmen gave for the delay of television was financial. A comparison with European conditions will illustrate this claim. For instance, in Britain, where in 1936 the publicly financed BBC provided funds for a single public telecasting facility in London, private industry had no need to win the confidence of potential advertisers for the new medium and therefore could continue to experiment with television technology after commencing public transmissions. But in America, where all financing was to be derived from the private sector, a nationally marketable system was required before public broadcasting could be expected to begin producing any significant return on initial capital outlay. Thus, in the

United States most advances in television technology and programming necessarily had to precede the marketing of the medium.

By 1936 the high-definition engineering component had been developed reasonably well enough to allow the programming potential to be explored fruitfully. Consequently, the major element in the failure of mechanical television could now be avoided. But ultimately, to be successful television would have to provide an attractive enough advertising medium to draw sufficient revenues to make the undertaking commercially rewarding. And this required a large audience. While the engineering obstacles to the creation of national television networks capable of servicing such an audience were being removed, enough transmitting stations still had to be constructed and receivers sold to provide those elements necessary to create a national audience in the first place. Additional financial support was also necessary to produce the expensive entertainment required to maintain sustained audience support.

RCA therefore set out to convince the advertising industry of the usefulness of television for their purposes. If the effort was successful, advertising would provide the means for generating the revenue needed to improve programming and to attract new investment in station construction. It was then expected that the problem of the availability of receivers would solve itself (as, in fact, it very quickly did).

That the industry had already invested heavily in television research without yet receiving any significant return is evident from a relatively conservative estimate of capital outlay published in 1939. This survey suggested that $13 million had so far been spent by the five leading companies. Of this sum, RCA had contributed between $5 and $10 million, with two other firms having invested $2 million each.[74] The scale of this investment particularly limited the revenue available for continuous lavish program productions and for the construction of new facilities. So, not surprisingly, the industry's representatives were eager to promote their new medium and begin finally to receive some substantial returns.

Already in 1934 Walter R. G. Baker, vice-president and general manager of RCA-Victor, had explained that the expense (that is, the cost of sets and the many stations necessary for national coverage) was the principal reason for television's continuing delay.[75] This view was repeated the following year by Alfred N. Goldsmith, long associated with RCA and the industry, and was reiterated once again in FCC hearings the following year.[76]

As *Business Week* commented in 1936, the difficulty was, "Who's going to pay the bill?" For the "public looks first of all to the big radio chains, and the chains look to the advertiser. And the advertiser and his agent are keeping mum, just watching."[77] And with good reason. As one commentator noted:

> If the United States has no television yet [in 1938] it is because it is not certain whether the advertiser can pay the cost of sponsoring the kind of

program that will appear. . . . An investment is involved that dwarfs anything to which even American capital is accustomed. . . .

The telecasting of a news event or a play by some sponsor will be preceded, followed, and interspersed with images of men and women smoking cigarettes . . . smacking their lips over a drink of whiskey or ginger ale, extolling the virtues of a hand cream, all to the accompaniment of advertising patter. Will the masses like it? Perhaps. They respond to printed advertising now. But they are volunteers. Television will make them conscripts.[78]

David Sarnoff naturally thought television just the answer for the advertiser: "Advertisers who sponsor radio programs will be given new possibilities of appeal through the medium of television."[79] And RCA had long before set out to convince potential sponsors that he was right. Shortly after the 1935 announcement of the firm's commitment to the development of public telecasting, it was noted that

a considerable amount of research was conducted on the advertising aspects of television. In fact, programs thought suitable for advertising purposes, involving products of many different industries, were tried. . . . A considerable number of manufacturing and advertising agencies cooperated in the production of these shows.[80]

As Noran E. Kersta, NBC assistant coordinator for television, explained:

A point has been made to keep advertisers and advertising agencies constantly informed on the progress of television broadcasting. This service is and has been in the form of lectures, monographs, personal meetings, and an open invitation of all qualified advertising men to visit the television plant. This policy reaped excellent response, with the result that there is now a considerable file of information on the advertising potentialities of television broadcasting. . . .

One phase of cooperation with the advertising industry was to issue an invitation to all advertising agencies to appoint a liaison post in each agency to act as a clearing house for the agency on television matters with N.B.C. There is now quite a long list of agencies who have responded.[81]

In fact, Kersta claimed that after public (but noncommercial) telecasting began in 1939, seventy-three different advertisers, representing seventeen major industries, cooperated with NBC during the first eight months of service, to account for 12 percent of total broadcast time.[82] Clearly the advertising industry had become convinced of television's potential for their purposes, a development already predicted by Edgar Felix as early as 1931.

Thus by the end of 1938 the difficulties of networking were being overcome, the programming possibilities were being rapidly explored, and the promotional campaigns to market the television medium to advertisers and to the public were successfully underway. In fact, for RCA there was only one significant problem remaining. Once again the engineering component was unable to meet the demands of the rest of the system. Or rather, *its* engineering component could not, at least not in the United States.

RCA STALLED

As was soon discovered, the iconoscope was not, after all, the perfect television pickup tube. Two technical articles published in 1937 discussed serious problems with the iconoscope. In the first place, while its general sensitivity was impressive and the iconoscope could provide good pictures of parades, races, and baseball games, it was not reliably useful for football games that were played near sunset, for instance. In part, this problem of insufficient sensitivity arose from the second difficulty: as a charge-storage system, the iconoscope's efficiency was extremely low.[83] A further problem with the iconoscope, not mentioned in these articles, was that aberrant nonuniform shading appeared even in low-light portions of its pictures. Thus viewers often noticed a dime-size dark spot in the middle of the receiver images.

That the iconoscope was only 5 percent efficient as a storage system and that it produced spurious signals was a result of secondary electron emission. That is, when the high-velocity scanning beam struck the mosaic, it not only released the photoelectrons necessary to generate the signal but also yielded secondary electron emissions. The collection of these secondary photoelectrons was inefficient, allowing some of them to fall back prematurely onto the mosaic, erasing part of the stored charge. This resulted in a loss of the degree of sensitivity one could have expected from the iconoscope's design. Secondly, a greater fraction of the redistributed electrons were concentrated in the center of the mosaic, resulting in the spurious shading signal produced.[84] Thus, although the iconoscope was the most satisfactory pickup tube available in America at the time, it clearly would not meet the programming needs and consumer expectations for a commercial system.

However, the difficulties with the iconoscope had been recognized for several years. In fact, in November 1937, in Britain, the BBC first used a much-improved pickup tube, the superemitron, developed by RCA's British associate, Marconi-EMI.[85] In Germany, RCA's associate, Telefunken, introduced its version, the Super-Ikonoskop, the following year.[86] Although not quite perfect, here was a pickup tube that did reduce significantly the difficulties experienced with the iconoscope. And yet RCA was unable to use its version of the improved pickup tube, the image iconoscope. The radio giant was trapped in a patent dilemma.

Unlike the Europeans, the American television industry had not created a patent pool, so that patents assigned to one firm could not be employed by another without first arriving at a licensing agreement. And it was then the policy of RCA not to enter into any such agreements where it would be required to pay someone else for a patent license; instead of paying for a license, RCA preferred to purchase the rights to the patent itself from the original assignee. But Philo T. Farnsworth, who owned the key patents necessary to the design of RCA's image iconoscope, did not intend to sell his patent rights.

PHILO T. FARNSWORTH AND HIS IMAGE DISSECTOR

Philo T. Farnsworth and his firm were the complete antithesis of Vladimir K. Zworykin and RCA. RCA was the dominant firm in radio broadcasting and manufacturing; Farnsworth Television Incorporated was, during most of the decade, a tiny research firm financed by a small group of Californians. Zworykin was an internationally educated engineer with a doctorate in his field; Farnsworth was an inventor who had never even attended college regularly. But these disadvantages did not prevent Farnsworth from developing the only pickup tube to present serious competition to Zworykin's iconoscope and, with his pickup tube, to pose a challenge to RCA in the United States, and to its associates in Britain and Germany. If RCA was to introduce a commercially viable television system in America it could not avoid, despite all its efforts, a reckoning with Farnsworth.

Philo T. Farnsworth was born in a small Utah town in August 1906 and spent his boyhood on a ranch in Idaho. In 1923 his family returned to Utah, to Provo, where Farnsworth took some courses in mathematics and electronics at Brigham Young University, while working to support the family after his father's death in 1924. Then, in 1926, he went to Salt Lake City to seek employment and soon set up his own radio service shop, in partnership with a friend, Clifford Gardner. But the business quickly failed, and the two were again out looking for jobs.

Having registered with the University of Utah employment bureau, Farnsworth was referred to George Everson and Leslie Gorrell, two fund raisers from California who had come to organize Salt Lake City's Community Chest drive. Soon he was working for the charity drive, along with Gardner and Gardner's sister Elma, shortly to be Farnsworth's wife. In conversations with his new employers, Farnsworth displayed his two most outstanding characteristics: his innovative engineering genius and his ability to inspire confidence in hardheaded businessmen to invest in the development of his designs. Detailing his conception of an all-electronic television method, the twenty-year-old Farnsworth convinced Everson and Gorrell to form a partnership with him: Everson and Gorrell agreed to supply $6,000 for a quarter interest each in the partnership, while Farnsworth would supply and develop his ideas for the other half of the partnership. The goal

Philo T. Farnsworth with his electronic television receiver, 1929. (Wide World Photos; used with permission)

was not merely to create a workable electronic television method, Farnsworth insisted, but to use his patent rights to acquire the financial power to be able to pursue research in other fields. This intention, clearly formulated by 1926, provided the guiding principle for the inventor's relations with all other firms, including RCA.

Farnsworth moved to Los Angeles to work on his television method, but it was soon apparent that his belief that a working apparatus could rapidly be perfected had been naive and that much more money would be required before that goal would be achieved. Everson therefore set about organizing an additional group of financial backers, the new group consisting of executives of the Crocker National Bank in San Francisco headed by the bank's vice-president, Jesse B. McCargar. The San Francisco investors acquired 60 percent of the concern, the remaining 40 percent being retained by the original partners.

Farnsworth relocated his laboratory in San Francisco at the Crocker Research Laboratories, at 202 Green Street. Contributing to the continued delay of the project was the fact that most of the equipment needed was not commercially available, so Farnsworth was forced to make his own, assisted by Clifford Gardner. But confident that his method was feasible, he filed disclosures of his patents for it in January 1927 (and the U.S. Patent Office awarded them in August 1930). Then finally, on 7 September 1927, at the Green Street laboratory, the twenty-one-year-old Farnsworth transmitted his first successful image by wire—a horizontal line. By January 1928 he was successfully able to send two-dimensional images, such as photographs of his wife and brother-in-law, and later a picture of Gardner smoking a cigarette.

However, these early achievements were marred by the fact that the received images suffered from two serious distortions: there was blurring caused by ghosting and there was a black smudge that appeared like a line down the center of the picture. Both of these, Farnsworth soon came to realize, were caused by using sine waves in the scanning process: the ghosting was produced after the left-to-right scanning by the returning electron beam, while the smudge was the result of the steep slope of the wave, which caused fewer electrons to be released in the center of the left-to-right scanning. To solve both of these difficulties, a sawtooth wave was introduced instead, for governing the scanning. Now the scanning ratio was 10 to 1 for left to right and right to left, thus blanking out the ghosting; the straight line of the sawtooth wave eliminated the smudge as well.[87]

With these improvements, Farnsworth, having already spent $60,000, decided he was ready to demonstrate his electronic method publicly. On 2 September 1928, a laboratory presentation, the first public display anywhere in the world of a completely electronic television system, was put on for representatives of the press, the "show" consisting of a man smoking a cigarette. Farnsworth enthusiastically predicted that the equipment would soon be available commercially and would sell for about $100.[88] The story was carried by a wire service, and national publicity followed. In January 1929 *Radio News* ran a brief feature on the Farnsworth electronic method, and in late 1930 Farnsworth visited New York to display his apparatus, which, he claimed, "makes commercial television practical at once."[89] Besides giving demonstrations, Farnsworth attracted attention by writing articles describing his method. In the first issue of *Television News*, in April 1931, he provided detailed explanations of his pickup and receiving tubes, including photographs and diagrams, as well as an explanation of his method of synchronization.[90] And, even before this, in 1930, he coauthored an article that not only insisted on the superiority of electronic over other means of accomplishing television but also displayed great insight into the eventual requirements of an American national television system:

> A practical system of television broadcasting that will satisfy the ultimate requirements is being developed and consists in having a local television transmitter for each metropolitan area on an extremely short wavelength. . . . This transmitter is located atop the highest building in the district. . . . Its range

will not be more than 10 to 15 miles . . . and thus it will not interfere with another transmitter on the same frequency located fifty or one hundred miles away. Chain broadcasting will be handled by beam transmitters operating in the six meter region which will connect various cities in a television network.[91]

The Green Street laboratory began to attract famous visitors eager to investigate the promise of the new medium. These visitors included film stars Mary Pickford and Douglas Fairbanks and producer Joe Schenck. But probably the most significant visitor was Vladimir K. Zworykin, who spent several days inspecting Farnsworth's apparatus. Although his backers were upset by this visit by Zworykin, Farnsworth, not interested in broadcasting and manufacturing in themselves, recognized that if television was to be a commercial success, RCA would eventually have to be involved.[92]

The reason Farnsworth had decided to attract attention to his achievement was primarily financial. Between 1926 and 1929, the project had cost $140,000, and it was felt that some public investment would be necessary for commercialization. So in March 1929 Farnsworth's financial backers decided to incorporate the venture as Television Laboratories, Incorporated. But at the coming of the depression, with expenses continuing to mount and with the system still not ready for marketing, even more capital became necessary. In June 1931 McCargar and Everson negotiated a contract with the parent company of Philco, RCA's chief manufacturing rival. Farnsworth and most of his staff agreed to move to Philadelphia (a skeleton crew of two remained at the Green Street laboratory) to continue their research at the Philco plant there, while Philco received a nonexclusive license to manufacture receivers of Farnsworth design.[93]

The apparatus Farnsworth brought to Philadelphia consisted of two components: a pickup tube, the image dissector (named for the process of breaking down the image for transmission); and a receiver tube, the oscillite (named for the glowing image at the end of the CRT, which was produced by the oscillation of the electron beam). The image dissector differed radically from the iconoscope. Cylindrical in shape, it was a nonstorage pickup tube and operated without a scanning beam. Instead, the optical image to be transmitted was focused through a lens onto a photosensitive surface coated with caesium oxide, which acted as the CRT's cathode and was located at the lens end of the tube. This photoelectric surface emitted electrons proportional to the light intensities of the optical image falling on it. These electrons were not focused into a beam, as in Zworykin's design, but rather formed an electron image on an imaginary plane at the opposite end of the tube, being focused there by means of a magnetic field created by a solenoid mounted around the outside of the tube. Into the plane of this electron image projected the finger-shaped target structure, within which was the tube's anode. In the target was a tiny aperture, the point at which the electron image was "dissected" into picture elements. For scanning pur-

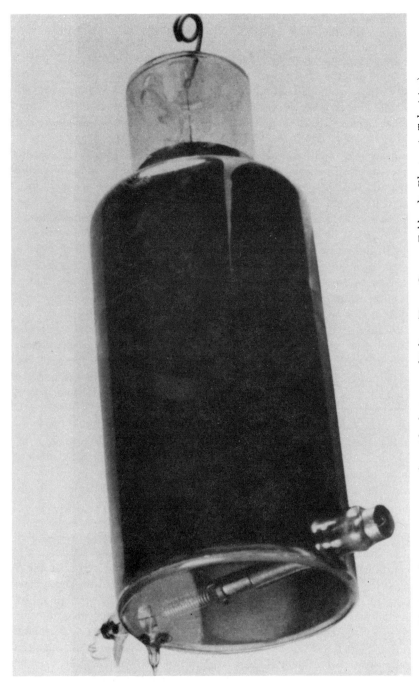

Farnsworth's image dissector camera tube with electron multiplier. (From George Eckhardt, *Electronic Television*)

poses, deflecting coils swept the entire electron image, horizontally left to right and vertically top to bottom, across this target aperture. As electrons successively entered the aperture, the sequential video signal was produced, after amplification.[94]

Very significant in the design of the dissector tube was the scanning of an electron image. That Farnsworth intentionally defined his pickup tube in terms of this technique is evident from his original 1927 disclosure, in which he described his device as "an apparatus for television which comprises means for forming an electrical image, moving the image in two directions over an electrical shutter having a small aperture, thus forming an electrical current which is a function of the intensity of the portion of the electrical image at said aperture."[95] This Farnsworth claim to primacy in the disclosure of the creation, focusing, and scanning of an electron image in a pickup tube was the main obstacle he represented to the introduction by RCA of the image iconoscope, as will be discussed below.

The image dissector's superiority to the iconoscope lay in the fact that it was completely linear in operation. This meant that the output signal would be proportional to the light intensities of the optical image that fell on the photosensitive surface. However, Farnsworth's original pickup tubes were too insensitive to operate except at very high light intensities, forcing him to limit his transmissions to film telecasts.[96] It was the necessity of solving this dilemma, primarily a result of the nonstorage nature of the tube, that so delayed the marketing of this design, for the experience of mechanical television had proven the need of direct and outdoor pickups for satisfactory and entertaining programming.

Farnsworth's receiver, the oscillite, generally resembled the kinescope, although Farnsworth consistently used electromagnetic deflection to focus and scan the beam across the fluorescent screen. The inclusion of the horizontal and vertical synchronizing pulses within the video signal was also a feature of the original disclosure of the design.[97]

The working relationship between Farnsworth and Philco was terminated after two years. Philco officials were disappointed that after this amount of time and an investment of $250,000, the image-dissector tube still had not been perfected. Furthermore, Philco officials saw research more as an adjunct to production requirements, while Farnsworth wanted to use his work to create a broad patent structure without regard to production. Philco, therefore, now established its own laboratory television staff, while Farnsworth reestablished his own independent research facility in the Chestnut Hill area of Philadelphia. To finance this venture, small blocks of the corporation's stock were sold privately.[98] With these new funds, he continued his efforts to develop a commercial television pickup tube.

Since 1930, Farnsworth had been concentrating on reducing the engineering deficiencies of the image dissector. At that time he explained that the principal weakness of his method lay in the fact that only a relatively small portion of the electrons emitted from the photo-sensitive surface are used at any given instant, and therefore extremely photosensitive screens and amplifiers are necessary in order to transmit satisfactory pictures.

When it is attempted to amplify the picture currents above a certain level, background noise, "Schottke effect" and other ordinarily negligible factors come in to make the amplified picture currents unsatisfactory and distorted.[99]

To meet this weakness and to increase the sensitivity of his pickup tube, Farnsworth developed his "multipactor," a secondary electron emission multiplier, which he first disclosed in a 1930 patent application. In operation, Farnsworth's multipactor was attached to the image dissector on the end opposite the photosensitive surface, behind the target anode. It was a cold cathode tube containing neither filament nor grid; instead it had two plates between which electrons would pass and bounce with sufficient force on the plates to release additional electrons; these, in turn, would then also bounce, producing a multiple of the same effect, thus greatly amplifying the

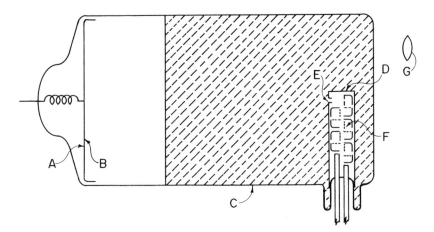

Image dissector with electron multiplier. When an object is focused through lens G onto the cathode A, the optical image formed on its photoelectric surface, B, emits photoelectrons, which are accelerated by the potential difference between A and the anode C, till they converge at the target aperture E, in a plane parallel to the cathode plane; this is the electron image. This image is then deflected horizontally and vertically past E in the multiplier housing D, causing a succession of the electrons composing the image to bombard the first segment, F, in the multiplier, where the remaining segments are further bombarded by primary and secondary electrons, thus greatly increasing the original input current at E. (Reprinted [adapted] with permission from *Electronics*, October 1939; copyright © McGraw-Hill, Inc., 1939. All rights reserved.)

current. The result of this innovation was that the sensitivity of the image dissector was sufficiently increased to allow for direct and outdoor pickups, providing there was adequate lighting.[100]

Receiving the patent for his secondary-emission multiplier in 1934, Farnsworth agreed to stage a demonstration for the Franklin Institute in August. A 220-line-frame, 30-frames-per-second, picture was produced by this camera, which, when used outdoors, showed "moving automobiles and passengers leaving their cars. The swaying leaves of nearby trees could easily be distinguished."[101] Farnsworth claimed that his improved apparatus made it possible, now, to televise satisfactorily football and baseball games, as well as tennis matches and news events.[102]

But the new pickup tube was, in fact, still not capable of the sensitivity necessary to meet adequately the requirements of a commercial system. The continuing insufficiency of the improved image dissector was primarily the result of the fact that only a small fraction of the electrons emitted by its photocathode at any one time were able to enter the multipactor.[103] Farnsworth, therefore, was forced to continue his research, while at the same time pressing ahead for commercialization of television as soon as possible.

Shortly after David Sarnoff announced RCA's commitment to a plan to develop public telecasting, Farnsworth staged another demonstration at his Chestnut Hill laboratory. The audience saw the film and direct pickups of the show on 5½-by-7-inch screens, and many viewers were impressed by the clarity of the images, which were now 240 lines, interlaced, 24 frames per second. Discussing the current status of television, Farnsworth claimed that commercial receivers could be immediately marketed and that the primary reason for the delay of television was the lack of transmitting stations. To help remedy this, his firm, he announced, intended to begin construction of several stations. And Farnsworth predicted that commercial television would be available within a year.[104]

In 1936 construction of the Philadelphia station began, and the facilities of W3XPF, in the suburb of Wyndmoor, were completed in early 1937. An "elaborate Hollywood-like studio" was designed to stage complicated live programming, which was broadcast by a 4-kw. transmitter. The picture, consisting of 441 lines, interlaced, at 30 frames per second, was demonstrated at the studios on receivers with horizontally mounted oscillites having 6-inch square screens. Although at first green-tinted images were still displayed, Farnsworth had already successfully tested receivers capable of producing black-and-white pictures.[105]

Then at the November 1938 meeting of the Institute of Radio Engineers–Radio Manufacturers Association in Rochester, New York, Farnsworth unveiled his new "image amplifier" pickup tube. While retaining essential features of the image dissector, the new tube also adopted Zworykin's storage principle and scanning beam. These greatly increased the sensitivity of the image amplifier, in fact allowing it to surpass that of the conventional iconoscope.[106] Unfortunately for Farnsworth, the new device had serious engineering deficiencies. These arose primarily because it employed a two-sided target in place of Zworykin's mosaic. However, while this allowed an electron image to be scanned, as in the image dissector, it was also a rich source of spurious signals, the result of the high velocity of its scanning beam, as well as because of the nonuniformities in structure, secondary-emission ratio, and amplification of the target. The entrance pattern of the electrons into the image amplifier's electron multiplier was also wide enough to create a further source of significant shading.[107]

But if the image amplifier was an eventual disappointment, the corporate successes generated by the improved image dissector certainly were not. In 1937 Farnsworth Television, Incorporated (as the firm was now called) concluded a deal to supply pickup equipment to CBS, now that CBS was preparing to reenter the public telecasting field.[108] Even more encouraging, in July 1937 AT & T agreed to a cross-licensing arrangement with Farnsworth.[109] Behind this latter deal was the influence of the banking firm of Kuhn, Loeb and Company, whose partner, Hugh Knowlton, had been involved with Farnsworth Television since 1935.[110]

The influence of the new financial investors soon became predominant. To the Kuhn, Loeb executives, it was evident that Farnsworth Television could no longer be successfully sustained by private investment. Without a new source of steady income to counterbalance the expenses incurred by the television research, the concern was doomed to collapse shortly. Although these bankers realized that Farnsworth's original conception of the firm had been frustrated by the long delay in perfecting his equipment, they also recognized the essential soundness of the plan to create a research and licensing organization based on his patents. The only question was from where to derive the capital necessary to sustain the mounting laboratory expenses. In the end, the solution arrived at was to transform the firm into a manufacturing enterprise.

In February 1939 Farnsworth Television and Radio Corporation was founded. It combined the research facilities of Farnsworth Television, Incorporated with the manufacturing plants of two other foundering firms: Capehart, Incorporated, in Fort Wayne, Indiana, famous for its record-changing phonographs, and General Household Utilities Company, owner of the Grigsby-Grunow Majestic radio plant in Marion, Indiana. Although the firm had a new name and a new task, its continuity with Farnsworth's original backers and with his original purpose was reflected in the composition of its officers. Jesse McCargar became chairman of the board, and George Everson, secretary-treasurer. The new president was Edward A. Nicholas, former manager of RCA's patent licensing division. Farnsworth himself became the firm's vice-president and director of research, although he had little to do with its day-to-day operation. Choosing to sell the Philadelphia facility, the new Farnsworth concern established its headquarters in Fort Wayne and soon began producing a full line of radios and Capehart phonographs. And by the eve of the Second World War, these manufacturing endeavors had become quite profitable, and more than offset the expenses of television research and development.[111]

But Farnsworth was succeeding not only in the United States. After 1933 he also became involved in the races for electronic television then taking place in Britain and Germany. As a result, the competition between his image dissector and Zworykin's iconoscope now acquired an international dimension.

THE TELEVISION RACE IS INTERNATIONALIZED

In 1935 the British government decided to terminate its mechanical low-definition experimental telecasts and to initiate broadcasting of high-definition television for regular public service. Two firms competed for government authorization to supply equipment to the BBC for the new service. One, Marconi-EMI, in which RCA held a financial interest, offered an all-electronic system based on their emitron pickup tube. This camera, closely resembling the iconoscope, was then capable of producing a 405-line frame, with interlaced scanning, at 25 frames per second.[112]

The other company was the pioneering independent British telecaster, Baird Television, which had provided the BBC with its original low-definition equipment. Now it offered two systems capable of producing a 240-line picture, 25 frames per second. One, a mechanical direct-pickup system, was intended for close-up shots, while the second, intended for more general programming, involved the "intermediate film system." In this technique, the scenes to be televised were first filmed; the film was very rapidly processed and then televised with a specially developed telecine scanner. The entire "intermediate film process" delayed the broadcasting of a scene by about forty seconds.[113]

The British government decided to allow the viewers themselves to choose between the competing techniques by providing broadcast facilities and time to both firms. Regular high-definition telecasting was thus inaugurated in London in November 1936, from the BBC's new television station at Alexandra Palace. Programs were carried daily, except Sunday, from 3:00 to 4:00 and 9:00 to 10:00 P.M. The competing systems alternated in these broadcasts.[114]

However, even before the telecasts had begun, Baird officials had begun to act in order to be able to adopt an all-electronic system of their own. In the fall of 1934 they contacted Farnsworth, who soon traveled to Britain to demonstrate his equipment to company officials. They were favorably impressed, and on 19 June 1935, a licensing agreement was signed between the British firm and Farnsworth Television that allowed Baird Television to employ the image-dissector pickup equipment for use in their Alexandra Palace telecasts.[115] However, the expected public contest between the image dissector and the iconoscope failed to materialize. As Baird engineers were preparing their new electronic equipment, a fire destroyed their studio and transmitting equipment at Crystal Palace. Before there was time to replace the damaged equipment, the government decided, in February 1937, to adopt the Marconi-EMI standards.[116] And by this time, an improved electronic pickup tube, the superemitron, combining features of the image dissector and the iconoscope, was being readied for introduction by Marconi-EMI engineers.[117]

But if the Farnsworth and Zworykin systems did not finally directly compete in field demonstrations in Britain, they did in Germany. There also two firms had come to dominate the television industry. The first of these was Telefunken, a large communications concern that by 1929 had introduced a mechanical low-definition system designed by A. Karolus of Leipzig. However, by 1934 Telefunken had abandoned mechanical television for an all-electronic system employing the "Ikonoskop-Kamera," derived from Zworykin's design, and in accordance with patent agreements with RCA.

Telefunken's primary competitor was Fernseh A. G., organized in 1929 as a partnership among Bosch, D. S. Loewe, Zeiss-Ikon, and Baird Television Company. Baird had been specially recruited by the German government to stimulate the development of German telecasting. Fernseh A. G. soon introduced its own version of mechanical television based on J. L. Baird's design. However, with the decline of mechanical methods and with the consequent introduction of the iconoscope by Telefunken, Fernseh A. G. also sought an effective electronic pickup device. Baird Television's recently established relationship with Farnsworth provided the route through which Fernseh A. G. and Farnsworth arrived at a cross-licensing arrangement, the inventor having demonstrated his apparatus in Berlin after his visit to Baird Television in London. In 1935 the continental concern introduced its "Farnsworth-Bildsondenröhre." As with its American counterpart, this German image dissector lacked the necessary sensitivity to compete with the iconoscope for direct pickups. Fernseh A. G. therefore adapted it to the intermediate film process, which it had previously introduced when Telefunken began developing mobile units for outdoor pickups. That Farnsworth benefited from this agreement is evident from the fact that he also employed a Fernseh telecine scanner and the intermediate film process in his telecasts from Philadelphia.[118]

In one of the earliest German demonstrations of the technique, a truck containing the film-processing equipment and a low-power VHF transmitter was sent to cover the May Day arrival of Adolph Hitler at Berlin's Templehof Airport in 1935. The scene was first recorded by means of a special motion-picture camera, the film was then processed in the truck, and the resulting images were relayed to the central station, from which it was finally transmitted. From live scene to final telecast, a total of about ninety seconds elapsed.[119] With the addition of the image dissector, a pickup tube particularly well suited for film scanning, Fernseh A. G. felt confident as it set out to compete with Telefunken in coverage of the 1936 summer Olympics.

For the Berlin games, a network of stations in five German cities was established, using coaxial cable interconnections. Telefunken and Fernseh A. G. each covered the various events for the network. Using its iconoscope cameras and the mobile van, Telefunken was able to cover both indoor and outdoor meets, as well as providing "color" with direct pickup of various street scenes. On the other hand, Fernseh A. G. was limited to indoor competition, such as swimming, for direct pickups with its image dissectors, while employing the intermediate film process in its telecasts of outdoor events, such as the marathon.

After the Olympics, German television technology continued to improve. By 1939 Telefunken had introduced its Super-Ikonoskop, capable of producing a 441-line picture, with interlaced scanning. Using cameras equipped with this tube, Telefunken was able to televise satisfactory pictures even from indoors without the necessity of artificial lighting.

Fernseh A. G. also increased the definition of the pictures produced by its equipment and, in 1937, introduced a new light scanner designed by Farnsworth. Using this apparatus, Fernseh covered the Nazi *Parteitag* in Nürnberg in the fall of 1938. However, restricted by the limited sensitivity of the image dissector, with its nonstorage design, the scenes still had first to be filmed, the motion pictures flown to Berlin, and there, after processing, telecast over the coaxial cable network.

Meanwhile, Telefunken was using its Super-Ikonoskop cameras to cover sporting events in Berlin. In 1939 the camera's versatility was impressively demonstrated in coverage of a German-Italian soccer match in the Olympic stadium in November, when good pictures were produced despite inclement weather. Thus it was not surprising that the German government chose to employ only the Super-Ikonoskop for its television coverage of the 1940 winter Olympics to be held in Helsinki.[120]

It was clear, in fact, by the outbreak of the Second World War, that the competition between Telefunken and Fernseh A. G. was over. Fernseh, unable to compete convincingly with its rival equipment and also without an income from other sources to offset the expenses incurred in its television experiments, was perilously close to financial collapse. Telefunken, on the other hand, had clearly emerged as the dominant firm in the German television industry.[121]

RCA'S PATENT DILEMMA AND FARNSWORTH'S VICTORY

The British and German experiences demonstrated to Farnsworth that the image dissector could not match the programming versatility of the iconoscope, and especially not that of the improved design of the tube being introduced in Europe. Farnsworth Television and Radio also required RCA licensing for its radio and phonograph manufacturing. On the other hand, RCA saw the European developments as confirmation of its own experience: the domestic model of the iconoscope was not a commercially acceptable pickup tube. But with a different patent structure for the industry in the United States than in Britain and Germany, RCA was unable to introduce the new pickup tube already being used in Europe without first acquiring a license from Farnsworth, an arrangement RCA was extremely reluctant to make.

All along Farnsworth had expected to be successful financially with his television apparatus not through his own manufacturing efforts, but instead by using his designs as a source for licensing production by other firms. And even in his earliest efforts, he had recognized the predominant position RCA would play in the industry. It was therefore necessary for him to devise a technique different from (and, he hoped, superior to) that of RCA and also to limit the patent claims of RCA where there might be any prospect of similarity between his designs and theirs. This would provide him with the resources to bargain with the communications giant from a position of strength. It was his ability to convince others of the feasibility of this plan which attracted such loyal financial backers for his venture.

For these reasons, Farnsworth had joined Harold J. McCreary's patent-interference suit against Zworykin's 1923 iconoscope disclosure. This action was brought by McCreary in 1927, the same year Farnsworth filed the first applications for his television system. McCreary finally lost his case in February 1932. Then in May of that year, Farnsworth filed his own patent-interference action against Zworykin. The case rested on Farnsworth's claim to priority in disclosing the concept of "electronic image" scanning in his 1927 patent application. On 27 July 1935, the patent examiner for the case found that Zworykin had no right to make the claim that his pickup method, disclosed in 1923, scanned an "electronic image," and that the iconoscope as it currently operated also did not scan an electron image (but instead relied upon the scanning of an optical image). Farnsworth had thus won his case. RCA, however, appealed the verdict. On 6 March 1936, the Patent Office's Board of Appeals announced that it upheld the original findings of the examiner that Farnsworth had priority to the claim of scanning an electron image.[122]

RCA now had three alternatives open to it: (1) it might appeal this decision in a civil court; (2) it might develop a satisfactory pickup tube without relying on the Farnsworth patent; or (3) it could arrive at some arrangement with Farnsworth. The first alternative was the least attractive: not only had RCA already lost twice on its presentation of the case, but a civil case, which might last several years, could seriously delay the introduction of commercial telecasting, or at least restrict it by limiting RCA to the use of the unsatisfactory iconoscope.

The second alternative was complicated by the fact that this was not the only patent at issue between Farnsworth and RCA. Still to be decided, particularly, was an interference claim concerning priority in the standard synchronization techniques employed in television. Involved in this case were the conflicting claims of Farnsworth against patents assigned to RCA by the principal researchers in Purdue University's television project, Roscoe H. George and Howard J. Heim. Furthermore, Farnsworth and RCA had counterclaims over the priority of the technique employed in interlaced scanning.[123]

Such financial and legal considerations, in addition to the increasing evidence of the limitations of the iconoscope, forced RCA to arrive at some settlement with Farnsworth. Of course, the former had not hesitated to offer previously to buy the rights to Farnsworth patents, a course often followed by RCA. But Farnsworth would not sell; all along he had intended only to agree to license RCA to employ his techniques. But it was RCA's policy not to purchase licenses from others. Still, too much had been invested by the communications giant to risk further delays when the necessary technology already existed for providing, immediately, the quality necessary to attract public and advertising support. The stalemate became intolerable once RCA initiated regular public telecasting in New York, in May 1939. So, in a precedent-breaking agreement, RCA and Farnsworth Television and Radio signed a nonexclusive cross-licensing arrangement in September 1939.[124] Farnsworth won his point, but RCA was now free to employ its image iconoscope.

RCA first introduced the image iconoscope in the United States at the thirteenth annual meeting of the Institute of Radio Engineers in June 1938; the first published account of it appeared in September 1939.[125] Central to the new design was the separation between the photoemission and charge-storage functions of the tube. In the new design, an optical image of the scene to be transmitted was focused on a semitransparent conducting photocathode. The photoelectrons emitted by this cathode traversed the tube to an insulating target, on which they were focused either electrostatically or electromagnetically. The high velocity at which the electrons struck the target produced secondary emissions that increased the charge of the target severalfold. The resulting amplified electron image was then scanned by a cathode-ray beam in a fashion similar to that of the original iconoscope. The result was that the image iconoscope was five to ten times more sensitive

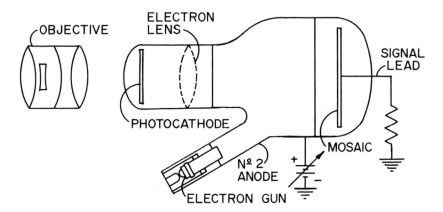

Schematic diagram of the image iconoscope. The object is focused on the photo-cathode, where an optical image forms. The photocathode emits electrons proportional to the light falling on it; these form the electron image. This, in turn, is focused on the mosaic by means of the electron lens. The mosaic is then scanned by the cathode-ray beam emitted by the electron gun. (© 1939 IRE, now IEEE. Reprinted, with permission, from Harley Iams, G. A. Morton, and Vladimir K. Zworykin, "The Image Iconoscope," *Proceedings of the IRE* 27, no. 9, September 1939)

than the iconoscope, and thereby greatly increased the programming potential available to RCA-NBC, especially for outdoor events occurring in the late afternoon and evening. It also significantly reduced the amount of studio lighting required for indoor pickups. But the image iconoscope still was subject to annoying spurious shading patterns.[126]

For this reason, RCA officials were particularly enthusiastic about an entirely new tube introduced in 1939, the orthicon. This name, a shortened form of *orthiconoscope*, was derived from the Greek word *orthos*, "straight," and the previously coined word *iconoscope*. The name reflected the fact that in this new tube there was a linear relationship between input light and output current, as in the image dissector but unlike the iconoscope.

However, the truly revolutionary feature of the orthicon was its low-velocity scanning beam.[127] In operation, light from the scene to be transmitted was focused on a mosaic target similar to that of the iconoscope. However, the charge of the target was equal to the charge of the cathode of the electron gun. Thus, electrons of the scanning beam approached the target surface at zero velocity, turned around at the target surface, and returned to a collector at the cathode: Where the light intensities of the scene focused on the target caused photoemission, the beam electrons landed without producing any appreciable secondary emissions and simply restored the original voltage. In this fashion, the target was charged uniformly, and there was no secondary emission. The signal was produced by impulses given to the signal

An RCA orthicon camera tube. (Courtesy of RCA)

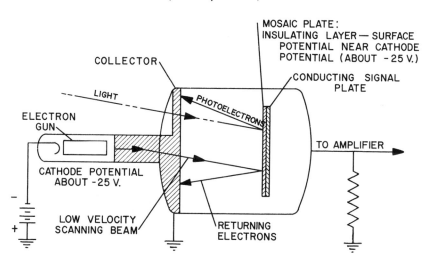

The orthicon. Light from the object falls on the mosaic plate, and all the photoelectrons are drawn to the collector. The plate is swept by the electron beam, reaching the plate at zero velocity. If the mosaic has been charged up by any light falling on it, the electron beam merely resupplies the electrons that were emitted as a result of photoemission, bringing the mosaic back to cathode potential. The signal is produced as each successive point of the mosaic is discharged. (Courtesy of the *RCA Review*)

plate by the beam electrons as they arrived at the lighted portions of the target. This meant that the transmitted signal was proportional to the light on the target and that the conversion of possible photoemission into signal was about 100 percent efficient. Thus the orthicon achieved three important advances over previous charge-storage pickup tubes: it eliminated spurious signals, it demonstrated an extremely high efficiency of conversion of photo-emission into video signal, and it produced a large signal output. These features eliminated the dark spot of the iconoscope and the image iconoscope; they also made it possible for the orthicon to operate in low-light, low-contrast scenes, because the orthicon was at least ten times as sensitive as the iconoscope.[128]

However, despite RCA's understandable enthusiasm for the orthicon, it did suffer from offsetting defects of its own. Primarily, it had neither the resolution of the iconoscope nor its wide-ranging capability of responding to contrasts. Only after the war, in 1946, was a "perfect" commercial pickup device finally introduced. This device, the image orthicon, integrated fea-

Coinventors of the RCA image orthicon camera tube, Albert Rose, Paul K. Weimer, and Harold B. Law, shown here with the first model, in 1945. (Courtesy of RCA)

tures of the image dissector, iconoscope, image iconoscope, and orthicon into one tube.[129] Its design combined the use of the electron image amplification of the image dissector, while eliminating the amplifier noise, with the high light stability of the iconoscope, the sensitivity of the image iconoscope, and the linearity of the orthicon. The result was that the image orthicon exceeded the sensitivity of the orthicon by a factor of at least 100, and closely matched that of the human eye in its operating range.[130] However, the key factor that made the development of this new device possible was the introduction of a thin sheet of semiconducting glass for the image orthicon's tube-sided target, an innovation that kept it completely free from the intolerable spurious signals that had plagued earlier designs.[131] Nevertheless, even with only the image iconoscope and the orthicon, RCA could feel confident of providing the picture quality and programming range necessary for a commercial television system.

THE INVENTORS OF ELECTRONIC TELEVISION

After tracing the engineering history of high-definition television in the United States and Europe, the purely speculative question arises: Who, then, is the inventor of electronic television? Pragmatic reasoning from the data dictates that there were, as with television itself, two coinventors: Philo T. Farnsworth and Vladimir K. Zworykin. Although their circumstances differed markedly from those of Baird and Jenkins in that Farnsworth and Zworykin did not work entirely independently of knowledge of each other's work and that they did not simultaneously demonstrate their techniques publicly, other considerations do force this conclusion. Six factors provide the basis of this judgment: each worked from a common fund of accumulated television research; each did, independently, develop a distinctive all-electronic technology during the same time-frame; each of these technologies was capable of providing high-definition television service; acceptable public telecasting required a combination of the technologies of both men; differences in the dates of the first public demonstration of each man were not dictated by engineering feasibility and quality, but rather by financial and corporate policies; and finally, such a conclusion provides an equitable historical evaluation of the contributions of both Farnsworth and Zworykin without yielding to subjective partisan squabbling over various specious definitions of "first invented," an exercise that can be continued ad infinitum, ad nauseam.

Even allowing for his organizational bias, David Sarnoff himself acknowledged and summarized the arguments for the coinvention of electronic television. When he testified before a U.S. Senate subcommittee in 1940, he said, "It is only fair that I should mention this—an American inventor who I think has contributed, outside R.C.A. itself, more to television than anybody else in the United States, and that is Mr. Farnsworth, of the Farnsworth Television System. . . . I believe the industry will require the license under the Farnsworth patents as well as the R.C.A. patents if they are to go ahead."[132]

The Race for Perfect Television

The mutually satisfactory resolution of the stalemate between RCA and Farnsworth did not terminate the television race nor remove all obstacles to the initiation of commercial telecasting. In fact, the competition actually intensified. Now other manufacturers attempted to prevent an RCA-Farnsworth monopoly of television engineering, while rival broadcast networks sought to force the pace of the introduction of public telecasting. At the same time, the FCC continued to adhere to its traditional policy of refusing authorization for fixed industry standards or for commercial service until there was unanimity among industry engineers and broadcasters that the entire system had been perfected. But as the television industry's competitive field broadened and the tempo quickened, this proved increasingly difficult to attain. So RCA, caught in this maelstrom of industrial rivalry and governmental inertia, quickened its own drive toward the introduction of a complete television system for public marketing.

RCA AND ITS COMPETITORS

If RCA and Farnsworth Television were, by 1939, the established leaders in the television race, they were certainly not unchallenged. In fact, it was in part because RCA officials felt the breath of their two primary competitors—one in manufacturing and the other in broadcasting—that they quickened their own pace to complete the development of a commercial television system. Philco, the leading independent radio manufacturer, and CBS, the leading radio network challenging NBC, both were intensively involved with television by the end of the decade, and both sought to block RCA's (and Farnsworth's) total triumph. And unlike the competition between RCA and Farnsworth, these were longstanding rivalries among fierce combatants. Throughout the decade of the 1930s RCA's most intense manufacturing rivalry was with Philco, a conflict that was not only intense but also emotional.

The hostility between the two firms preceded their mutual involvement with television by several years. Philco had been founded in 1892 as the

Helios Electric Company. In 1906 it adopted the name Philadelphia Storage Battery Company, and by the 1920s, though still a small firm, it conducted a thriving national business producing the storage batteries and "B" (that is, battery) eliminators then required to operate ordinary home radios. But the development of an AC tube would end the need to employ B eliminators. However, Philadelphia Storage Battery, believing they had received firm assurances from the management of RCA that they did not intend to bring out the new tube, built up a large inventory of storage batteries and B eliminators for its fall selling season. Shortly thereafter, RCA did introduce the AC tube, and Philadelphia Storage Battery's business collapsed, its executives convinced they had been deliberately betrayed.

But the firm's management did not despair; instead it decided, in 1927, to enter the home-radio market as the means for recouping its losses. Through its existing national distributor-dealer network, Philadelphia Storage Battery already possessed the necessary marketing capability for the new venture. As RCA was then limiting the total number of licenses it granted for radio production, to enter the radio market rights to an existing license had to be purchased; this was done in February 1928. At the same time, because Philadelphia Storage Battery's personnel were primarily electrochemists and because it was necessary to recruit a new staff with engineering competence in radio, an arrangement was also made with Hazeltine Laboratories. To compete successfully with RCA, Philadelphia Storage Battery officials conceived the idea of producing radios that would be attractive as furniture pieces, and so further arrangements were made with furniture designers. In all, the firm had to borrow about $7 million for its conversion to radio manufacture. But by 1933 the gamble had paid off, and Philadelphia Storage Battery was outselling RCA in home radios.[1]

In the meantime, the firm reorganized, in 1932, in order to reduce to a minimum its license payments to RCA. Although located within the same plant, two corporate entities replaced the parent concern. Philadelphia Storage Battery continued as the production firm and so was obliged to pay royalties to RCA, but the new Philco Radio and Television Company took over the engineering and marketing functions and claimed exemption from RCA licensing fees.[2]

The firm's officials had also decided early on to enter the competition to develop a commercial television system. For this reason the arrangement was made with Farnsworth in 1931. In the same year Philadelphia Storage Battery applied to the FRC for permission to construct an experimental visual broadcast station. The license was granted, and the all-CRT VHF station, W3XE, located at the plant at C and Tioga streets, in Philadelphia, began operating in the summer of 1932.[3] When the contract with Farnsworth was terminated in 1933, the firm organized its own television research staff. Although work was also conducted on transmitters, Philco concen-

trated its primary development efforts on producing commercial home receivers.

At the beginning of 1936 Philco president Lawrence E. Gubb told the
press that he did not expect commercial television that year.[4] However, a
month after RCA staged its first television demonstration in New York,
Philco staged its own press show from W3XE. The fifty-five-minute program
on 11 August included a boxing match and soloists performing before iconoscope cameras, sending a 345-line picture. The audience viewed the black-
and-white images reflected in a 9-by-8-inch mirror in the receiver's cabinet
lid, the Philco-designed CRT also being mounted vertically in the set. Viewers were impressed by the pictures and noted especially their clarity and
lack of shimmer; additionally, the Philco sets operated well in a lighted
room. However, it was felt by many that the images were still too small and
that there remained some distortion at the picture's edges. Not surprisingly,
Gubb told the audience, "We don't believe that television is right around
the corner, but we do believe it will result in a tremendous industry when it
does arrive. We do not believe in doing anything premature."[5] This was
exactly RCA's attitude.

In February 1937 Philco staged a second demonstration. An elaborate
program was presented, including singer Helen Hughes, a newsreel of
midwestern flooding, a Bonwit Teller fashion show, and an interview with
Philadelphia Athletics manager Connie Mack. The pictures were now of 441
lines, and the receivers had only ten, instead of fourteen, control knobs.
Still, viewers felt that while the pictures were clear, they were not equal to
the quality of theater and home motion pictures.[6]

These demonstrations occurred at a time when Philco's decade-old conflict with RCA intensified even further. As the first demonstration was being
readied, Philco filed suit in New York Supreme Court charging RCA with
unfair trade practices. The suit charged that RCA had obtained valuable
"confidential information" on Philco's latest television patents from some of
the firm's female employees, who had been lavished with "expensive entertainment and intoxicating liquors at hotels, restaurants and nightclubs."
RCA was alleged to have sought to "involve them in compromising situations
and did induce, incite and bribe said employees."[7] Philco also filed a second
suit in Wilmington, Delaware, to restrain RCA from withdrawing its access
to their licenses. RCA denied both charges.[8] Besides these direct confronta-
tions, Philco shortly thereafter also entered into joint television research
with RCA's main rival as a patent-holding company, the Hazeltine Corporation, to try to develop a synchronizing method superior to that employed in
RCA equipment.[9] These efforts would all culminate in moves by Philco to
block RCA's effort to win government authorization for commercial television. In this endeavor Philco was joined by CBS.

After abandoning mechanical low-definition television, CBS retained its experimental VHF television station, W2XAX. Spurred on by Sarnoff's May 1935 announcement of RCA's television plan, CBS's William Paley decided to revitalize his own network's program. In December 1935 Hungarian-trained engineer Peter Goldmark was hired to rebuild CBS television, employing the latest technology.[10] And in April 1937 CBS announced plans to install a 30-kw. transmitter in the Chrysler Building, connected by coaxial cable to elaborate studios to be constructed in the Grand Central Terminal, above the waiting room.[11] CBS had also arrived at an agreement with Farnsworth, although iconoscopes and an RCA transmitter were also purchased.[12] At the same time Paley agreed to Goldmark's suggestion in 1938 that CBS endeavor to develop its own equipment.[13] Although CBS originally intended to compete with NBC only as it did in radio, that is, as a rival network, Goldmark's suggestion led to a technological innovation that encouraged CBS, along with Philco and newcomer Allen B. DuMont, to press the FCC, in 1940, not to authorize the RCA–Farnsworth Television system. But no sign of this bitter struggle was yet on the horizon.[14]

THE DON LEE SYSTEM IN LOS ANGELES

Although the most extensive CRT television experimentation occurred during this decade in the Philadelphia and greater New York areas, research was also being conducted in several other areas of the country. The most active work among these more modest operations was being done in Los Angeles.

There the Don Lee Broadcasting System had begun operating a mechanical visual station, W6XK; in December 1931 it began also broadcasting simultaneously over VHF electronic station W6XAO. The television equipment necessary for this new station had been developed by Harry R. Lubcke.

Lubcke, a graduate of the University of California at Berkeley, had first been employed by Farnsworth in his San Francisco laboratory in 1929. However, when the Crocker Laboratories' financial situation worsened in 1930, several members of its staff were discharged, including Lubcke. In November of that year, Don Lee hired the twenty-five-year-old engineer as his director of television.

The earliest programming, scheduled for one hour daily, except Sunday, was limited to films, which were obtained from Paramount and Pathe Newsreel.[15] At this time Lubcke employed a CRT to generate the "flying spot" of light which scanned the film. That is, the cathode-ray beam was directed outside the tube to provide the light beam that affected the photocells after having scanned the film.[16] The signal produced by these cells was then transmitted to a CRT-equipped receiver synchronized with the transmitter. In March 1933, with television demonstrations now being conducted by two local department stores, W6XAO provided coverage of the Long Beach earthquake disaster for three consecutive days, employing the intermediate film process. At the same time, the station televised a current full-length motion picture, World Wide's *The Crooked Circle*.[17]

In 1936, after adopting more conventional CRT pickup equipment, W6XAO expanded its schedule to four hours daily, transmitting a 300-line picture at 24 frames per second. Programming now included live telecasts as well as film. Typical of these telecasts was the feature "Living-Room Education," consisting of live demonstrations from the University of Southern California on such topics as pottery making, first aid, golf strokes, and cake decorating. W6XAO also introduced classroom educational television, with four local schools participating in the experiment. Public demonstrations of television were now also staged in a variety of settings, and a receiver was made available to the public in the Don Lee Building.[18] At the same time, the station conducted experiments on the suitability of motion pictures for television for the American Society of Cinematographers, which, in August 1937, issued seven rules for the filming of motion pictures intended for television.[19]

During the following year W6XAO began telecasting four dramatic sketches a week. These included the first televised serial, "Vine Street," a fifty-two-episode comic drama of Hollywood life from the poverty of park benches to the riches of the motion picture studios, written by Maurice Ashley and Wilfred Pettitt, and starring Shirley Thomas and John Barkeley.[20] Such programming allowed for a further expansion of the broadcast schedule, so by the spring of 1939 the station was transmitting seven hours daily, except Sunday, of which five hours and fifteen minutes were of live subjects and one hour and forty-five minutes, of film.[21]

At the same time, work was begun on moving W6XAO from its original location on the eighth floor of the Don Lee Building, at Seventh and Bixel streets in Los Angeles, to a new location, purchased from the Mack Sennett estate. At this new site, now renamed Mt. Lee, located between Hollywood and Burbank, a two-story building was erected to house the modern transmitter room and large sound stage, the sound stage modeled after those of motion-picture studios. In October the new facility was inaugurated by the mayor of Los Angeles, Fletcher Bowron.[22] The station's transmitter remained at Mt. Lee for over a decade, well into the era of commercial telecasting.[23]

THE SMALLER TELEVISION EXPERIMENTERS

Besides W6XAO, three small CRT stations operated experimentally outside the Philadelphia–New York area during this decade. In 1932 First National Television, Incorporated, of Kansas City, Missouri, began operating W9XAL in conjunction with a school organized to train students in television techniques. W9XAL originally operated as a shortwave mechanical station from 106 West Fourteenth Street, but later converted to CRT equipment on VHF and moved to the thirty-fourth floor of the Fidelity Building. From this location the station continued to function until January 1941.[24]

In Jackson, Michigan, W8XAN operated from 1932 to 1938. Located at plant number one of the Sparks-Withington Company, the station was evidently used by the firm's engineering department to determine the feasibility of entering the field of television broadcasting. Although Sparks-Withington did not pursue the project into the following decade, it did employ the experience gained from its telecasts over W8XAN in the manufacture of its Sparton television sets, produced from 1948 through 1956.[25]

The fourth small CRT station also telecasting during this decade was W1XG in Boston—the only survivor of those independent telecasters of the boom years of mechanical television. W1XG had been introduced as Shortwave and Television's VHF outlet; it was eventually converted to CRT equipment and continued to operate without any audio from 70 Brookline Avenue under the same firm, now reorganized as General Television Corporation. This station would continue until its application for a commercial telecast license was dismissed by the FCC in 1945.[26]

ELECTRONIC HIGH-DEFINITION TELEVISION STANDARDS EXPLORED

The experimental transmissions conducted by the nation's CRT stations were essential elements in developing the engineering technology and production techniques necessary to introduce successfully a commercial television system. Furthermore, the demonstrations conducted by the stations in New York, Philadelphia, and Los Angeles were also an important means for arousing the public's interest in the endeavor, and therefore they were essential if television was to become financially feasible. Similarly, as has been evident from the earliest years of mechanical telecasting, standardization of equipment was a prerequisite for the introduction of commercial television. And so to this task the Radio Manufacturers' Association once again turned its attention.

In fact, the RMA had reconstituted its original Television Committee as early as 1933, in order to reflect the new trend toward electronic apparatus. Representatives of the mechanical telecasters were replaced by officials from radio manufacturers that had expressed interest in entering the television market: RCA Victor Company, whose Elmer T. Cunningham chaired the committee, Stromberg-Carlson Company, Philadelphia Storage Battery Company, and Crosley Radio Corporation.[27] However, it was not until

RCA's 1935 announcement of its commitment to the development of a public television service that RMA instructed its engineering department to determine when it would be advisable to adopt uniform television standards. This action came to the attention of the FCC's chief engineer, Tunis A. M. Craven, who proposed that the RMA first adopt an agreement on standardization that would provide that all American-made television sets be able to receive the transmission from all stations in the country; he also suggested that special frequency allocations be specifically assigned for television's use. These recommendations from the FCC reflected the traditional practice of allowing private interests to determine the technical specifications for the communications industry, with governmental action being limited to regulatory matters. In response to Craven's suggestions, the RMA established two committees.[28] At FCC hearings on television standardization convened in 1936, the RMA Allocations Committee recommended that the commission establish seven 6-MHz. television channels between 42 and 90 MHz., in addition to experimental authorization above 125 MHz. The RMA Standards Committee recommended 441 lines, interlaced, with 30 frames per second, double-sideband negative picture modulation, with a 2.5-MHz. video bandwidth, and FM audio signal, the video and audio carriers spaced approximately 3.25 MHz. apart, the audio carrier being the higher in frequency.[29]

In May 1936 the FCC issued television frequency allocations divided into three groups: Group A, 42–56 MHz.; Group B, 60–86 MHz.; and Group C, any two adjacent frequencies above 110 MHz., except 400–401 MHz.[30] Then, the following year, these allocations were revised, and television was assigned seven channels: 44–50, 50–56, 66–72, 78–84, 84–90, 96–102, and 102–108 MHz.[31] However, the commission did not consider that television engineering possessed the necessary stability required for the government to act on the RMA recommendations on standardization.

The RMA committee therefore continued its deliberations into 1938, when it recommended that several new elements be included in the list of standards and also altered two previous recommendations: the video bandwidth was raised to 4.0 MHz. and double-sideband transmission was replaced by a system of vestigial sideband transmission instead.[32] However, the FCC again concluded that "television is not ready for standardization or commercial use by the general public" because of the continuing danger of rapid obsolescence of equipment, and it therefore decided to continue its policy of not acting on the RMA recommendations.[33]

But in April 1938 the FCC did act decisively in a manner that affected the future status of television: it issued a revised set of Rules of Practices of Procedure. Included in this new code was Rule 103.8 limiting experimental television licenses to stations engaged in research and experimentation in the technical phases of television broadcasting. This rule eliminated those stations that had previously engaged only in program development (for example, W9XAT in Minneapolis, W9XD in Milwaukee, and W8XAN in Jackson, Michigan).[34] This was still another blow to those in the industry who were pressing for rapid commercialization.

However, most telecasters chose to modify their equipment to conform to the RMA standards, and RCA announced plans to inaugurate regular public transmissions on 30 April 1939 in New York. Receiver sets were also being retailed in accordance with these standards. In response to these developments, the FCC appointed a Television Committee consisting of Tunis A. M. Craven, chairman, Norman S. Case, and Thad H. Brown to investigate the current conditions of television technology and to recommend commission policy. The committee suggested that further experimentation be encouraged in order to provide "a stable television service of good technical quality, without too rapid obsolescence of the instruments it [the public] has purchased."[35] Therefore the committee warned against the danger of "freezing" television's improvement by premature official adoption of standards.[36]

These recommendations actually reflected a new division that had occurred within the ranks of the industry itself. While RCA, GE, and Farnsworth continued to support the RMA position, in 1939 Philco, Zenith, and DuMont (and soon CBS) now strongly dissented. The latter group claimed that the proposed standards were not "sufficiently flexible to permit certain future technical improvements without unduly jeopardizing the initial investment of the public in receivers."[37]

This conflict in the industry led FCC officials to conclude that adoption of the RMA standards, besides "freezing" further engineering improvements, might also lead to the creation of a monopoly of the industry by one group of manufacturers at the expense of all others, an eventuality the commission was determined to avoid.[38] Therefore the Television Committee recommended that the FCC continue to withhold any action on the RMA standards in order to allow engineering flexibility, which might foster further technical improvements and also reduce the retail price of receivers.[39] But underlying this decision was the commission's determination not to act so long as all the major industry interests could not arrive at agreement over standardization, a policy reflecting the federal government's general concern over corporate monopolies. This FCC policy meant that in 1939 regular public telecasting would be inaugurated, and receivers retailed, without the commission's acceptance of television standardization. And this promised still further delay in the FCC's final authorization of commercial service.

RCA INTRODUCES PUBLIC TELECASTING

Several factors account for RCA's decision to proceed with regular public telecasting in April 1939, even without the prospect of immediate authorization of commercial service. First, the inauguration was timed to coincide with the opening of the New York World's Fair, an event guaranteed to provide massive publicity for the new service. In this way, public telecasting was simply a natural extension of the television-development plan announced by David Sarnoff in 1935, the last stage in the process before commercialization could be reasonably expected. To inaugurate this service in the spotlight of World Fair publicity was an opportunity too valuable to ignore.

The second consideration, a corollary of the first, was that such regular telecasting would convince the public of television's potential for providing attractive home entertainment. RCA could be even more confident of this potential as it moved to conclude its licensing agreement with Farnsworth. And once public support had been achieved, more intense pressure could be applied to the FCC to authorize commercial service.

Such authorization was the prerequisite for RCA's finally marketing its television system. However, this system itself was now being seriously challenged. Pressure from industry rivals thus provided the third incentive for RCA to initiate its regular public telecasts. Three challenges to RCA's system existed in 1939. First, rival telecasters, particularly CBS in New York and Don Lee in Los Angeles, were clearly intent on inaugurating their own regular services sometime later that year, and it would be a serious blow to RCA's desire for television leadership if it found itself following others from the very beginning. This situation became more intolerable as RCA found Philco and DuMont both working to produce technologies that would provide alternatives to the technology developed by RCA. At the least, this might cause still further delays in commercial authorization, since the FCC could be expected to await industry unanimity on standardization before acting; at the worst, RCA might find itself actually required to purchase licenses from these rivals if their efforts were allowed enough time to mature. And third, RCA had found that already in 1938 rival manufacturers were retailing television receivers before its own sets were available to the public and that its share of this potential market was already being jeopardized.

This last issue was the only one that RCA faced as an actuality, and the response to it reflects RCA's intention to defend its commanding position in the television industry. The challenge to its manufacturing plans arose in May 1938. At that time the Empire State Building telecasts had been extended to four afternoons and two evenings a week. Taking advantage of the availability of these programs, Communicating Systems, Incorporated (later renamed American Television Corporation) announced plans to begin retailing television sets in the New York and Boston areas (where the telecasts of W1XG were available for viewers). The firm would thus be the first to retail CRT television receivers in the United States. Already two models were in production, a set with a 3-inch screen, to sell at $150, and one with a 5-inch screen, at $250. Both models received video only, although a sound adapter could be purchased for an additional $15 to $17. Demonstrations of the sets were held at Bloomingdale's in Manhattan, Abraham Straus in Brooklyn, and Piser and Company in the Bronx.

Shortly thereafter, DuMont announced it also intended to market television receivers, one with a 10-by-8-inch screen for $650 and one with a 8¼-by-6½-inch screen for $395. These sets reproduced both the video and audio portions of the transmissions. Davega City Radio Stores had arranged to demonstrate the DuMont equipment at its Madison Square Garden store.

Reacting only a few hours after Communicating System's announcement, RCA restated its position that television receivers should not be retailed until technical perfection had been achieved, in order to guarantee the public both quality entertainment and protection against set obsolescence.[40] This policy reflected RCA's long-held view that premature marketing of television might discourage public enthusiasm for the new medium. To emphasize further its position that television was still experimental, RCA terminated its telecasts for two months, ostensibly for technical adjustments. This action did, in fact, hurt Communicating Systems' plans, but the firm announced, once the transmissions were resumed, that it would guarantee against obsolescence for one year every set it sold.[41]

However, by the time RCA-NBC inaugurated their regular public service in April 1939, the atmosphere had changed considerably. Now not only were American Television and DuMont marketing their receivers, but RCA, GE, and Andrea Radio Corporation also made their sets available, with several other firms announcing plans to do so soon. These sets varied widely in almost every important feature: in price, in screen size, in channels available (from three to seven), in channel bandwidth (2.5 MHz. to 4 MHz.), in channel number assigned to each frequency, in color of picture (black and green or black and white), and in design (direct-view console with video and audio, direct-view table model with video only, or video and audio console with picture viewed in a mirror on the inside of the cabinet lid).[42] Expressing the change in RCA's policy, Oscar B. Hanson, vice-president of NBC, wrote that "American television has been delayed to assure the adoption of the best possible group of transmission standards," and urged their adoption by the FCC to avoid the danger of obsolescence (a danger that, it was feared, might now discourage receiver sales).[43]

This change in RCA policy had been announced by David Sarnoff at an RMA meeting the previous October. There Sarnoff had said that NBC would begin regular public telecasts the following April, to coincide with the opening of the World's Fair, and that at the same time RCA would place its television sets on the market.[44] In his remarks, Sarnoff did not explain what had caused the change in RCA policy between May and October, as no significant technical development had occurred, apparently, nor had FCC

An RCA television receiver, its picture viewed in a mirror in the upraised cabinet top, 1940. (Courtesy of the Library of Congress)

policy on standardization been altered. In fact, besides the obvious motive of responding to the competition, Sarnoff was acting from an awareness of both the serious flaws in the iconoscope and of the impending introduction of improved pickup tubes. And with this announcement by Sarnoff, the 1935 decision by RCA to develop a feasible television system was finally to be realized with the introduction of a regular television service in New York and with the retailing of receivers to the public.

For the 30 April 1939 inauguration of regular public telecasting, by NBC, a mobile unit was sent to the fairground, for the ceremonies. Here the iconoscope camera, connected to the pickup van by coaxial cable, was stationed about fifty feet from the speakers' podium. The program began at 12:30 P.M. with a view of the Trylon and Perisphere in the distance; the camera then swept across the Court of Peace for a panoramic shot of the crowd. The fair's opening parade followed, the camera also occasionally turning to the grandstand in order to survey the notables attending. And unexpectedly, during the parade, Mayor Fiorello LaGuardia walked directly up to the camera, inspiring NBC's engineers to declare him "the most telegenic man in New York." Finally, President Roosevelt's automobile came into view, with the speeches of the visiting dignitaries closing the three-and-a-half-hour program.[45]

It was estimated at the time that between one hundred and two hundred sets were then available in the New York area, and that this first program in NBC's new service was viewed by about one thousand persons. Although some viewers complained that the camera was too far from the speakers, resulting in images too small to be interesting, the producer in charge of the mobile unit declared the telecast to be a success and explained that the difficulties experienced by the audience would be corrected in the future by employing additional cameras.[46]

Following this initial telecast, NBC announced that along with continued demonstrations of television at the fair itself, regular telecasts were scheduled from the fair on Wednesday, Thursday, and Friday afternoons, and from the Radio City studio from 8:00 to 9:00 P.M. Wednesday and Friday evenings.[47] Thus, a decade after the beginning of regular television service in New York by mechanical means, a new era of regular service began, completing the triumph of electronic technology.

COMMERCIAL TELECASTING STALLED

In 1939 it appeared that the race for perfect television was over and that RCA and Farnsworth had both won. All three of the component television subsystems seemed ready. A high-definition technology had been successfully demonstrated; the image iconoscope and the orthicon promised to eliminate the final difficulties encountered with the iconoscope and image dissector. Networking was now also clearly feasible as coaxial cable and microwave interconnecting techniques had been developed. In addition, video stations were either already operating or being constructed across the country to provide service to the largest potential markets.

Because of the development of high-definition, light-sensitive pickup equipment, the telecasting of a wide range of entertaining programs became practical. An elaborate studio facility already existed in New York; others were being built in New York, Philadelphia, and Los Angeles, and still more were planned elsewhere. Furthermore, mobile unit coverage of a variety of indoor and outdoor events was already possible, greatly diversifying the types of entertainment television could present to its viewers.

With the creation of high-definition television and entertaining programming and with the simplification of receivers, the public could reasonably be expected to begin purchasing sets in large numbers, thereby creating the sizable audience required to induce already-eager advertisers to channel funds into the new medium. The promise of realizing profits from sales of transmission equipment to new stations, receiver sales to an expanding

market, and especially advertising revenue boded well for still further program improvement and expansion of television service.

Thus in 1939, a second television boom was expected. All that now
seemed necessary was astute marketing of the various components of the
complete system. But there was one looming obstacle, in fact exactly the
obstacle that had been the immediate cause of the collapse of the television
boom of the previous decade: commercial telecasting still had not been
authorized by the FCC. The commission continued to insist on general
unanimity within the industry on standards before acting. But Philco and
DuMont strongly dissented from several of the RMA recommendations that
RCA had already adopted. And in 1940 CBS unexpectedly entered the field
of television engineering with the introduction of a radical innovation that
threatened the entire existing technological structure and even seemed, to
some, to be a return to mechanical devices.

Therefore, the events of 1939 did not signal the beginning of a new boom.
Instead they initiated a period of bitter struggle within the industry and
between elements of the industry and the federal government. Only after
two more years could a truce be achieved, while the conflict over standards
would not be finally settled for still another decade. Thus in 1939, with the
components of the television system satisfactorily developed, a new ingre-
dient—intraindustry competition—intensified to such a degree that it became the primary source of delay in the authorization of commercial service
in the United States.

The Struggle for Commercialization

By the summer of 1939 most spectators believed that the great race was about over and that television had finally rounded the corner. After over a decade of competition and more than a score of early contenders, RCA and Farnsworth were well ahead. Another television boom, this one commercially viable, loomed just on the horizon. But all these appearances were belied by the unexpected. Late entries suddenly were making extraordinary gains and even threatened to capture the lead. The race's ultimate arbiters, the members of the Federal Communications Commission, seemed mesmerized into confused inaction by this unexpected renewal of intense industry rivalry. And yet at the finish of the race two years later, when the television system was finally completed and monochromatic commercial telecasting was officially authorized, the pundits of 1939 were not so very far wrong after all.

But the years between RCA's introduction of regular public television at the New York World's Fair and the FCC's authorization of commercial service witnessed the fiercest struggle yet within the new industry and between members of the industry and the commission. Essentially it was a conflict between the established television manufacturers and the newcomers. That is, RCA and Farnsworth found their combined engineering techniques challenged at major points by Philco and DuMont. Yet all of these advocates of monochromatic television suddenly faced a challenge to their method from CBS, which introduced color television in 1940. Further complicating these issues was a renewed challenge to television launched by the growing number of champions of FM radio. Caught in the midst of these contending forces was the FCC.

Considering the scope and complexity of all this contention, it is not surprising that the television boom, which had seemed so imminent in 1939, did not occur until 1947. Delayed until 1941, when the commission had successfully arbitrated between the television and FM radio interests, achieved mediation of the struggle among the television manufacturers, and arrived at a truce between monochrome and color advocates, it was still further postponed by American entry into armed conflict. Nevertheless, with the exception of further frequency reallocations, the system authorized in 1941 is the system that was marketed to both advertisers and the public in 1947 and that has continued to the present.

A NEW BOOM

The expectation of many in 1939 that the television industry was about to experience a boom was not merely an exercise in optimistic logic, but rather was derived from palpable evidence. As with the first boom, in the previous decade, there was a large number of license applications submitted to the FCC, many construction permits granted, and several new stations actually beginning to operate. Capital was certainly available again to invest in the new medium, from which profits seemed assured, despite the tremendous escalation in initial outlay required by the new electronic technology. As *Fortune* informed its readers, "Television is the best advertising medium yet discovered."[1] Many of these promising developments even occurred in the same locations that had experienced the first wave of television excitement during the mechanical era.

By the end of 1939, in New York City, NBC already was transmitting programs over W2XBS from the Empire State Building. CBS was completing its construction of facilities for its W2XAB at the same time.[2] In addition, Allen B. DuMont Laboratories was already operating W2XVT in Passaic, New Jersey, and would soon begin work on W2XWV in New York City itself.[3] And within a year Bamberger Broadcasting Service, a subsidiary of R. H. Macy and Company and operator of radio station WOR, and Metropolitan Television, owned by Bloomingdale's and Abraham and Straus, would also be granted construction permits in New York.[4]

Three other cities closely associated with New York during the first boom also were prominent during this period. First, in Schenectady, New York, GE had once again entered the television field and was operating W2XB (GE also had construction permits for stations in Albany and Bridgeport, Connecticut).[5] In Boston, General Television Corporation continued to operate W1XG, although the firm was soon to come under new ownership and move to enlarge facilities in the Sears Tower.[6] And finally, in Washington, D.C., NBC soon received a construction permit for W3XNB, while DuMont was authorized to operate W3XWT.[7]

In Philadelphia, Philco, of course, continued to telecast over W3XE. At the same time, local radio station WCAU had received a construction permit for W3XAU, while NBC had been authorized to begin work on W3XPP.[8] The Farnsworth facility in Philadelphia had been sold when the firm was relocated in Ft. Wayne, Indiana, but there it entered the telecasting field with experimental outlet W9XFT.[9]

The Midwest also began to witness a revival of VHF television activity.

Chicago once again became a center for telecasting, although entirely new interests were involved. In February 1939 W9XZV went on the air, operated by the independent radio manufacturer Zenith.[10] The following year Balaban and Katz, associated with Paramount Pictures, received a construction permit for W9XBK. And shortly thereafter, CBS was authorized to begin work on W9XCB.[11] However, in Milwaukee it was the Journal Company which again pioneered television broadcasting, receiving a license in 1941 for W9XMJ.[12] And in Cincinnati, which had not participated in the first boom, the Crosley Corporation also received a television license.[13]

But it was in California that suggestions of a boom were strongest. For Los Angeles and San Francisco, a total of nine stations were licensed. The oldest station in Los Angeles, W6XAO, was operating from its new facilities on Mt. Lee by the end of 1939. In the same city, automobile dealer and operator of radio station KFI, Earle C. Anthony, Incorporated, had received a construction permit for W6XEA; Hughes Tool Company had received one for W6XHH, and Television Productions, Incorporated, a subsidiary of Paramount Pictures, was acting on its construction permit for W6XYZ, while CBS had a permit for W6XCB; by 1941, Leroy's Jewelers and Mays Department Stores also held television construction permits. And in San Francisco, Don Lee and Hughes Tool both had received construction permits from the FCC.[14]

In all, by the end of 1941 there were thirty-two licensed VHF television stations either already operating or under construction.[15]

The accompanying list suggests that, as in the era of the mechanical television boom, so during this nascent electronic boom, interest in the new medium, outside of the South, was quite widespread. In addition it is also evident that incipient networks were already being created. Both of the national radio chains, NBC and CBS, held licenses in three major markets each, and both had already announced their intention of creating national television networks.[16] Furthermore, Don Lee, Hughes Tool, DuMont, and Paramount's Balaban and Katz and Television Production held licenses in two major markets each. And still other licensees had announced their interest in network affiliation. This departure from the trend of the previous decade reflected not only the growing importance of networks in the communications industry but also the engineering, programming, and financial constraints of VHF telecasting. Only the combination of Jenkins Laboratory in Washington, Jenkins Television in New York, and De Forest Radio in Passaic approaches this pattern of multicity ownership; in 1931 such an arrangement was thus the exception, while in 1941 it was quite typical.

Another departure from the previous era can be observed by comparing the licensees of the two periods. At first glance, similarities seem to predominate: during both, networks, manufacturers, universities, radio broadcasters, and specialized television firms were the predominant holders of licenses. However, the contrasts hidden within these apparent uniformities illustrate the significant changes that had occurred in the industry over the intervening decade. First, no new specialized television firms received licenses, nor did any new universities. And although manufacturing interests were still represented, they were all larger, established firms, even DuMont and Farnsworth. Finally, only during the later period were motion-picture interests represented. That is, television already, at this time, combined manufacturing, retailing (for example, department stores), network, radio broadcasting, firm, and newspaper interests. And, in addition to these AT & T was involved in providing possible interconnection equipment to stations. In other words, by 1941 television had come to represent a heavy investment of capital for the entire range of communications and media industries, a sign of their confidence and their influence within the new medium.

NBC Experiments in Television Programming

While these interests were investing impressive amounts, during these years, in the erection of television's engineering component on a national scale, still others were concerned with developing the kind of programming that would attract advertising capital to the medium and also win it a large sustained audience. Describing this programming to its stockholders, RCA's management summarized NBC's first regular television schedule, in 1939, as consisting of "drama, fashion, variety shows, round table discussions, demonstrations of art, music, and domestic science, sports of all kinds, and movies."[17] This array of programs was at first compressed into a mere ten hours a week. However, by the fall, W2XBS's weekly offerings had been expanded and included:[18]

Sunday	2:30–5:00 P.M.	Football: New York Giants v. Brooklyn Dodgers, Ebbets Field
	8:30–9:30 P.M.	*Captain Bob Bartlett*, motion picture of Arctic explorations; talk of explorers
Wednesday	2:30–3:30 P.M.	Elizabeth Watts, stylist; film serial, *The Lost Jungle*, episode 11, with Clyde Beaty; film, *Oberon Overture:* Alison Skipworth, actress, interviewed
	9:30–11:00 P.M.	Boxing at Madison Square Garden
Thursday	2:30–3:45 P.M.	Film, *Two Minutes to Play;* variety show: Gaige's Cooking Scandals; Buffano's marionettes; fashion show
Friday	2:30–4:00 P.M.	Film, *Forty Girls and a Baby*
	8:30–9:40 P.M.	Film, *Young and Beautiful*
Saturday	2:30–5:00 P.M.	Football: NYU v. Lafayette College
	8:30–9:45 P.M.	*Treasure Island*, dramatized

Stations Licensed by the End of 1941

City	Call Letters Experimental (Commercial)	Original Licensee	Original Channel	Current Call Letters
New York	W2XBS (WNBT, WRCA-TV)	NBC	1	WNBC-TV
	W2XAB (WCBW)	CBS	2	WCBS-TV
	W2XWV (WABD)	DuMont[a]	4	WNEW-TV
	W2XBB	Bamberger	6	WOR-TV
	W2XMT	Metropolitan Television	8	
Schenectady	W2XB	GE	3	WRGB-TV
Passaic	W2XVT	DuMont	4	
Camden	W3XEP	RCA	5	
Boston	W1XG	General Television	1	
Washington	W3XWT	DuMont[a]	1	WTTG
	W3XNB	NBC	2	WRC-TV
Philadelphia	W3XE (WPTZ)	Philco	3	KYW-TV
	W3XAU	WCAU Broadcasting	5	WCAU-TV
	W3XPP	NBC	7	
Cincinnati	W8XCT	Crosley	1	WLWT
Chicago	W9XZV (WTZR)	Zenith[b]	1	
	W9XBK (WBKB)	Balaban and Katz[c]	2	WBBM-TV
	W9XCB	CBS	3	
Milwaukee	W9XMJ (WMTJ)	The Journal Company	3	WTMJ-TV
Fort Wayne	W9XFT	Farnsworth	3	
West Lafayette	W9XG	Purdue	3	
Iowa City	W9XUI	State University of Iowa	1	
Manhattan	W9XAK	Kansas State College	1	

City	Call Letters Experimental (Commercial)	Original Licensee	Original Channel	Current Call Letters
Los Angeles	W6XAO (KTSL)	Don Lee[d]	1	KNXT
	W6XHH	Hughes Tool	2	
	W6XYZ	Television Productions	4	KTLA
	W6XEA (KSEE, KFI-TV)	Earle C. Anthony	6	KHJ-TV
	W6XCB	CBS	8	
	W6XLJ	Leroy's Jewelers	10	
	W6XMC	Mays Department Store	12	
San Francisco	W6XDL	Don Lee	1	
	W6XHT	Hughes Tool	2	

a. WABD was named for Allen B. DuMont, while WTTG was named for the firm's research director, Thomas T. Goldsmith.

b. Although commercial call letters were assigned, Zenith never employed such a format for its station, which was always operated only as an experimental outlet.

c. With the merger of ABC and United Paramount Theaters, Balaban and Katz sold WBKB to CBS, which had the call letters changed to WBBM-TV. ABC's WENR-TV then assumed the call letters WBKB, before adopting its present designation, WLS-TV.

d. During this period the president of the Don Lee System was the founder's son, Thomas S. Lee.

This schedule reflects several adjustments of broadcast times and days since the inauguration of regularly public telecasting on 1 May in an attempt to attract the largest possible audience. Nevertheless, despite the lapse of time and the sophistication of technology, the program schedule and content were quite reminiscent of what had been offered by the better mechanical attempts.

But this similarity decreased as NBC began to alter the emphasis of its programming after several months of experimentation. An increasing reliance on sports to fill up airtime is reflected in this March 1940 W2XBS weekly schedule, in which sporting events were telecast on four of the five days listed:[19]

Sunday	3:45–5:30 P.M.	Hockey: New York Rovers v. Valley Field of Quebec at Madison Square Garden
	8:30–10:30 P.M.	Play, *When We Are Married*, comedy at the Lyceum Theatre currently
Wednesday	3:30–4:30 P.M.	Film shorts
	6:45–7:00 P.M.	News, Lowell Thomas
	9:00–11:00 P.M.	Boxing: Golden Gloves Tournament at Madison Square Garden
Thursday	3:30–4:40 P.M.	Film, *The Phantom Fiend*
	6:45–7:00 P.M.	News, Lowell Thomas
	8:45–10:30 P.M.	Hockey: Boston Bruins v. New York Americans at Madison Square Garden
Friday	3:30–4:30 P.M.	Film shorts
	6:45–7:00 P.M.	News, Lowell Thomas
	8:30–9:30 P.M.	Play, *Dangerous Corner*
Saturday	3:30–4:30 P.M.	Children's matinee; film travelogues
	7:30–8:00 P.M.	"Art for Your Sake"
	9:30–10:30 P.M.	Knights of Columbus track meet at Madison Square Garden

This reliance on sports was quite deliberate on the part of NBC. It had found that this was the single most popular subject for program material.[20]

In order to evaluate its programming, NBC devised ratings based on a three-point system. Beginning in 1939, members of the audience were asked to fill out and send in post cards rating program categories; later a four-point system was introduced. And consistently the results showed that sporting events were rated as the most popular category, closely followed by drama. Film features and film variety were the least popular categories.[21]

The success of both sports and drama depended heavily on the effectiveness of the mobile unit, which had been criticized rather strongly in W2XBS's inaugural public telecast of 30 April 1939.[22] It was again used for an outdoor event to provide play-by-play coverage for the Columbia-Princeton baseball game of 17 May 1939. Again the criticism was rather severe. The single-camera coverage would follow the pitcher's wind-up and then follow the ball to the batter, but it could not show a hit to the outfield until the fourth inning because of the lack of sunlight, a typical problem with the iconoscope. Viewers felt that the commentator "saved the day," since without his remarks there was no way to follow the play or tell where the ball was.[23]

However, by the Fordham-Waynesburg football game of 14 October 1939, the criticism had metamorphosed into praise. "So sharp are the pictures and so discerning the telephoto lens as it peers into the line-up that the televiewer sits in his parlor wondering why he should leave the comforts of home," commented one critic.[24] This change was not the result of any new pickup equipment (the orthicon was not introduced into the mobile unit until the following year), but rather a revision of coverage techniques. Now two cameras were being employed, one on the rim of the stadium and a second, on a dolly, on the sidelines. Such coverage made football a "natural" for television, particularly with its "cavorting cheerleaders, the band and panoramic views of the grandstands."[25] However, even with such visual improvements, one reviewer acknowledged the necessity of retaining a good commentator, though also noting that television required calm and factual reporting, not the emotional style then common on radio.[26]

About the same time that the popularity of televised sports was being confirmed, a more general proposition about the relationship existing between programming and audience size was being formulated. As one version of this proposition put it, "the only way to catch the public fancy with television is to put such events on the air that will irk people to think that they missed the show, while neighbors with tele-radios saw it in their home."[27] This was, of course, a formula for special-events telecasting.

Although sports constituted a major portion of such events, there were many other possibilities. For instance, for Easter 1940 W2XBS telecast a special two-and-a-half-hour program of religious services—one Protestant and one Catholic—from its Radio City studio, and then followed these with Cecil B. DeMille's *King of Kings*.[28] But 1940 was also an election year, and so politics elicited much of the same sort of excitement as sports and religion. To take advantage of this, NBC arrived at an agreement with RKO-Pathe Newsreel to have the July Democratic convention in Chicago filmed and the newsreels broadcast the following day in New York.[29]

But even more impressive had been NBC's coverage of the Republican convention in Philadelphia during the previous month. A mobile unit was sent to Convention Hall by NBC to cover the event both outside the building and within, where the television cameras (an iconoscope and an orthicon) were mounted on the newsreel platform, along with special lighting equipment. The resulting pictures were sent from Convention Hall via cable to the Philadelphia terminal for AT & T's interconnection to New York, where it was relayed for transmission from the Empire State Building. In a further refinement W2XBS's signal was received on special equipment at GE's Schenectady facility, where it was then rebroadcast over W2XB, which functioned here as a VHF translator.[30] More political coverage followed, including separate Democratic and Republican rallies at Madison Square Garden.

Concerning the effect of television on the American political style, Orrin E. Dunlap, Jr., a media commentator, observed: "Sincerity of the tongue and facial expression gain in importance. . . . Naturalness is the keystone of success. . . . The sly, flamboyant or leather-lunged spellbinder has no place on the air. Sincerity, dignity, friendliness and clear speech . . . are the secrets of a winning telecast. More than ever, the politician must picture himself in the living room, chatting heart-to-heart with a neighbor. . . . How they comb their hair, how they smile and how they loop their necktie become new factors in politics."[31]

David Sarnoff agreed. Addressing the American Academy of Political and Social Science in 1941, he said: "Political addresses are certain to be more effective when the candidate is both seen and heard and when he is able to supplement his address with charts or pictures. Showmanship in presenting a political appeal by television will become more important than mere skill in talking or possession of a good radio voice, while appearance and sincerity will prove decisive factors with an audience which observes the candidate in closeup views."[32]

Television Programming Experiments Beyond New York

While NBC was aggressively exploring programming possibilities in New York, others were conducting similar experiments elsewhere. In Philadelphia Philco's W3XE introduced its sports coverage in 1939 with a night telecast of the Temple v. Kansas football game. And in 1940 regular telecasts of the University of Pennsylvania home football games began. That same year, W3XE also covered the Republican national convention at Philadelphia's Convention Hall.[33]

And in Boston, struggling W1XG, not having a mobile unit, was nonetheless able to present a varied schedule, as this listing from Monday, 6 January 1941, suggests:[34]

2:30–2:45 P.M.	Selected travel and educational films
2:45–3:00 P.M.	Film, *Maine Recreation: News and Views of Vacationland*
3:00–3:20 P.M.	W1XG cooking demonstration and food exhibit
3:20–3:30 P.M.	Weather forecast, test pattern, and visual novelties
8:30–8:45 P.M.	The Boy Scout Program: demonstration of scouting techniques

8:45–9:00 P.M.   Bob Henry Presents: humorous sketches on the current scene
9:00–9:15 P.M.   TBA
9:15–9:30 P.M.   Twinkling Toes: Claire William, tap dancer and popular vocals

In Chicago Zenith's W9XZV was on the air weekday afternoons from noon to 1:00 P.M. and Monday, Wednesday, and Friday evenings from 7:00 until 10:00. The afternoon "show" consisted merely of a still picture, telecast so that local televisions could be tested, there being no other station in the area at first. The evening telecast included both film and live productions and included such personalities as Pat Buttram, Tommy Bartlett, Les Tremaine, the Dinning Sisters, the Vagabonds, and puppeteer Burr Tillstrom. On Wednesday evenings, a forty-five-minute show, "Time on Television," was presented in cooperation with *Time* magazine.[35]

Don Lee's W6XAO, in Los Angeles, was a most aggressive experimenter, comparable to NBC in its programming. Furthermore, like W2XBS, W6XAO possessed an RCA mobile unit, at first equipped solely with icono-scopes, but later also including orthicons.[36] Employing this equipment, the refurbished Los Angeles telecaster covered Pasadena's New Year's Day Tournament of Roses Parade in 1940. Following this an Easter sunrise ser-vice was broadcast from the Hollywood Bowl in March 1940, as were boxing and wrestling from the American Legion Stadium in Hollywood. In July of that year a beauty contest, sponsored by the Junior Screen Actors Guild at the Ambassador Hotel, was telecast, while the following year a race from the Southern Ascot Speedway, Southgate, was featured.[37]

Programming without an Audience

All of these coast-to-coast efforts among telecasters exemplify the initia-tives being undertaken to identify, and then to provide, the type of program-ming which would secure for television the sizable audience necessary to make the medium a financial success. But although such programming was being developed, television was not obtaining a very significant audience for itself: the nascent boom was apparently stillborn. This became quite evident from the statistics on receiver sales.

For instance, originally the idea had been to retail between 10,000 and 40,000 sets in the greater New York area during the first year of regular public telecasting. Once such an audience had been created, sponsored programs could be expected to follow, and the television industry could begin to recoup its expenses and expand further.[38] But after three months, only about 800 sets had been sold in the country, while another 5,000 were idling on dealer's shelves.[39] By October 1939 some firms were introducing discounts in an attempt to stimulate sales, and in March 1940 RCA

A 1939 RCA Victor television adapter, with a 5-inch kinescope for direct viewing of
its 3⅜-by-4⅜-inch picture. The 16-tube unit utilized the chassis and loudspeakers of
a standard radio. (Courtesy of RCA)

announced that it planned to reduce receiver prices by about one-third in
the hope that sales in the New York–New Jersey area could be raised from
2,500 to 25,000.[40] GE, DuMont, and Andrea soon followed.[41]

Three factors were identified as the cause of this surprising failure of the
public to purchase television receivers. First, there was the problem of the
sets' high cost, the immediate reason for the price reductions. Second, there
was the lack of adequate programming: the schedule was still too limited and
offered too many repeated programs for most families to feel justified in
investing in such a costly apparatus.[42] And third, there was the continuing
lack of standardization of equipment. This meant that while one set might
receive W2XBS when its channel selector was set at number one, another
might show the same station only when set at channel five.[43] It also meant
that while NBC's transmissions might conform to the RMA recommended
standards, DuMont did not. Such discrepancies did not merely confuse the
public but also reminded them of FCC and earlier RCA warnings concerning

the dangers of obsolescence. Such confusion and fear could only be resolved with standardization of transmission and receiving equipment.

The last factor, standardization, was really the crux of the problem of receiver sales. Prices could not be permanently reduced until there was successful mass marketing of sets. But sets could not be sold in large quantities until there was attractive programming. And there would not be such programming until sponsors were available to absorb the high production costs. And sponsors could not invest until commercial telecasting had been authorized by the FCC. However, the commission would not act until there existed general agreement within the industry on what standards should finally be accepted. But while some firms, such as RCA, GE, and Farnsworth, were eager to reach agreement, others, such as Philco and DuMont, were not, or at least not yet. It was the desire to help resolve this dilemma which eventually led the FCC into assuming a more active role in arriving at technical policy formulation than was usual for government in the United States.

The FCC and Television Standardization

FCC action in the case of the commercialization of television's rival, FM radio, however, followed the more traditional exercise of administrative, not discretionary, power. This was possible because this medium had not suffered from the engineering uncertainties arising from the turmoil in the television industry. Thus FM's commercialization would fall within the accustomed purview of the commission, satisfy the demands of one of the contending media, allow the FCC to demonstrate its effectiveness after failing to solve the television dilemma, and apparently settle the rivalry between the television and FM radio advocates over VHF frequency allocations.

In the spring of 1940 the commission held hearings to determine the feasibility of allowing FM radio to operate on a sponsored basis. In May 1940 the authorization was granted, to be effective 1 January 1941. At the same time, to facilitate the success of this new medium, the FCC reallocated the VHF band in order to accommodate an anticipated expansion in FM license requests. In this reallocation, the 42–44-MHz. band, previously used by standard stations, the government, and educational services, was combined with the 44–50-MHz. band, previously television's channel one, to provide the necessary FM frequency assignments. Television's previous channel two, 50–56 MHz., was now redesignated as channel one—to which any station earlier licensed to channel one moved—and a new channel two, 60–66 MHz., was assigned for television service. This allowed television seven channels, each 6 MHz. wide, between 50 and 108 MHz. As a result of a further reallocation television lost its 156–162-MHz. channel, but retained its remaining eleven channels between 162 and 294 MHz.[44]

This FCC decision was made in the absence of any significant concern about possible obsolescence of FM consumer receiver equipment, the predominant theme in concurrent debates about television's commercialization. Evidently it was not apparent that obsolescence could be caused not only by actions within the industry, for example, from a conflict over standards, but also by actions of the FCC, for example, its allocations policy. Of course, existing FM radios and television sets would both now need adjustments in order to receive the new frequencies, but the public had been forewarned that these services had been only experimental. The FCC seemed to insist, in the case of television particularly, that commercialization could be interpreted by the public as a guarantee against early equipment obsolescence.

It is therefore rather surprising that in May 1945 the FCC again reallocated VHF frequencies, this time completely moving FM to 88–108 MHz. and also creating new assignments for television's channels seven through thirteen, between 174 and 216 MHz. (Channel one was soon once again deleted, but this time without the confusion of the 1940 station reassignment.) The FCC action made all existing FM radios obsolete and contributed to the meager utilization of this medium for long afterward. However, the postwar action of the FCC can be interpreted as largely the result of altered perceptions of these media by the commission and also of altered priorities. No doubt the lack of manufacture and sale of receivers for these services during the war years also contributed to the justification of this decision, although policy anticipated with UHF assignments and color television must cast some doubt that such an explanation is entirely adequate. At any rate, authorization of commercial FM service in 1940 did, for a time, ease tension between it and television, although it did nothing to resolve the commission's quandary over the authorization of a commercial television service amidst intense industry rivalry over standards. In fact, it actually contributed to the disarray already rife within the industry.

Following the VHF reallocations, NBC announced it would temporarily close down W2XBS in order to make the shift to the new frequency and also to allow service agents to adjust receivers. Simultaneously, NBC announced that it would also change its picture standards from 441 to 507 lines, a significant departure from the original RMA standards.[45] In defense of this change, RCA engineers suggested that the optimum number of lines in a television system lay in a continuum between 441 and 507, 30 frames per second; hence, NBC was merely shifting from the lower level of the continuum to the upper.[46] However, it became evident that NBC's move would not satisfy its opponents when the Don Lee System announced that, after W6XAO was similarly closed down for frequency adjustment, its line definition would be increased from 441 to 525.[47] And, in fact, the upper limit of

RCA's optimum was even further from those demanded by Philco and DuMont.

Conflict within the Industry. Philco had by this time already demonstrated a receiver with a 605-line picture, 24 frames per second; later it would propose a standard with even higher values.[48] At the same time, Philco had allied with RCA's primary rival as a patent-holding company, Hazeltine Corporation, to develop a new method of synchronization that they hoped would substitute for the RCA technique currently employed and found to be subject to serious disturbance from the urban environment.[49] To secure the time needed to perfect their equipment, Philco argued that standards become immutable through public investment and that it was insufficient simply to adopt any workable system; rather, only the best possible system within the frequency and bandwidth limitations should be authorized, a position endorsed by FCC inaction. Philco further insisted that the line definition and synchronization system adopted in the RMA proposals were clearly not the best.[50] As a warning against adopting standards precipitously, Philco pointed to the British experience, where a 405-line picture had been standardized prematurely.[51] Zenith, another of the independent radio manufacturers, strongly agreed.[52]

Even more extensive criticisms of the RMA proposals were made by the Allen B. DuMont Laboratories, a newcomer to the field and not a member of the RMA. DuMont had been chief engineer of De Forest Radio Company until 1931, when he resigned to found his own experimental laboratory in Upper Montclair, New Jersey; here he concentrated on the production of cathode-ray tubes and oscillographs. Then in 1938 Paramount Pictures invested in the firm, allowing it to expand into television research, manufacture, and broadcasting.[53]

DuMont quickly proceeded to challenge not only the proposed RMA standards but the entire concept of fixed standards itself. Instead, it was argued, transmitting and receiving equipment should be manufactured with the capability of operating anywhere between 400 and 800 lines per frame within a 6-MHz. bandwidth; the frame rate would also be variable, between 15 and 30 per second, depending upon the line definition being transmitted at the time. The firm's engineers had already developed a new type of vertical synchronizing pulse capable of controlling the receiver automatically at any rate required within the line-definition rate, although manual width and height controls would still be required to adjust the size of the picture as it altered according to the number of lines. A cathode-ray screen that minimized flicker at low frame rates had also been developed in order to facilitate acceptance of the technique.[54]

DuMont claimed that the RMA's proposed standards were qualitatively unsatisfactory and threatened to freeze the medium's engineering at an unnecessarily low level. Rather than prematurely authorize any standard, flexibility was offered as an alternative, and as early as December 1939 a demonstration of DuMont's equipment was staged for the RMA Television Committee. However, the committee members remained skeptical and were particularly critical of the quality of some of the pictures shown at 15 frames per second, depending on the subject matter.[55] Undaunted, DuMont continued to advocate its flexible system as the best means for accommodating all competing techniques and also for providing the highest-quality service to the public.

The rancor existing in the industry exploded into public view during hearings held in April 1940 by the U.S. Senate Committee on Interstate Commerce. In the course of these hearings, representatives of some of the smaller firms, and particularly DuMont, launched bitter attacks on RCA, while representatives of the established firms vigorously defended their position and launched counterattacks against their opponents. For instance, the DuMont representative testified that RCA controlled the RMA, intended to "freeze" standards at the RMA's proposed levels, and even pressured its licensees to support its position.[56] For its part, Philco had already temporarily withdrawn from RMA activity; its position was that although the RMA Standards Committee had accepted the proposed standards, the RMA Board of Directors had evidently disavowed them. Therefore, Philco argued that they should not be forced on the smaller firms needing more time to prepare fully to participate effectively in television manufacture.[57]

David Sarnoff vehemently denied these charges. Instead, he accused DuMont of advocating a technology it still had not put on the air. Sarnoff also suggested that Philco had originally accepted the soundness of the RMA standards and only later opportunistically joined with nonmember DuMont in unexpectedly rejecting them to divide the industry.[58] A representative for Farnsworth Television supported Sarnoff's contention that RCA did not control the RMA. He also quoted Philo T. Farnsworth as saying that there was "nothing worthwhile" in the DuMont proposals.[59]

The FCC's Mistake. Out of this maelstrom of industry strife, the FCC had to construct a coherent policy for standardization and commercialization. That the members of the commission recognized that any action they initiated would be perilous helps explain why they delayed four years before authorizing any change in the status of television. That the FCC's forebodings were justified was immediately confirmed when its action resulted in more industry confusion, a public uproar, and the Senate's 1940 television hearings.

The commission had been faced with the demand for television standardization since the formation of the RMA's Allocations and Standards committees in 1936. The FCC did agree to establish VHF channel allocations the following year; however, because of the uncertain state of the engineering development at the time, the commission was unwilling to ratify the proposed standards. Much the same policy had been pursued by the FRC during the era of mechanical telecasting.

In 1938 pressure from the industry appeared in a new guise. The *Milwaukee Journal* management, bypassing the issue of standardization, applied for the first commercial television license in the country's history. The Journal Company had previously operated VHF mechanical station W9XD, but a change in FCC rules forced termination of these transmissions. So the firm now argued that "experiments and investigation have shown that television has developed beyond the laboratory stage and is now ready as a service to the public."[60] And in support of this claim, the firm suggested that "adoption by radio manufacturers of RCA specifications for television equipment as trade standards is further justification for The Journal's new undertaking."[61] The application was warmly applauded by David Sarnoff.[62] But the FCC refused to act, in 1938, either on the Journal Company's application for a commercial license or on the revised RMA proposals.[63]

Pressure on the commission increased with RCA's announcement that W2XBS would inaugurate regular public telecasting in the spring of 1939. However, the FCC's Television Committee, formed in response to RCA's initiative, recommended that standards not be authorized until the public could expect "to purchase receivers of a stable television service of good technical quality, without too rapid obsolescence of the instruments it has purchased."[64] Because of continuing engineering innovations, the Television Committee warned against "freezing" developments by authorizing standards before general industry agreement had been achieved.[65] James L. Fly, chairman of the FCC echoed this sentiment when he explained later that year that the main obstacle to commercialization was the continuing danger of equipment obsolescence.[66]

Nevertheless, pressure was mounting on the commission to take some action, even in the absence of any engineering consensus. Of particular concern was the increasing need to provide some source of revenue to allow adequately for both station and program development, the prerequisites for the successful public introduction of the new medium. In order to try to promote these conditions while the industry remained seriously stalemated over several technical issues, the FCC chose to accept the distinction between commercialization and standardization, and the priority of the former, suggested in the *Milwaukee Journal's* 1938 application. By making this distinction, it also sought to maintain the traditional policy of limiting its own activity to regulatory functions, leaving technical decisions to the industry itself. But the results of this reversal of the priority between standardization and commercialization resulted only in worsening the prospects of the medium, in intensifying the strife already raging within the industry, and in increasing pressure on the commission.

This first approach to sponsored television in the United States was the debacle the FCC called "limited commercial service." After holding hearings in January, in which both Philco and DuMont strongly objected to the RMA proposals, the commission adopted new rules on 29 February 1940, to become effective 1 September, allowing sponsors to bear the expense of program production. However, stations would still have to cover the cost of the use of their telecasting facilities themselves; it was this restriction that qualified this commercialization plan as "limited."[67] The arrangement would allow for some defraying of production costs and was thus aimed at improving the quality of programming, a necessity for the widespread public acceptance of television. In fact, this really authorized NBC's existing practice, although allowing for its expansion as well.

At the same time, on the issue of standards, the FCC warned against freezing television at its current level of technical development: "That research should not be halted and that scientific methods should not be frozen in the present state of the art are fairly to be deduced from the engineering testimonies of representatives of the companies."[68] Addressing itself to the paradox of how standards could remain unfixed while a commercial service was being authorized (the latter obviously requiring the retailing of receivers), the commission adopted the DuMont position and suggested that sets marketed should be designed to receive "any reasonable changes in methods of synchronization or changes in the number of frames or lines."[69] To institutionalize the distinction between engineering standards and commercial programming, two classes of stations were created: one to continue technical investigations and one to experiment in program production. The FCC stressed, however, that both classes of stations remained experimental.[70]

Telecasters responded enthusiastically to the new rules. Although they expected no increase in their income, they did anticipate that limited commercialization would stimulate receiver sales and encourage construction of new stations.[71] Plans were immediately formulated by manufacturers, therefore, to launch sales campaigns. On 20 March 1940, a full-page RCA advertisement ran in New York newspapers announcing that television was now ready for the home and that the public could expect more exciting and extensive programming from NBC. In the *New York Times* large advertisements for RCA receivers at significantly reduced prices appeared for Bloomingdales, Davega City Radio, and Abraham and Straus on the pages flanking the RCA statement.[72]

Furious at what it claimed was a blatant violation by RCA of the purpose of limited commercial service, the FCC suspended the order authorizing such service on 22 March. Explaining its precipitous decision, the commission said:

> The current marketing campaign of the Radio Corporation of America is held to be at variance with the intent of the commission's television report of February 29. . . . Such action is construed as a disregard of the commission's

findings and recommendations for further improvement in the technique and quality of television transmission before sets are widely sold to the public. . . . Promotional activities directed to the sale of receivers not only intensifies the danger of these instruments being left on the hands of the public, but may react in the crystallizing of transmission standards at present levels.

Moreover, the possibility of one manufacturer gaining an unfair advantage over competitors may cause them to abandon the further research and experimentation which is in the public interest.[73]

To decide what should be done next, new hearings were scheduled by the FCC for 8 April.

A public outcry against the FCC now ensued. It was accused of attempting to impose an "alien theory of merchandising" on the United States by attempting to protect consumer interests beyond "acceptable bounds."[74] To respond, Chairman Fly, a controversial New Deal activist, was granted an hour of free time by the Mutual radio network to defend the commission's decision; in his defense, he attacked "Big Business's bullying of the little fellows."[75] Fly also met with President Roosevelt, who announced that the problem would soon be resolved.[76]

For his part, David Sarnoff denied that RCA had ever intended to freeze standards, and he also denied that the commercialization of television would adversely affect future research. He argued that "a greater public interest will be served at this time by research toward the methods that would extend television service to as many homes as possible than by improvements that merely add to the size or definition of the picture now enjoyed by the few."[77]

A fierce exchange between the spokesmen for the FCC and RCA occurred during Senate hearings called at the request of Minnesota's Ernest Lundeen to investigate the commission's actions and allegations that it had exceeded its authority by interfering with the freedom of public and private enterprise.[78] After arguing that there was still a need for engineering flexibility, Chairman Fly, defending the decision of the commission to withdraw authorization for limited commercial service, explained, "The thing that is halted, I hope, for the time being is an intensive and extensive sales-promotion campaign, which would have locked these standards down."[79] He then admitted, "I think we misjudged the situation in our first opinion [authorizing limited commercial service]. We expressed all the cautions, all the warnings, carried all the conservative expressions we could. We begged the industry then not to fix the standards, not to let them become frozen. . . . I must say we misjudged the situation, because within 3 weeks—well, came the blitzkrieg."[80]

Denying Fly's charges that RCA was trying to freeze development and force its standards on the industry, Sarnoff argued, "The purchaser of such a [television] set knows exactly what he is paying for. He is paying for the

unique privilege of seeing what is important or interesting today in a program of news, information, entertainment, education, and sports-events
which he cannot witness tomorrow or next year, however great the technical
improvements. . . . The miracle of sight transmitted through the air should
not be treated on the basis of obsolescence as a spring hat or furniture."[81]
Sarnoff also explained that any receiver built to RMA specification and later
requiring alterations to some new standard would need no more than forty
dollars for servicing. Finally, in rejecting the suggestion that RCA sought to
create a television monopoly, he claimed that his firm had already issued
forty-five licenses to others for receiver manufacture and itself had to acquire
Farnsworth licenses.[82]

After allowing all views to be expressed, the Senate hearings ended without any action being taken. However, in its own hearings held concurrently,
the commission, faced with the continued opposition of Philco and DuMont
to the RMA proposals, concluded that no form of commercial operation
should be permitted because of "its possible adverse effects on technical
experimentation."[83] Thus, annulling its previous decision to separate commercialization from standardization, the FCC now announced a return to its
original policy: "that a single uniform system of television broadcasting was
essential and that the Commission would authorize full commercialization
whenever the industry agreed upon standards insuring a satisfactory level of
performance."[84]

Yet if the FCC returned to its traditional policy of allowing the industry to
agree on standards before authorizing them, it also recognized that the
industry was deadlocked, caught between two opposing interested factions.
Until the deadlock could be broken, commercialization would be impossible, and the industry would languish, a situation certain to discourage television's acceptance by the public and by advertisers, although the deadlock
did benefit those interests which favored the delay of commercialization till
they achieved a more competitive position in the field.

Nevertheless, such an impasse was not unprecedented in the history of
the communications industry. A similar deadlock had paralyzed radio at the
time of the First World War; in fact, only the active, albeit surreptitious,
intervention of the federal government to organize the creation of RCA had
finally produced a solution. Once again, the federal government, this time
through the FCC, would have to move beyond its merely regulatory function and devise a mechanism by which the industry could resolve its differences. The mechanism created to achieve this was the National Television
System Committee (NTSC).

THE NATIONAL TELEVISION SYSTEM COMMITTEE

The NTSC was organized after the report on the April hearings was issued
the following month, and after the FCC had officially eliminated the cate-

David Sarnoff, by Karsh. (Courtesy of RCA)

gory of Class II stations that had been planned for experimentation in television programming. At a meeting of Chairman Fly and Walter R. G. Baker, director of engineering for the RMA, it was decided to form a committee on standardization; representatives from the entire industry, if technically qualified, would be invited to participate, whether they were members of the RMA or not. The FCC suggested that it would accept the recommendations of the NTSC as constituting an industry consensus, thus providing the basis for commercialization.

Although the FCC served as the catalyst for the formation of the NTSC, the new committee operated under the auspices of the RMA. Members were appointed by the RMA's president, subject to the approval of its Executive Committee. They were selected from those firms interested and experienced in television, along with representatives of related national technical organizations. Eventually, the NTSC came to have a membership of 168, divided into nine panels, each assigned the task of investigating a particular phase of standardization (namely, system analysis, subjective aspects, television spectra, transmitter power, transmitter characteristics, transmitter-receiver coordination, picture resolution, synchronization, and radiation polarization). Although the NTSC was thus a technical body, it was designed to operate according to parliamentary procedure; in this way, it was hoped, an industry-wide engineering consensus could be fairly created.[85]

The first meeting of the NTSC was held on 31 July 1940. Organizational work continued; then in September the panels began meeting. At the time of the initial meeting, three issues most seriously divided the industry: that of the lack of the picture-definition value; that of the method of synchronization; and that of whether, in fact, fixed standards should be established at all, or whether a flexible number of lines and frames per second should be allowed. However, when the panels began operating in September, a new, and very serious, technical controversy had arisen: during the intervening two months, CBS staged an impressive demonstration of color television, although employing a method not compatible with any of the existing monochrome alternatives. The CBS achievement thus threatened to alter radically the structure of the entire industry.

On 3 September CBS first publicly demonstrated its color television apparatus, designed by Peter Goldmark. After seeing the color film *Gone with the Wind*, Goldmark convinced CBS officials that a method for color television could be quickly developed and that such a technique would prove superior to any of the contending monochromatic methods. Responding to this inducement, CBS approved Goldmark's project.

Borrowing from the early mechanical color television experiments of John L. Baird, Goldmark created his "field sequential system" of color television. Standard electronic transmitting and receiving apparatus formed the basis of the technique. Color was introduced in both the transmitting and receiving apparatus by a motor-driven rotating disc containing a set of filters for the three primary colors. At the transmitter, the disc was spun behind the camera lens in synchronization with the scanning beam. The basic idea was that the electronically scanned picture was transmitted in a rapid sequence of red, blue, and green fields; that is, each picture was scanned in each color, the complete image being transmitted sequentially in three scanning fields. These fields were sent at a rate of 120 per second, or 60 interlaced per second. This means only two fields were included in a complete frame; the third color would appear as the first field in the next frame. Thus at the end of six fields two complete pictures would be transmitted and received. To allow for the doubling of the field rate per second within a 6-MHz. bandwidth, the line-definition value had to be reduced from the RMA recommendation of 441 to 343. However, CBS officials argued that the loss in picture definition was more than compensated for by the introduction of color.[86]

FCC representatives were quite impressed by the demonstration; however, they were concerned that the method could operate successfully only with film, a serious encumbrance for program development. This limitation was the result of needing a linear conversion of optical to electronic signal in the pickup tube, a characteristic then available only in the rather insensitive image dissector. But Goldmark was soon able to adapt the new orthicon to his color method, thus acquiring direct-pickup capability for the technique.[87]

However, most industry representatives were not so sanguine. RCA, GE, Farnsworth, Philco, and DuMont, all with heavy investments in monochrome apparatus, were highly critical of the field sequential color system. They were particularly concerned about the lowering of picture definition and about the reintroduction of mechanical devices into television engineering. On the other hand, Zenith and Stromberg-Carlson, firms which were just entering the television field, defended the idea.[88] Tension over the issue further increased when reports began circulating that CBS, which had no manufacturing interest, was willing to wait until enough television sets had been sold to attract sponsors to meet broadcast costs, even if this meant an additional five to ten years till commercialization.[89] DuMont even came to maintain that CBS was using its color method merely as a device for stalling commercial service until it had improved its competitive position in the industry.[90]

Following the introduction of color television by CBS, the NTSC was faced with the difficult task of considering two types of flexibility in standards, besides determining which standards to set. First, there was the "continuous flexibility" advocated by DuMont; here monochromatic scanning rates would vary along a continuum. Second, there was the "discontinuous flexibility" advocated by CBS: here receivers would be required to adjust to two different standards—monochrome and color.[91] Although these issues involved genuine technical considerations, they arose out of rival corporate interests. Hence, recommendations on flexibility would not only determine the nature and quality of American television (as with other standards controversies), but would also help to regulate future corporate relations within the industry.

On 27 January 1941 the NTSC presented the FCC with its tentative report. After much deliberation, it decided to reject the DuMont proposal for continuous flexibility in standards; this decision was based on the disadvantages arising from the increase in receiver cost entailed by this approach, the inconvenience of manual adjustment of picture size, and the inevitable flicker that would result in the lower portion of the proposed frame range.[92] On similar grounds, the CBS proposal for discontinuous flexibility was also rejected for the present.[93] However, the NTSC did believe the field sequential color system should be encouraged and therefore recommended that: "(a) a full test of color be permitted and encouraged; and that (b) after successful field test, the early admission of color transmissions on a commercial basis coexistent with monochromatic television be permitted employing the same standards as are herewith submitted except as to lines and frame and field frequencies."[94]

If no definitive settlement between monochrome and color television had been achieved, at least a truce which temporarily satisfied both sides, and allowed for immediate standardization, had been negotiated. But authorization of a noncompatible color system (that is, discontinuous flexibility) remained for the future, and with it remained the grounds for more potential conflict.

On particular standards, the January report generally followed the RMA proposals. But on two major issues a consensus had not yet been achieved: no agreement had been arrived at concerning the competing RCA, Philco, and DuMont methods of synchronization; and no single position had been achieved with regard to the number of picture lines to be recommended.[95]

These remaining two points of contention were decided in NTSC meetings held over the course of the following two months. On the question of which type of synchronizing signal to authorize, it was recommended that since commercial sets were able to receive all of the signals under consideration interchangeably, all three should be permitted. Thus the RMA amplitude-modulation synchronizing and picture signals of the vertical synchronizing pulse type, the synchronizing signals of the alternative carrier type with AM picture signals, and the FM picture and synchronizing signals were all to be permitted and to compete commercially.[96]

To resolve the contentious issue of the number of picture lines to be recommended, Chairman Baker of the NTSC asked an engineering expert,

Donald G. Fink, to prepare a paper in which he would provide a compromise solution. Fink proposed 525 lines as the standard and defended his position with arguments drawn from an important study that had recently been published by Millard W. Baldwin of the Bell System.[97] Basing his position on this article, Fink explained that it had been shown

> by careful observation of viewers' reaction to the sharpness of television images that, in effect, *any number of lines*, within the range then proposed would suffice, so long as the video bandwidth was fixed. This [is] so, because increasing the number of lines, for a fixed bandwidth, decreases the horizontal resolution proportionately, and the total number of picture elements remains constant, being fixed by the video bandwidth. The only change is the ratio of the vertical resolution to the horizontal resolution, and Baldwin showed that the typical viewer is not sensitive to the value of this ratio, over a fairly wide range.[98]

That is, as long as the bandwidth remained 6 MHz., little objective benefit could be derived from arbitrarily increasing the number of lines per picture at the expense of frames per second.[99] Fink's line value and his rationale for it were accepted by the NTSC, and a 525-line picture, interlaced, 30 frames per second, was recommended.

The NTSC approved the recommendations on synchronization and line value at its final meeting, 8 March 1941. Assessing the work of this committee, Philco's representative, David B. Smith, reflected the general satisfaction felt by most of its members when he said that "the NTSC was an excellent example of how in these socio-economic-technological public issues, a group of engineers can get together, forget their industry rivalries and arrive at sound answers to the technological issues."[100]

Between 20 March and 24 March, the FCC conducted hearings on the NTSC report. After the testimony of the final witness, television pioneer Ulises S. Sanabria, it was evident that a general industry consensus had been achieved on engineering standards. The only significant dissenter from the NTSC report had been DuMont Laboratories, which continued to advocate its technique of flexible standards.[101]

In fact, at the hearings emphasis was already shifting from technical questions to regulatory ones. Some firms, such as Farnsworth and General Television, called for immediate and rapid commercialization, while others, particularly RCA-NBC, Zenith, and Hughes Tool advocated a slower pace.[102] Since the positions of those who supported a rapid pace for commercialization and those who opposed it generally reflected the length of their experience with television, RCA's view was surprising. In fact, RCA's caution was dictated less by its status within the television industry than by its assessment of the current international political situation.

Reacting to the general engineering consensus, the FCC approved the

NTSC proposals and authorized full commercial telecasting in new rules issued 30 April 1941.[103] Channels one through seven were allowed to provide sponsored service, while channels eight through eighteen remained limited to experimental and television relay uses. The third group of frequencies, above 300 MHz., also remained available for relays and for UHF experimentation. The commission also opted for rapid commercialization. The rules specified that each commercial station was to operate a minimum regular program schedule of fifteen hours weekly, of which two hours had to be between 2:00 and 11:00 P.M. daily, except Sunday, with at least a one-hour program telecast on five weekdays between 7:30 and 10:30 P.M.[104] At the same time, to increase competition, ownership or control of more than three commercial stations was prohibited.[105] These new rules became effective 1 July 1941, and on that day commercial telecasting finally became a reality in the United States.

AMERICAN COMMERCIAL TELECASTING AUTHORIZED

A commercial television system had been ready in 1939. During the following two years, its subsystems, particularly the engineering and programming components, had been still further refined. Now the FCC had authorized full commercial service for the new medium, which meant that full promotion of television might now be possible.

Between the commission's action on 2 May and the 1 July starting date for commercial telecasting, several technical adjustments were necessary to meet the NTSC standards. While their transmitter was being readied, RCA announced that it would establish ten special service centers to adapt all receivers in the New York area so that they would be able to operate under the new specifications; these modifications would be made without charge.[106] Although several other stations were also preparing to adopt the new sponsored format, on the first day that it was authorized only the Empire State Building facility was ready. On 1 July 1941, NBC's New York station, WNBT, carried the first American commercial television broadcasts.

The first commercial to be telecast was a test pattern in the form of a Bulova clock face. The image remained on the screen for a minute, while the second hand made its sweep. This commercial cost $4. The first sponsored program was a USO fundraising show. This hour program cost the USO $120, NBC's regular evening rate; weekday afternoon broadcasts cost $60 an hour, while the weekend afternoons were $90 an hour.[107]

But there was to be no boom in commercial telecasting in 1941. Once again industry expectations were belied by reality. War-caused shortages of parts and material made the manufacture of equipment first difficult and then impossible. At the same time, engineering personnel and production facilities were being diverted to military use as the nation prepared for a more active role in the world war. By April 1942 all radio and television production had been banned as part of the war effort, and in May 1942 the FCC allowed commercial television's weekly program minimum to be reduced from fifteen hours to four.[108] Television languished as the country turned to other concerns.

However, with the approach of peace, interest in television began to revive. And by 1947 the boom that had been eagerly anticipated since 1927 arrived at last: after more than twenty years, television finally rounded the corner. The great television race was over. Or at least this first race was.

Commercial television was now an operating reality in the United States. First conceptualized in 1873, following the discovery of the light-sensitive property of selenium, it was finally actualized sixty-eight years later, in 1941. During the intervening years, the three subcomponents of the television system—the engineering, the programming, and the marketing—had been successfully developed. But the history of this final achievement of a marketable television system in America had been fraught with delays—because of false starts, inadequate technologies, bitter industrial strife, and governmental aloofness.

It was only in 1925 that the engineering component had been sufficiently refined to produce successful television demonstrations, in the United States by C. Francis Jenkins and in Britain by John L. Baird. Yet although successful as a curiosity, the television demonstrations by both Jenkins and Baird employed cumbersome mechanical equipment to produce low-definition results. Still, even this was an exciting beginning, and soon a minor television boom sprang up in America, only to collapse, by 1933, amidst technical and financial difficulties too complex for most of the pioneering television firms to master.

But building on the experiences of these low-definition telecasters, new men introduced an electronic television technology capable of producing the high-definition pictures necessary to meet public expectations for a visual medium, and so attract the sizeable audience needed to secure the capital required to allow television to succeed financially. Vladimir K. Zworykin and Philo T. Farnsworth invented rival electronic cameras, each possessing uniquely attractive capabilities, but each also suffering from debilitating limitations. After international competition between the two, RCA departed from its traditional policy of refusing to purchase licenses from others and acquired one from Farnsworth. This departure from tradition then allowed RCA to introduce its commercial-quality camera tube, the image iconoscope.

At the same time, RCA had already initiated public telecasting in New York, had introduced one version of interconnection networking technology, started to develop its programming skills, and had begun recruiting commercial sponsors for the new medium.

Yet at the very time RCA and Farnsworth arrived at their mutual victor-
ies, they were suddenly challenged by new rivals, particularly Philco,
DuMont, and CBS. A bitter industrial struggle ensued, primarily revolving
around the question of television standardization. This conflict paralyzed all
governmental efforts to authorize commercial telecasting. But amidst
mounting pressures, the FCC finally instigated, in 1940, the formation of the
NTSC by all segments of the industry to arrive at standards agreeable to the
vast majority of the interested firms. And on 1 July 1941, with the engineering, economic, and political issues resolved, commercial high-definition
electronic telecasting commenced in the United States.

Although temporarily interrupted by the disruptions of the Second World
War, this television system introduced in 1941 has since become the most
pervasive communication medium ever conceived by man. The race to produce this system ended in 1941; the race to market it is still being run today.

Notes

CHAPTER 1

1. *System* is employed in the technical sense, defined "as an ordered set of methods, procedures, and resources designed to facilitate the achievement of an objective or objectives." Robert J. Thierauf, *Systems Analysis and Design of Real-Time Management Information Systems* (Englewood Cliffs, N.J.: Prentice-Hall, 1975), p. 4.

2. The ensuing attitudes will be discussed in the appropriate chronological sequence. *Postindustrial* is used as defined by Daniel Bell in *The Coming of Post-Industrial Society* (New York: Basic Books, 1976).

3. U.S., Federal Communications Commission, *The Historical Evolution of the Commercial Network Broadcast System*, Network Inquiry Special Staff Report (Washington, D.C., October 1979), p. 7.

4. Christopher H. Sterling and John M. Kittross, *Stay Tuned* (Belmont, Calif.: Wadsworth Publishing Co., 1978), p. 40.

5. Ibid., p. 43.

6. FCC, *Evolution of Broadcast*, pp. 8, 11.

7. For further details of the creation of RCA, see FCC, *Evolution of Broadcast*, pp. 10–14; Sterling and Kittross, *Stay Tuned*, pp. 52–58; and Robert C. Bitting, Jr., "Creating an Industry," p. 1055, in *Technical Development of Television*, ed. George Shiers (New York: Arno Press, 1977).

8. Sterling and Kittross, *Stay Tuned*, pp. 61–63, 66.

9. Erik Barnouw, *Tube of Plenty* (New York: Oxford University Press, 1975), pp. 38–39.

10. FCC, *Evolution of Broadcast*, pp. 19–22.

11. Sterling and Kittross, *Stay Tuned*, p. 68.

12. Ibid., p. 107; FCC, *Evolution of Broadcast*, p. 23.

13. Erik Barnouw, *A History of Broadcasting in the United States*, vol. 1 (New York: Oxford University Press, 1966), pp. 194, 220–22; and Sterling and Kittross, *Stay Tuned*, pp. 109–10.

14. Barnouw, *History of Broadcasting*, p. 220.

15. Ibid., pp. 232, 251.

16. Eugene Lyons, *David Sarnoff* (New York: Harper and Row, 1966), pp. 160–61.

17. Gleason L. Archer, *Big Business and Radio* (New York: American Historical Co., 1939), p. 381.

18. Bitting, "Creating an Industry," pp. 1016–17.

19. Thomas E. Will, *Telecommunications Structure and Management in the Executive Branch of the Government, 1900–1970* (Boulder, Colo.: Westview Press, 1978), p. 3.

20. Sterling and Kittross, *Stay Tuned*, p. 39.

21. Will, *Telecommunications Structure*, p. 4.

22. Sterling and Kittross, *Stay Tuned*, pp. 51–52.

23. Ibid., pp. 84–88, 126–27; Will, *Telecommunications Structure*, pp. 8–11.

24. FCC, *Evolution of Broadcast*, p. 26.

25. Sterling and Kittross, *Stay Tuned*, pp. 187–88.

26. FCC, *Evolution of Broadcast*, pp. 62–66.

27. Radio was not a prerequisite for television, which could have utilized wire transmission, as several early systems actually did and as is common in today's cablevision.

28. Gerald R. M. Garrat and Albert H. Mumford, "The History of Television," p. 25, in *Technical Development of Television*, ed. Shiers.

29. Alexander Bain, "Electric Time-Pieces and Telegraphy," British patent no. 9,745, issued 27 November 1843; "Automatic Telegraphy," *English Mechanic and Mirror of Science* 2, no. 46 (9 February 1866): 273–74. See also George Shiers, "Early Schemes for Television," *IEEE Spectrum* 17, no. 5 (May 1970): 24.

30. George Shiers, "Historical Notes on Television before 1900," *SMPTE Journal* 86, no. 3 (March 1977): 130; David T. MacFarland, "Television: The Whirling Beginning," in *American Broadcasting*, ed. Lawrence W. Lichty and Malachi C. Topping (New York: Hastings House, 1975), p. 47.

31. Willoughby Smith, "Effect of Light on Selenium during the Passage of an Electric Current," *Journal of the Society of Telegraphy Engineers* 2 (12 February 1873): 31; *Nature* 7, no. 173 (20 February 1873): 303; *The American Journal of Science and Arts* 5, no. 28 (1873): 301. Historians dispute whether credit for the discovery should be assigned to May or Smith. See Shiers, "Historical Notes," pp. 129–30, for a discussion of the evidence.

32. Shiers, "Historical Notes," p. 131.

33. Harry W. Sova, "A Descriptive and Historical Survey of American Television, 1937–1948" (Ph.D. diss., Ohio University, 1977), pp. 19–23.

34. "The Telectroscope," *English Mechanic and World of Science* 28, no. 723 (31 January 1879): 509; "The Telectroscope," *Scientific American* 40, no. 20 (17 May 1879): 309.

35. Denis D. Redmond, "An Electric Telescope," *English Mechanic and World of Science* 28, no. 724 (7 February 1879): 540.

36. Ibid.

37. "Seeing by Electricity," *Scientific American* 42, no. 23 (5 June 1880): 355; "Seeing by Electricity," *English Mechanic and World of Science* 31, no. 795 (18 June 1880): 345–46. J. George Knapp and Julian D. Tebo, "The History of Television," *IEEE Communications Society Magazine* 16, no. 3 (May 1978): 8. George Shiers, in "Historical Notes," pp. 130–31, shows that those who credit Carey with pioneering research in 1875 have been misled.

38. John Perry and William E. Ayrton, "Seeing by Electricity," *Nature* 21, no. 547 (22 April 1880): 589.

39. Ibid.

40. For a full list see Shiers, "Early Schemes," p. 25, and John C. Wilson, "Twenty Five Years' Change in Television," pp. 92–93, in *Technical Development of Television*, ed. Shiers.

41. William Lucas, "The Telectroscope; or, 'Seeing by Electricity,' " *English Mechanic and World of Science* 35, no. 891 (21 April 1882): 151–52. Lucas's "Telectroscope" was the receiver for the system only.

42. Ibid., p. 151.

43. Ibid.

44. Ibid.

45. Ibid., p. 152.

46. Paul Nipkow, "Electrisches Teleskop," German patent no. 30,105, issued 6 January 1884. Notice that in this proposed method very few picture elements per line are possible, while in other techniques one line may be analyzed into several hundred picture elements.

47. John V. L. Hogan, "The Early Days of Television," in *A Technological History of Motion Pictures and Television*, ed. Raymond Fielding (Berkeley and Los Angeles: University of California Press, 1967), pp. 232–33.

48. Shiers, "Historical Notes," p. 133, and Garratt and Mumford, "History of Television," p. 29. Both articles note that this design evidently was first advanced by Llewelyn B. Atkinson in 1882, although not publicly.

49. Albert Abramson, *Electronic Motion Pictures* (Berkeley and Los Angeles: University of California Press, 1955), p. 30.

50. "Seeing by Electricity," *Electrician* 24 (7 March 1890): 448–50.

51. Abramson, *Electronic Motion Pictures*, p. 21; Knapp and Tebo, "History of Television," p. 10.

52. However, in 1950 the commercially highly successful Vidicon transmitting tube, based on photoconductivity, was introduced by RCA.

53. Hogan, "Early Days," p. 223. De Forest's audion, developed before the First World War, was also an important element in the development of a workable television receiver, serving to amplify the weak incoming signal from the transmitter.

54. Knapp and Tebo, "History of Television," p. 10; Gerald R. M. Garratt and Geoffrey Parr, eds., "Television," (London: H. M. Stationery Office, 1937), p. 31, in *Technical Development of Television*, ed. Shiers.

55. Max Dieckmann and Gustav Glage, "Verfahren zur Übertragung von Schriftzeichen und Strichzeichnungen unter Benuntzung der Kathodenstrahlröhre," German patent no. 190,102, issued 12 September 1906. See also Axel G. Jensen, "The Evolution of Modern Television," in *A Technological History*, ed. Fielding, p. 235.

56. See also Jensen, "Evolution of Television," p. 175; Knapp and Tebo, "History of Television," pp. 10, 16; and Garratt and Parr, "Television," pp. 12–13.

57. Boris Rosing, "Verfahren zur Übertragung von Lichtbildern in elektrischen Apparaten, bei welchen auf der Gebestelle die von den einzelnen Punkten des Bildfeldes ausgehenden Strahlen durch ein optisches System in bestimmter Reihenfolge auf einen gemeinsamen photoelektrischen Empfänger gelenkt werden," German patent no. 244,746, issued 3 March 1911. Rosing quoted in P. K. Gorokhov, "History of Modern Television," p. 75, in *Technical Development of Television*, ed. Shiers.

58. Knapp and Tebo, "History of Television," p. 16.

59. Robert Grimshaw, "The 'Telegraphic Eye,' " *Scientific American* 104, no. 13 (April 1911): 151.

60. Ibid.

61. A. A. Campbell Swinton, "Distant Electric Vision," *Nature* 78, no. 2016 (18 June 1908): 151.

62. A. A. Campbell Swinton, "Presidential Address," *Journal of the Röntgen Society* 8, no. 30 (January 1912): 7.

63. Ibid., p. 11.

64. Ibid., pp. 10–12.

65. Ibid.

66. Ibid., p. 9.

67. A. A. Campbell Swinton, "Electronic Television," *Nature* 118, no. 2973 (23 October 1926): 590.

68. The history of the development of electronic television after the First World War will be presented in Chapter 4.

69. *Television* seems to have occurred in French in 1900. Apparently it was first employed in English in the 25 September 1909, issue of *Athenaeum*, p. 367, where it appears in an article translated from the French. Its first American use is attributed to Hugo Gernsback in a December 1909 article in *Modern Electrics*. Until the early 1930s, however, alternative terms were sometimes still used.

70. Sova, "Survey of American Television," p. 43.

71. "Charles Francis Jenkins," vol. B, *The National Cyclopaedia of American Biography* (New York: James T. White and Co., 1927), p. 246; and C. Francis Jenkins, *The Boyhood of an Inventor* (Washington: National Capital Press, 1931).

72. C. Francis Jenkins, *Vision by Radio, Photographs, Radio Photograms* (Washington: Jenkins Laboratories, 1925), pp. 25, 118.

73. Ibid., p. 118.

74. Ibid., pp. 25, 95–99.

75. Ibid., p. 118.

76. Ibid.

77. "Charles Francis Jenkins," *National Cyclopaedia*, p. 246.

78. Carl H. Claudy, "Motion Pictures by Radio," *Scientific American* 127, no. 5 (November 1922): 320. It is interesting to note that 1922 was also the year radio received full commercial authorization.

79. Jenkins, *Vision by Radio*, p. 119.

80. "Radio Shows Far Away Object," *New York Times*, 14 June 1925, p. 1.

81. George L. Bidwell, "Television Arrives," *QST*, July 1925, p. 9.

82. Jenkins, *Vision by Radio*, p. 12.

83. Ibid., p. 34; Claudy, "Motion Pictures by Radio," p. 13; and Alfred Dinsdale, *First Principles of Television* (New York: John Wiley and Sons, 1932), pp. 46–47, 50.

84. "The 'Televisor,' " *Times* (London), 28 January 1926, p. 9. Accounts of Baird's earliest work are sketchy but can be found in J. D. Percy, "John L. Baird," (London: Television Society, 1952), pp. 3–5, reprinted in *Technical Development of Television*, ed. Shiers. George Shiers, "Television Fifty Years Ago," *Journal of Broadcasting* 19, no. 4 (Fall 1975): 387–400; and Garratt and Parr, "Television," pp. 14–15. P. Waddell, W. V. Smith, and J. Sanderson, in "John Logie Baird and the

Falkirk Transmitter," *Wireless World* (January 1976): 43–46, suggest that Baird distorted details of much of his work between 1925 and 1928 to hide his progress from possible competitors, thus making reconstruction of his research even more hazardous. Britain's John Logie Baird should not be confused with Hollis S. Baird, an American television pioneer working in Boston, who will be discussed in Chapter 3.

    85. Percy, "John L. Baird," pp. 8–9.

CHAPTER 2

    1. Letter from William D. Terrell, chief of the Radio Division, Department of Commerce, to Grosvenor K. Glenn, president of Television Publishing Company, publisher of *Television*, "America's First Television Magazine," dated 26 November 1928.

    2. The mechanical type of television, as noted in Chapter 1, operated on the same technical principles as electronic television, but incorporated mechanical moving parts as the cathode-ray tube method did not. And the label *low-definition* was applied only subsequently, comparing it to later achievement as a biplane was slow only when compared to later jet aircraft.

    3. Conflict between the industry and the government over what constituted acceptable quality also existed from the television industry's inception until 1941. This will be discussed in chapters 5 and 6.

    4. The result of such competition is not a foregone conclusion, as will be seen in Chapter 4.

    5. Herbert E. Ives, "Television," *Bell System Technical Journal* 6 (October 1927): 551.

    6. "Far Off Speakers Seen As Well As Heard Here in a Test of Television," *New York Times,* 8 April 1927, p. 1.

    7. Ibid.

    8. Ibid. Accounts of the AT & T demonstration besides those listed in notes 5 and 6 include Edward L. Nelson, "Radio Transmission System for Television," *Bell System Technical Journal* 6 (October 1927): 633–52; in the same issue is Danford K. Gannett and Estill I. Green, "Wire Transmission for Television," pp. 616–32; Louis S. Treadwell, "Practical Television Demonstrated," *Scientific American* 136, no. 3 (June 1927): 385; and "Television Developments," *Engineering* 124 (19 August 1927): 247–50; Herbert E. Ives, "Television: Twentieth Anniversary," *Bell Laboratories Record* 25, no. 6 (May 1947): 190–93.

    9. "Colored Films, Talking Movies, and Television," *Literary Digest* 98, no. 6 (11 August 1928): 9; "Out-of-Door Television—The Latest Advance," *Scientific American* 139, no. 3 (September 1928): 255–56.

    10. Herbert E. Ives, "Television in Colors," *Bell Laboratories Record* 7, no. 11 (July 1929): 439–44. See also Herbert E. Ives, "Radio's Flickering 'Eyes' Now Sensitive to Color," *New York Times,* 7 July 1929, p. ix, 15.

    11. "Television in Color Shown First Time," *New York Times,* 28 June 1919, p. 25.

    12. Ives was not the first to demonstrate color television, however. John L. Baird unveiled his method in July 1929. J. D. Percy, "John L. Baird," pp. 7–8, in *Technical*

Development of Television, ed. George Shiers (New York: Arno Press, 1977). A version of Baird's technique was advocated in the U.S. in 1940, as discussed in Chapter 6.

13. Captioned photograph, *New York Times*, 19 December 1926, p. viii, 15. The device, however, seems to have at first been limited to facsimile.

14. "Radio Vision Takes Another Step toward the Home," *New York Times*, 22 January 1928, p. ix, 14.

15. "Radio Television to Home Receivers Is Shown in Tests," *New York Times*, 14 January 1928, p. 1.

16. Accounts of the telecast appear in "Play Is Broadcast by Voice and Acting in Radio-Television," *New York Times*, 12 September 1928, pp. 1, 10; "Television Makes the Radio Drama Possible," *Radio News* 10, no. 6 (December 1928): 524–27, 587–88; and William J. Toneski, "How We Staged the World's First Television Plays," *Television News* 1, no. 4 (September–October 1931): 260–63, 315.

17. "Play Is Broadcast," *New York Times*, 12 September 1928, pp. 1, 10; "Radio Drama Possible," *Radio News* 10, no. 6 (December 1928): 524–27, 587–88.

18. Edgar H. Felix, "Television Advances from Peephole of Screen," *Radio News* 12, no. 3 (September 1930): 228–30, 268–69.

19. "Says His Television Has Spanned Ocean," *New York Times*, 9 April 1927, p. 5.

20. Edgar T. Larner, *Practical Television* (New York: D. Van Nostrand Co., 1928), p. 172.

21. "Persons in Britain Seen Here by Television As They Pose before Baird's Electric 'Eye'," *New York Times*, 9 February 1928, p. 1.

22. In fact, in Chapter 4 it will be shown that Baird provided a means for an American firm to enter the British market. Baird was, however, more successful in his German venture, as will also be discussed in that chapter.

23. Theodore H. Nakken, "Picture Broadcasts Create Interest in Television," *New York Times*, 27 May 1928, p. ix, 12. WGY broadcast on 380 meters. Nakken also indicates that station WMCA broadcast still pictures on a regular schedule.

24. Editor, *Radio News* 10, no. 1 (July 1928): 84.

25. "Performers at WRNY to be Seen over Radio," *New York Times*, 16 June 1928, p. 10.

26. "WRNY to Start Daily Television Broadcasts," *New York Times*, 13 August 1928, p. 19.

27. Hugo Gernsback, "What to Expect of Television," *Radio News* 10, no. 2 (August 1928): 1; and Robert Hertzberg, "Successful Television Programs Broadcast by *Radio News* Station WRNY," *Radio News* 10, no. 5 (November 1928): 412–15, 490.

28. Hertzberg, "What to Expect," p. 415. See also Ralph P. Clarkson, "What Can We See by Radio?" *Radio Broadcasting* 13, no. 5 (August 1928): 185–87; and Theodore H. Nakken, "Television: Practical Demonstration over WRNY," *Radio News* 10, no. 1 (July 1928): 20–21, 84. "Televisor" was the receiver popularized by John L. Baird.

29. Clarkson, "What Can We See?" p. 185. "Television Experiments in Boston Create Great Interest," *Radio News* 10, no. 2 (August 1928): 118; and "Several Wavelengths Used for High-Frequency Radio Movies and Television," *Radio News* 10, no. 6 (December 1928): 535.

30. "Broadcast Scene and Sound," *New York Times*, 21 June 1928, p. 28.

31. "Successful Television Accomplished on Broadcast Band," *Radio News* 10, no. 3 (September 1928): 219–20, 277.

32. "Radio Standard Movies," *New York Times*, 18 December 1928, p. 34.

33. C. Francis Jenkins, *Radiomovies, Radiovision, Television* (Washington: Jenkins Laboratories, 1929), pp. 10–11; C. Francis Jenkins, "Radio Vision," *Proceedings of the IRE* 15, no. 11 (November 1927): 958–64; and "The Jenkins 'Radio-Movie' Reception Methods," *Radio News* 10, no. 5 (November 1928): 420, 492–93.

34. "Stations Licensed for Television," *New York Times*, 21 July 1928, p. 16.

35. Howard E. Rhodes, "Television: Its Progress To-day," *Radio Broadcasting* 13, no. 6 (October 1928), p. 332.

36. Terrell to Glenn, 26 November 1928.

37. Letter from Albert Cloutier to the supervisor of radio, Boston, 10 April 1928.

38. Letter from Atlanta supervisor of radio to the Radio Division, Department of Commerce, 20 February 1929. This same motivation explains many television applications after 1939 and also following the end of the Second World War.

39. However, this may also be a question of definition. For two of these stations telecasting was interrupted for a good while, in one case for fourteen years. In the third case, its call letters were actually reassigned to another later station operated by the same firm.

40. "Images Dance in Space Heralding New Radio Era," *New York Times*, 14 April 1929, p. xi, 17; "Radio Dealers Foresee Harvest in Television," *New York Times*, 22 March 1931, p. viii, 16.

41. U.S., Congress, Senate, Committee on Interstate Commerce, *Development of Television*, 76th Cong., 3rd sess., 10–11 April 1940, p. 48.

42. Personal communication from Hollis S. Baird.

43. U.S., Federal Radio Commission, *First Annual Report*, 1927, p. 13. Also see *Outlook* 145, no. 16 (20 April 1927): 489.

44. U.S., Federal Radio Commission, *Second Annual Report*, 1928, pp. 252–53. Goldsmith's brief represents the views of RCA, which he represented.

45. Ibid., pp. 21–22.

46. U.S., Federal Radio Commission, *Third Annual Report*, 1929, p. 2.

47. It was at this time that Westinghouse and GE terminated experimental telecasting as part of the unification scheme with RCA.

48. FRC, *Third Annual Report*, 1929, p. 2.

49. U.S., Federal Radio Commission, *Fifth Annual Report*, 1931, p. 54.

50. Ibid., pp. 53–54. By 1937 authorization of the shortwave frequencies for television was withdrawn, except for three stations granted special permission to operate on the 2000–2100-kHz. channel, as will be discussed in Chapter 3. Currently American television stations are allocated a bandwidth of 6 MHz. (that is, 6000 kHz.)

51. FRC, *Third Annual Report*, 1929, p. 28. Also W. E. Downey, acting director of radio, to Chapman Television Company, 13 July 1932.

52. U.S. Federal Radio Commission, *Report on the Application by WJR, the Goodwill Station, Inc. and the WGAR Broadcasting Company, Cuyahoga Heights Village, Ohio, for Visual Station Construction Permit*, 26 February 1932. Although eventually granted operating licenses, these stations do not seem to have actually broadcast very long, if at all.

53. U.S., Federal Radio Commission, *Report on Construction Permit Applica-*

tion of Radio Vision Company, Pittsburgh, Pa., 19 February 1932, and U.S., Federal Radio Commission, *Report on Construction Permit Application of Shreveport, La., Broadcasting Company*, 17 June 1932.

54. FRC, *Second Annual Report*, 1928, p. 21.

55. U.S., Federal Radio Commission, *Fourth Annual Report*, 1930, p. 68.

56. U.S., Federal Radio Commission, *Sixth Annual Report*, 1932, pp. 42–43.

57. U.S., Federal Radio Commission, Files. Press release, 7 December 1930, by Shortwave and Television Corporation.

58. A. M. Morgan to the Boston radio supervisor, 23 December 1930. Morgan, president of W1XAV, quoting the ruling of the FRC general counsel, assured the commission that his station would comply. It should be noted that if a sponsor were assured television exposure as well as the normal radio audience for his commercial, he might be convinced to pay a higher fee, even if not directly to the television station, although this was not the central concern of either W1XAV or the FRC in this case.

59. U.S. supervisor of radio, Chicago, to the director of radio, Department of Commerce, 30 December 1931.

60. Julius Weinberger, Theodore A. Smith, and George Rodwin, "The Selection of Standards for Commercial Radio Television," *Proceedings of the IRE*, 17, no. 9 (September 1929): 1584.

61. Ibid., p. 1585.

62. Ibid.

63. Jenkins, *Radiomovies*, p. 42; and Alfred Dinsdale, *First Principles of Television* (New York: John Wiley and Sons, 1932), p. 205.

64. Sanabria and Western Television Corporation will be discussed in Chapter 3.

65. A receiving apparatus with a 48-aperture disc could not receive a 60-line picture, and vice versa, except by changing discs.

66. Although the latter was the most common method of synchronization at the time, it suffered from the lack of a uniform power standard in the United States.

67. "RMA Optimistic in Television Review," *Broadcasting* 2, no. 6 (11 March 1932): 11. The RMA Television Committee represented the views of RCA, Jenkins Television, Philco, Sanabria, Baird Television, Shortwave and Television Laboratory, Radio Pictures, Freed Radio and Television, Stromberg-Carlson, and Kolster, according to *Broadcasting* 2, no. 1 (1 January 1932): 35. The committee was reconstituted in autumn 1933, after mechanical television had declined, to reflect the interests of electronic television. See Chapter 5.

68. FRC, *Fifth Annual Report*, 1931, p. 54.

69. David Sarnoff, *Looking Ahead* (New York: McGraw-Hill Book Co., 1968), p. 88.

70. David Sarnoff in "Radio," ed. M. M. McBride, *Saturday Evening Post*, 14 August 1926, pp. 24–25.

71. Sarnoff, *Looking Ahead*, p. 96.

72. Ibid., p. 97.

73. William S. Paley, "Radio and the Movies Join Hands," *Nation's Business* 17, no. 11 (October 1929): 237. Paley here was describing the advantages of the new alliance between CBS and Paramount.

74. Jenkins, "Radio Movies," p. 964.

75. Ibid.

76. C. Francis Jenkins, "Radio Finds Its Eyes," *Saturday Evening Post*, 27 July 1929, p. 12.

77. Edgar H. Felix, *Television: Its Methods and Uses* (New York: McGraw-Hill Book Co., 1931), p. 206.

78. William S. Hedges, "Need Develops for Censorship of Television," *Chicago Daily News*, 28 March 1931, p. 20.

79. "Picture Broadcasting Must Contain No 'Ads,' " *Radio Broadcasting* 13, no. 1 (May 1928): 11.

80. *The Zenith Story* (Chicago: Zenith Radio Corporation, 1955), p. 19. In 1947 Zenith would announce its "Phonevision" subscription system.

81. Felix, *Television*, p. 222.

82. Ibid., pp. 223–24.

83. Sarnoff, *Looking Ahead*, pp. 89, 95.

84. "Leaders Dispel Television Fears," *New York Times*, 16 December 1928, p. x, 18.

85. "Images Dance in Space Heralding New Radio Era," *New York Times*, 14 April 1929, p. xi, 17.

86. Paley, "Radio and the Movies," p. 22.

CHAPTER 3

1. Editorial Comment, *Television News* 1, no. 1 (March–April 1931): 28.

2. A copy of the invitation is in the files of the television reports of the FRC papers.

3. Quarterly Report for W3XK, quarter ending 30 September 1929.

4. Quarterly Report for W3XK, quarter ending 30 September 1930; Report on Television Transmission by G. E. Sterling, associate radio inspector, to U.S. supervisor of radio, 24 November 1930.

5. All of these reception reports included in W3XK Quarterly Report, 30 September 1930.

6. Ibid.

7. Quarterly Report for W3XK, quarter ending 31 March 1931.

8. Letter from Jenkins to L. C. Herndon, U.S. supervisor of radio, Baltimore, 27 June 1930.

9. Quarterly Reports for W3XK, quarters ending 30 June 1931 and 30 September 1931.

10. Quarterly Report for W3XK, quarter ending 30 September 1931.

11. Quarterly Report for W3XK and W3XJ, quarter ending 31 December 1931.

12. Jenkins to Herndon, 27 June 1930.

13. C. Francis Jenkins, "The Drum Scanner in Radiomovies Receivers," *Proceedings of the IRE*, 17, no. 9 (September 1929): 1577.

14. These sets are illustrated in A. Dinsdale, *First Principles of Television* (New York: John Wiley and Sons, 1932), facing pp. 186, 194.

15. Howard Rhodes, "Television: Its Progress To-day," *Radio Engineering* 13, no. 6 (October 1928): 331.

16. Jenkins, "The Drum Scanner," pp. 1579–81.

17. D. E. Replogle, "Where Television Is Today," *Radio News* 11, no. 7 (January 1930): 631, and "A 'Scanning Drum' Television Perfected by Jenkins," *Television News* 1, no. 1 (March–April 1939): 60–61, 68.

18. L. C. Herndon, U.S. supervisor of radio, Baltimore, to director of radio, 2 February 1932; and memorandum to Federal Radio Commission on experimental stations in the Third Radio District from W. D. Terrell, director of radio, 30 March 1932. In a memo to the director of radio dated 4 December 1931, Herndon reported that Jenkins had been confined to bed and did not intend to renew his broadcast license.

19. "Ten-Million-Dollar Concern to Push Television," *New York Times*, 5 December 1928, p. 3; "De Forest Radio Makes Offer," *New York Times*, 28 September 1929, p. 27. De Forest Radio operated its own separate television station, W2XCD, from 1930 until the station was destroyed by fire in January 1932. A description of programming can be found in "Television Programs to Be Given Daily," *New York Times*, 24 February 1931, p. 32. But this station did not attempt to compete with its sister operation of Jenkins Television.

20. "Television Movies to Start in Month," *New York Times*, 11 March 1929, p. 30. The station later was moved to Passaic and then to New York City.

21. August P. Peck, "Television Advances," *Scientific American* 140, no. 6 (June 1929): 527.

22. Advertisement in *Television News* 1, no. 1 (March–April 1931): 67.

23. Advertisement in *Television News* 2, no. 1 (March–April 1932): 45.

24. A photostory in Radio Broadcasting 16, no. 2 (December 1929): 87.

25. "Television Program in Times Square Area," *New York Times*, 24 August 1930, p. 19.

26. All quotations are from a Report on Television Transmission and Reception by G. E. Sterling, associate radio inspector, to the U.S. supervisor of radio, 24 November 1930.

27. George H. Waltz, Jr., "Get In on Television," *Popular Science Monthly* 119, no. 1 (July 1931): 16–17, 136; Delbert E. Replogle, "Television Now on Schedule," *Scientific American* 145, no. 1 (July 1931): 33; Delbert E. Replogle, "Jenkins with New Lighting System," *Television News* 1, no. 4 (September–October 1931): 246–48; and "Radio Talkie Put on Program Basis," *New York Times*, 27 April 1931, p. 24.

28. "Radio Dealers Foresee Harvest in Television," *New York Times*, 22 March 1931, p. ix, 16.

29. Quarterly Report of W2XCR, quarter ending 16 October 1931.

30. Ibid. See also "Hearst to Get WGBS and Offer Television," *New York Times*, 10 October 1931, p. 10. WGBS, originally founded by Gimbel Brothers in 1924, was assigned the call letters WINS after being acquired by the Hearst subsidiary.

31. Report on Inspection of Several Visual Broadcast Stations to the director of radio, Radio Division, Department of Commerce, 30 January 1932.

32. "De Forest in Jenkins Deal," *New York Times*, 1 February 1932, p. 15.

33. "De Forest to Take Over Assets of Jenkins Corporation," *Broadcasting* 2, no. 7 (1 April 1932):12.

34. "Receivers for De Forest," *New York Times*, 23 June 1932, p. 19; "De Forest Radio Bid Approved," *New York Times*, 7 March 1933, p. 9; "Considers Sale of De Forest Radio," *New York Times*, 25 March 1933, p. 27.

35. "Columbia Projects Television Station," *New York Times*, 14 August 1930, p. 12. WABC's call letters were later changed to WCBS. The current WABC was formerly WJZ.

36. "Columbia Looks Ahead to Television Programs," *New York Times*, 12 October 1930, p. ix, 11.

37. Ibid.; "Experimental Vision Broadcaster Ready for WABC in 1931," *New York Times*, 21 December 1930, p. ix, 10.

38. "Columbia Is Telecasting," *Television News* 1, no. 4 (September–October 1931): 252–53, 317.

39. Quarterly Report for Visual Broadcast Station W2XAB, quarter ending December 1931.

40. Report on Inspection of Several Visual Broadcast Stations to the director of radio, Radio Division, Department of Commerce, 30 January 1932.

41. "Sight-and-Sound Broadcasting on One Wavelength," *Television News* 2, no. 4 (September–October 1932): 167.

42. Quarterly Report for Visual Broadcast Station W2XAB, quarter ending December 1931.

43. "Sight-and-Sound Broadcasting," *Television News*, p. 167; also Samuel Kaufman, "Television and Sound," *Radio News* 14, no. 5 (November 1932): 270–71, 314–15.

44. U.S., Federal Communications Commission, Deleted Television License File.

45. "Television Placed on Daily Schedule," *New York Times*, 22 March 1929, p. 20; also Robert C. Bitting, Jr., "Creating an Industry," p. 1019, in *Technical Development of Television*, ed. George Shiers (New York: Arno Press, 1977).

46. "Columbia Projects Television Station," *New York Times*, 14 August 1930, p. 12.

47. Quarterly Report on Visual Broadcast Station W2XBS, quarter ending 20 February 1932. NBC also operated portable television station W2XBT in the New York area.

48. Statement from L. A. Briggs, manager, RCA Central Frequency Bureau, to FRC, 4 March 1931.

49. "Television Studio for Empire State," *New York Times*, 10 July 1931, p. 24.

50. Elmer W. Engstrom, "An Experimental Television System," *Proceedings of the IRE* 21, no. 12 (December 1933): 1652–54; Ray D. Kell, "Description of Experimental Television Transmitting Apparatus," *Proceedings of the IRE* 21, no. 12 (December 1933): 1674–91. The call letters of this new VHF station in the Empire State Building were W2XF, which were later changed to the previous call of the original NBC New York station, W2XBS.

51. George Waltz, Jr., "Television Scanning with the Cathode Ray Tube," *Popular Science Monthly* 120, no. 3 (March 1932): 82–83.

52. Letter from John V. L. Hogan to New York supervisor of radio, 30 December 1929.

53. A Report on Television Transmission and Reception, by G. E. Sterling, associate radio inspector, to the U.S. supervisor of radio, 24 November 1930.

54. Report on Inspection of Several Visual Broadcast Stations to the director of radio, Radio Division, Department of Commerce, 30 January 1932.

55. FCC, Deleted Television License File, and personal communication from John V. Hogan, the researcher's son.

56. "Broadcasters Get Ninety Days' Extension," *New York Times*, 25 June 1929, p. 34.

57. At this time the commercial medium-wave band extended from 550 to 1500 kHz.

58. Hollis S. Baird, "The Boston Television Station," *Television News* 2, no. 1 (March–April 1932): 11, 58, 60.

59. "Seeing a Radio Teacher," *New York Times*, 2 August 1931, p. 9.

60. "Television's Dilemma," *Literary Digest* 110, no. 1 (4 July 1931): 20.

61. U.S., Federal Radio Commission, Experimental Visual Broadcast Stations File. The FRC required audio identification because it lacked the equipment to monitor video identifications. See Chapter 2, note 59.

62. Personal communication from Hollis S. Baird.

63. Kenneth A. Hathaway, "Hathaway Sees Television Set Made in Boston," *Chicago Daily News*, 27 April 1931, p. 23.

64. Advertisement in *Television News* 1, no. 2 (May–June 1931): inside cover.

65. Frank W. Murphy, Boston, to FRC, 5 February 1931.

66. Jennie A. Glover, Boston, to FRC, 23 January 1931.

67. Charles C. Kolster, supervisor of radio, Boston, to the director of radio, 20 February 1931.

68. See Glover to FRC, for instance.

69. Personal communication from Hollis S. Baird.

70. W1XG, however, never received commercial authorization, as will be discussed in the following chapters.

71. William S. Hedges, "National Chains Both Increasing Activities Here," *Chicago Daily News*, 7 February 1931, p. 7.

72. WCFL chief engineer to the acting director of radio, 19 September 1930.

73. Quarterly Report for Experimental Relay and Television Station W9XAA, quarter ending 6 April 1931.

74. Letter from H. S. Hays, U.S. supervisor of radio, Chicago, to Radio Division, 4 March 1931.

75. Ulises A. Sanabria, "Method and Means for Scanning," U.S. patent no. 1,805,848, issued 19 May 1931 (filed 7 June 1929). A form of interlaced scanning is now part of American television standards.

76. The State University of Iowa's station will be discussed below. For Montreal's station, see "Television in Canada," *Broadcasting* 1, no. 3 (15 November 1931): 29.

77. Kenneth A. Hathaway, "Six Hundred Teachers Given Insight into Television," *Chicago Daily News*, 19 January 1931, p. 24.

78. Kenneth A. Hathaway, "Television Used in Transmitting Stock Reports," *Chicago Daily News*, 27 January 1931, p. 30.

79. See Kenneth A. Hathaway, "Television Put on Big Screen in Successful Test," *Chicago Daily News*, 7 April 1931, p. 36; "Enlarged Television Here," *New York Times*, 23 June 1931, p. 34; and "Television Draws Big Crowd at Fair," *New York Times*, 23 September 1931, p. 18.

80. W9XAO official log sheets, January–May 1931.

81. Quoted in Quarterly Report for W9XAO, quarter ending 4 January 1932.

82. Kenneth A. Hathaway, "Honeymoon Skit with Music on W9XAO Tonight," *Chicago Daily News*, 12 January 1931, p. 27.

83. Quarterly Report for W9XAO, quarter ending 29 June 1931. Evidently the sound portion of these plays consisted only of music from a live orchestra. Occasional log entries include remarks about the orchestra "failing to show."

84. For details see *Broadcasting*, 1 December 1932, p. 16; 15 December 1932, p. 114; and 15 May 1933, p. 5.

85. "Station WMAQ Will Supplement Its Broadcasts with Images," *New York Times*, 13 July 1930, p. ix, 11. Also see "Asks Radio Power for World Service," *New York Times*, 16 October 1929, p. 26.

86. *Chicago Daily News*, 29 September 1950. These same studios were later used for a time by WGN-TV when it began telecasting after the Second World War, and then by WENR-TV (now WLS-TV). W9XAP's sister station, W9XAO, only used 500 watts for its transmitter.

87. Kenneth A. Hathaway, "Take New Step Tonight in Art of Television," *Chicago Daily News*, 7 January 1931, p. 28.

88. Ibid. See also Kenneth A. Hathaway, "See and Hear First Television Play on W9XAP," *Chicago Daily News*, 8 January 1931, p. 26, and "Television's First Play," *Television News* 1, no. 2 (May–June 1931): 158.

89. "Television Drama Tonight," *Chicago Daily News*, 3 April 1931, p. 45.

90. "Television Offered by Chicago If Democrats Will Go There," *New York Times*, 9 January 1932, p. 10.

91. *Chicago Daily News*, 22 April 1931, p. 41.

92. Quarterly Report for W9XAP, quarter ending 29 February 1932; Kenneth A. Hathaway, "Western Cities Report Getting W9XAP Clearly," *Chicago Daily News*, 9 March 1931, p. 23.

93. "Chicago Steps Ahead in Television," *Television News* 1, no. 5 (November–December 1931): 332.

94. "NBC Gets Station WMAQ November 1," *New York Times*, 29 August 1931, p. 16; *Broadcasting* 1, no. 5 (15 December 1931): 32. NBC later acquired full ownership of WMAQ.

95. Personal communication from Walter R. Lindsay, former W9XAP station engineer.

96. Memo from Thad H. Brown, FRC general counsel, to Radio Director Terrell, 11 February 1931; Hedges, "National Chains." Unlike WMAQ, WENR was not a clear-channel station; in fact, it shared its Chicago frequency with then-independent WLS, which helps explain why WMAQ became the Red network affiliate and WENR, the Blue affiliate. NBC also acquired the company's shortwave audio station, W9XF. Great Lakes Broadcasting, with its headquarters in Chicago, had transmitted from suburban Downers Grove.

97. William D. Terrell, director of radio, to U.S. supervisor of radio, Chicago, 13 August 1929; "WENR Is Granted Television License," *New York Times*, 8 September 1929, p. x, 17; J. F. Morris, control room engineer, Great Lakes Broadcasting Company, to W. E. Downey, acting director of radio, Radio Division, Department of Commerce, 12 September 1930.

98. S. W. Edwards, U.S. supervisor of radio, Detroit, to the Radio Division,

Department of Commerce, 14 November 1929; memo to the radio supervisor from F. W. Sloan, U.S. radio inspector, Chicago, 24 January 1930.

99. Briggs to FRC, 4 March 1931; William D. Terrell, director of radio to U.S. supervisor of radio, Chicago, 21 August 1931.

100. "Open Station For Television," *The Milwaukee Journal*, 9 September 1931.

101. Personal communication from Jack Krueger, public affairs manager, WTMJ.

102. George W. Young, a jewelry-store owner and operator of radio station WDGY in Minneapolis, also had a VHF video outlet, W9XAT, from approximately 1933 to 1938. See U.S., Federal Radio Commission, *Construction Permit Application for Experimental Television Station*, 9 February 1932; U.S., Federal Communications Commission, *Reports* 6 (Washington: U.S. Government Printing Office, 1940), p. 867; and *Broadcasting* 8, no. 12 (1 July 1935): 108.

103. Memo from William D. Terrell to James W. Baldwin, secretary of the FRC, 24 June 1931; memo from Baldwin to Terrell, 27 June 1931.

104. Edwin B. Kurtz, *Pioneering in Educational Television* (Iowa City: State University of Iowa, 1959), pp. 10–11. Personal communications from Carl H. Menzer and James L. Potter.

105. Kurtz, *Pioneering in Educational Television*, p. 165; personal communications from Mrs. Edwin B. Kurtz, Carl H. Menzer, and James L. Potter.

106. Kurtz, *Pioneering in Educational Television*, pp. 20–24, 53.

107. Ibid., p. 70.

108. Ibid., pp. 80–115; quotation from p. 111.

109. Ibid., pp. 141–46.

110. Ibid., p. 164.

111. Charles F. Harding, Roscoe H. George, and Howard J. Heim, *The Purdue University Experimental Television Station*, Purdue Engineering Bulletin, Research Series no. 65, vol. 23, no. 2 (March 1939): 5–8, 14. Also "Report of the Research and Extension Activities of the Engineering Schools and Departments for the Sessions of 1934–35," Purdue University Engineering Experimental Station Research Series no. 51, vol. 19, no. 4 (July 1935): 25.

112. Harding, George, and Heim, *Purdue University*, pp. 10, 15.

113. Ibid., p. 9. This important agreement will be further discussed in Chapter 4.

114. "Report of the Research and Extension Activities of the Engineering Schools and Departments," Purdue University Engineering Experimental Station Research Series no. 91, vol. 27, no. 6 (November 1943): 32.

115. FCC, Deleted Television License File.

116. U.S., Federal Communications Commission, *Third Annual Report*, 1937, p. 36; Harding, George, and Heim, *Purdue University*, p. 9. In July 1936 the FCC assigned 2100–2200 kH. to these stations, but upon request, modified their order to substitute 2000–2100 kH. The FCC actually allowed a new fourth station, operated by National Television Corporation in New York, to operate its W2XMT on this channel as well for several months in late 1936 to test a new mechanical transmitting system. But they denied continuation of the tests as they did not seem promising. See U.S., Federal Communications Commission, *Reports* 4 (Washington: U.S. Government Printing Office, 1938), pp. 414–20.

117. Two technical accounts of this station can be found in a Report on Inspection of Pioneer Mercantile Company's W6XAH from Herbert H. Smith, assistant radio

inspector, San Francisco, May 1932, and Ralph D. Lemert, "Single Side Band Television Transmission," *Television News* 2, no. 3 (July–August 1932): 122–23, 152. Charles Schamblin, current president of Pioneer Mercantile Company, also provided information from *The Kern County Centennial Almanac*. Lemert later became vice-president of De Forest Television Corporation, in Los Angeles; see *Broadcasting* 11, no. 1 (1 July 1936): 111. (In Bakersfield, Humboldt Street was also named Twenty-first Street.)

118. "Most Powerful Transmitter in West Completed," *Radio Review and Television News* 2, no. 6 (January–February 1933): 295. W6XAO will be discussed in Chapter 5, along with the three other electronic stations already on the air by 1933: W3XE, Philadelphia; W8XAN, Jackson, Michigan; and W9XAL, Kansas City, Missouri.

119. In fact, by 1938 a Nipkow-disc technique had been developed for transmitting a 405-line picture. See Herre Rina and C. Dormsman, "Television System with Nipkow Disc," *Philips Technical Review* 2, no. 3 (March 1937): 72–76; H. Rina, "Television with Nipkow Disc and Interlaced Scanning," *Philips Technical Review* 3, no. 10 (October 1938): 285–91.

CHAPTER 4

1. In Chapter 6 it will be seen that by 1940, RCA also faced two new competitors—DuMont and CBS. The engineering rivalry between RCA and DuMont was also settled by 1941, while the conflict with CBS continued until 1953.

2. Alexander McLean Nicholson, "Television," U.S. patent no. 1,470,698, issued 16 October 1923 (filed 7 December 1917).

3. W. Rupert Maclaurin, *Invention and Innovation in the Radio Industry* (New York: Macmillan Co., 1949), pp. 200–201.

4. Vladimir K. Zworykin, "The Early Days: Some Recollections," in *American Broadcasting*, ed. Lawrence W. Lichty and Malachi C. Topping (New York: Hastings House, 1975), p. 55. That Zworykin was aware of the importance of the storage principle from the start is evident from the fact that he stressed it several times in his 1923 claims: for example, "in a light-sensitive device, an image plane divided into individual light-sensitive elementary areas, an impulse storing element for each of said elementary areas, and adopted to be energized in accordance with the characteristics of the associated areas, and means for connecting said storing element in succession in a common circuit." Vladimir K. Zworykin, "Television System," U.S. patent no. 2,141,059, filed 29 December 1923. The concept evidently originated in a C. Francis Jenkins patent (personal communication from Hollis S. Baird).

5. Zworykin, U.S. patent no. 2,141,059.

6. Ibid. Note that this double transmission of each frame is similar to a motion-picture projector's shutter; it should not be confused with the interlaced scanning later introduced.

7. Zworykin, "Early Days," p. 54.

8. *Harold J. McCreary v. Vladimir K. Zworykin*, 8 February 1932, U.S. Court of Customs and Patent Appeals, Interference no. 54922. *Court of Customs and Patent Appeals* 19 (Washington: Government Printing Office, 1932), pp. 991–99.

McCreary was employed by Associated Electric Laboratories, Incorporated, of Chicago, with a contract promising to finance his television research. Besides his patent for color television (U.S. patent no. 2,013,162), he also received television patents for a mosaic field (U.S. patent nos. 1,935,649 and 1,849,679). McCreary's relationship with Associated Electric was evidently terminated in 1930. Personal communication from Harold J. McCreary.

9. *Westinghouse Electric and Manufacturing Company* v. *RCA*, 6 October 1936, Equity no. 1183, *U.S. Patent Quarterly* 39:206–17.

10. Vladimir V. Zworykin, "Television System," U.S. patent no. 1,691,324, issued 13 November 1928 (filed 13 July 1925).

11. Zworykin, "Early Days," p. 55.

12. "New Cathode Ray Tube Pushes Television Ahead," *New York Times*, 24 November 1929, p. ix, 12. Accounts of the demonstration can also be found in "Cathode-Ray Television Receiver Developed," *Scientific American* 142, no. 1 (February 1930): 147; and "How Cathode-Ray Eliminates the Scanning Disc," *Television News* 1, no. 1 (March–April 1931): 58–59, 77–78.

13. Vladimir K. Zworykin, "Television with Cathode-Ray Tube for Receiver," *Radio Engineering* 9, no. 12 (December 1929): 39–41.

14. Eugene Lyons, *David Sarnoff* (New York: Harper and Row, 1966), pp. 207–9.

15. *Annual Report of the Radio Corporation of America*, 1930, p. 26.

16. Zworykin, "Early Days," p. 55.

17. Zworykin, "Television with Cathode-Ray Tube," pp. 38–39.

18. Vladimir K. Zworykin, "The Iconoscope: A Modern Version of the Electric Eye," *Proceedings of the IRE* 22, no. 1 (January 1934): 19–20.

19. Zworykin, "Early Days," p. 56.

20. Vladimir K. Zworykin, "Television," *Journal of the Franklin Institute* 217, no. 1 (January 1934): 1.

21. Ibid., pp. 1–32. Notice that in the operation of the pickup tube five distinct steps are involved: conversion of light, storage, scanning, erasure, and noiseless amplification. It is how these five steps are accomplished that distinguishes differing tube designs. For a discussion of these concepts, see Albert Rose, "Television Pickup Tubes and the Problem of Vision," in *Advances in Electronics*, vol. 1, ed. Ladislaus Marton (New York: Academic Press, 1948), pp. 133–34.

22. Zworykin, "Iconoscope," p. 31.

23. Elmer W. Engstrom, "An Experimental Television System," *Proceedings of the IRE* 22, no. 11 (November 1934): 1241–44.

24. Ibid., p. 1244.

25. Ibid., p. 1243. Its competitor originally could do neither as successfully.

26. Ray D. Kell, Alda V. Bedford, and M. A. Trainer, "An Experimental Television System," *Proceedings of the IRE* 22, no. 11 (November 1934): 1250–51.

27. Ralph S. Holmes, W. L. Carlson, and William A. Tolson, "An Experimental Television System," *Proceedings of the IRE* 22, no. 11 (November 1934): 1284–85.

28. Lewis M. Clement and Elmer W. Engstrom, "RCA Television Field Tests," *RCA Review* 1, no. 1 (July 1936): 38. RCA's interlaced system was evidently based on a design by Randall C. Ballard, of Marion, Indiana, filed with the U.S. Patent Office in July 1932, and issued 28 March 1939 as patent no. 2,152,234. Robert C. Bitting,

Jr. ("Creating an Industry," in *Technical Development of Television*, ed. George Shiers [New York: Arno Press, 1977]), attributes the idea to Alda V. Bedford of the Camden group. But in Ray D. Kell, Alda V. Bedford, and M. A. Trainer, "Scanning Sequence and Repetition Rate of Television Images," *Proceedings of the IRE* 24, no 4 (April 1936): 564, interlaced scanning is admitted to be an even older idea. In Chapter 3, Sanabria's system, disclosed in 1929, was shown to depend on interlacing.

29. It should be noted that interlaced systems will have an odd number of lines in a frame (for example, 343, 405, 441, 525). The half-lines at the top and the bottom of each frame are the result of the fact that the left-to-right movement of the electron beam is at a slight downward angle. The 30-frames per-second rate was deliberately chosen so that the scanning rate of 60 fields would coincide with the 60-cycle rate adopted as standard for electrical current in the United States.

30. *Annual Report of the Radio Corporation of America*, 1935, pp. 6–7.

31. Ibid., p. 7.

32. *Annual Report of the Radio Corporation of America*, 1933, p. 4.

33. *Annual Report of the Radio Corporation of America*, 1934, p. 15.

34. Ibid.

35. *Television: Collected Addresses and Papers on the Future of the New Art and Its Recent Technical Development*, vol. 1 (New York: RCA Institutes Technical Press, 1936), p. 2.

36. Ibid., p. 3.

37. The complications arising from this situation is a central topic of Chapter 6.

38. "Million-Dollar Plan Brightens Television Outlook," *New York Times*, 12 May 1935, p. x, 11.

39. "Television Tasks," *Business Week*, 8 June 1935, pp. 20–21; "Television for Millions," *Popular Mechanics* 64, no. 3 (September 1935): 321–23, 142A.

40. For some discussion of the interaction between RCA and Armstrong, see Erik Barnouw, *Tube of Plenty* (New York: Oxford University Press, 1975), pp. 80–82; Lyons, *David Sarnoff*, pp. 213–14; and Lawrence Lessing, *Man of High Fidelity: Edwin Howard Armstrong* (Philadelphia: J. B. Lippincott Co., 1956), chapter 12.

41. A further consideration for RCA, no doubt, was that whereas they controlled several necessary patents for television, Armstrong, an independent, controlled the key FM patents. It should also be noted that in several countries FM has, in fact, virtually replaced AM radio.

42. "Television Tasks," *Business Week*, 8 June 1935, p. 20.

43. "Transmit Movies by Coaxial Cable," *New York Times*, 10 November 1937, p. 6.

44. It was estimated that coaxial cable cost $5,000 per mile to manufacture and install. "Recent Television Gains Here and in Europe Revive Hope of Regular Programs," *Newsweek*, 5 September 1938, p. 24.

45. Charles J. Young, "An Experimental Television System," *Proceedings of the IRE* 22, no. 11 (November 1934): 1286–94. It is interesting to note that these tests were also used to compare the differences between the 120-line transmissions from the mechanical system still employed in the Empire State Building and the 240-line pictures being sent out with the iconoscopes in Camden.

46. The system is fully described in George H. Eckhardt, *Electronic Television* (Chicago: Goodhart-Wilcox Co., 1936), pp. 147–52.

47. Clement and Engstrom, "RCA Field Tests," p. 38.

48. "Tests of Television's 441-Line Images Begun," *New York Times*, 24 January 1937, p. x, 12.

49. Ibid.

50. "RCA Describes Television System," *Electronics* 10, no. 1 (January 1937): 8–11, 48. The ten knobs on the receiver were for tuning, sound volume, sound high-frequency tone, sound low-frequency tone, sight detail, sight brightness, sight contrast, horizontal scanning, vertical scanning, and synchronization.

51. "Television Unit Ready," *New York Times*, 9 December 1937, p. 26.

52. George L. Beers, Otto H. Schade, and Robert E. Shelby, "The RCA Portable Television Pickup Equipment," *Proceedings of the IRE* 28, no. 10 (October 1940): 450–58.

53. "Television Stages First Real 'Show,' " *New York Times*, 8 July 1936, p. 21.

54. "Telefilmed Faces," *New York Times*, 20 September 1936, p. ix, 13.

55. "Television Show Seen by Two Hundred Here," *New York Times*, 7 November 1936, p. 19; "Television Gives a Real Show," *Business Week*, 14 November 1936, pp. 44–48.

56. "1937 Stirs New Hopes," *New York Times*, 3 January 1937, p. x, 10.

57. "Television Extension Planned for New York," *New York Times*, 25 July 1937, p. x, 10.

58. "Shadowing A Sleuth," *New York Times*, 28 November 1937, p. xi, 12.

59. "Tele-booths Are Expected," *New York Times*, 30 January 1938, p. x, 12.

60. *Annual Report of the Radio Corporation of America*, 1938, p. 18; "1939: Television Year," *Business Week*, 31 December 1938, p. 31.

61. David Sarnoff, "Probable Influences of Television on Society," *Journal of Applied Physics* 10, no. 7 (July 1939): 428.

62. Ibid., p. 429.

63. Ibid., p. 430.

64. "Television for the British Public," *Radio News* 18, no. 7 (January 1937): 391.

65. "One Family in Eight Eager for Television," *New York Times*, 30 April 1939, pp. 1, 36.

66. Editorial, "Television to the Front!" *Radio News* 17, no. 1 (July 1935): 4.

67. "Television Show Seen by Two Hundred Here," *New York Times*, 7 November 1936, p. 19; "Television Gives Real Show," *Business Week*, 14 November 1936, p. 46.

68. Orrin E. Dunlap, Jr., "Unreeling a Science," *New York Times*, 18 July 1937, p. x, 10.

69. Ibid.

70. Ibid.

71. *Annual Report of the Radio Corporation of America*, 1935, p. 8.

72. "Television Not to Replace Broadcasting but Be Supplementary, Says Mr. Sarnoff," *Broadcasting* 11, no. 2 (15 July 1936): 19, 55.

73. "Television Gains Reported by RCA," *New York Times*, 27 February 1935, p. 21; "Tomorrow's Plan," *New York Times*, 25 February 1937, p. x, 10.

74. "Television I: A $13 Million 'If,' " *Fortune* 19, no. 4, (April 1939), p. 172.

75. "Home Television Held Five Years Off," *New York Times*, 29 May 1934, p. 21.

76. "Television: Only Expense Keeps It 'Just Around the Corner,' " *News-week*, 16 February 1935, p. 28; "Television Faces Economic Hurdles," *New York Times*, 13 May 1936, p. 17. Goldsmith was past president of the Institute of Radio Engineers, as well as a consultant to RCA.

77. "Making Room for Television," *Business Week*, 16 May 1936, p. 26.

78. Waldemar Kaempffert, "Big 'Ifs' Cloud the Television Screen," *New York Times*, 5 June 1938, pp. vii, 6, 21.

79. Sarnoff, "Probable Influence of Television," p. 428.

80. Noran E. Kersta, "The Business Side of Television," *Electronics* 13, no. 2 (March 1940): 90.

81. Ibid., p. 91.

82. Ibid.

83. Harley Iams, R. B. Jones, and W. H. Hickok, "The Brightness of Outdoor Scenes and Its Relation to Television Transmission," *Proceedings of the IRE* 25, no. 8 (August 1937): 1034–47; Vladimir K. Zworykin, George A. Morton, and L. E. Flory, "Theory and Performance of the Iconoscope," *Proceedings of the IRE* 25, no. 8 (August 1937): 1071–92.

84. Albert Rose, *Vision, Human and Electronic* (New York: Plenum Press, 1973), p. 59; Paul K. Weimer, "Television Camera Tubes: A Research Review," in *Advances in Electronics and Electron Physics*, ed. Ladislaus Marton (New York: Academic Press, 1960), p. 391.

85. James D. McGee, "Distant Electric Vision," *Proceedings of the IRE* 38, no. 6 (June 1950): 602. The British counterpart to the iconoscope was the emitron; McGee claims it was independently developed by EMI Laboratories engineers (p. 598).

86. Gerhart Goebel, "Das Fernsehen in Deutschland bis zum Jahre 1945," *Archiv für das Post-und Fernmeldewesen* 5, no. 5 (August 1953): 293.

87. This account of Farnsworth's early career is derived from George Everson, *The Story of Television* (1949; reprint ed., New York: Arno Press, 1974), pp. 15–107; and personal communication from Mrs. Philo T. Farnsworth.

88. "New Television System," *New York Times*, 4 September 1928, p. 20; personal communication from Mrs. Philo T. Farnsworth.

89. "A Radio Idea from the West," *New York Times*, 14 December 1930, p. x, 14; "New Television System," *Radio News* 10, no. 7 (January 1929): 637.

90. Philo T. Farnsworth, "Scanning with an Electric Pencil," *Television News* 1, no. 1 (March–April 1931): 48–50.

91. Philo T. Farnsworth and Harry R. Lubcke, "The Transmission of Television Images," *California Engineer* 8, no. 5 (February 1930): 22.

92. Everson, *Story of Television*, pp. 122–28; personal communication from Mrs. Philo T. Farnsworth.

93. Everson, *Story of Television*, pp. 132–33; Maclaurin, *Invention and Innovation*, pp. 207–08. A discussion of Philco's television activities will be found in Chapter 5.

94. Philo T. Farnsworth, "Television by Electron Image Scanning," *Journal of The Franklin Institute* 218, no. 4 (October 1934): 412–18; Albert Abramson, *Electronic Motion Pictures* (Berkeley and Los Angeles: University of California Press, 1955), pp. 71–72; Alfred Dinsdale, *First Principles of Television* (New York: John Wiley and Sons, 1932), pp. 213–19.

95. Philo T. Farnsworth, "Television System," U.S. patent no. 1,773,980, issued 26 August 1930, filed 7 January 1927, claim no. 15.

96. Rose, "Television Pickup Tubes," p. 150; Weimer, "Television Camera Tubes," p. 389.

97. Philo T. Farnsworth, "Television Receiving System," U.S. patent no. 1,773,981, issued 26 August 1930, filed 7 January 1927.

98. Everson, *Story of Television*, pp. 135–36; Maclaurin, *Invention and Innovation*, p. 208. The San Francisco laboratory, with its skeleton crew, also continued to operate (personal communication from Mrs. Philo T. Farnsworth).

99. Philo T. Farnsworth, "Electron Image Amplifier," U.S. patent no. 2,085,742, issued 6 July 1937, filed 14 June 1930.

100. Farnsworth, "Television by Electron Image Scanning," pp. 418–34; Everson, *Story of Television*, pp. 137–40; Archibald H. Brolly, "Television by Electric Means," *Electrical Engineering* 53, no. 8 (August 1934): 1153–69; personal communication from Mrs. Philo T. Farnsworth.

101. "An Electron Multiplier," *Electronics* 7, no. 8 (August 1934): 243.

102. "Tennis Stars Act in New Television," *New York Times*, 31 July 1935, p. 15.

103. Weimer, "Television Camera Tubes," p. 390.

104. "Television Transmitters Planned," *Electronics* 8, no. 9 (September 1935): 28–29; "Gain in Television Is Demonstrated," *New York Times*, 31 July 1935, p. 15.

105. "Farnsworth Television," *Radio News* 18, no. 11 (May 1937): 654-55, 679, 688.

106. "Rochester 1938," *Electronics* 11, no. 12 (December 1938): 8–9; Knox McIlwain, "Survey of Television Pick-up Devices," *Journal of Applied Physics* 10, no. 7 (July 1939): 441–42. Farnsworth had first disclosed the image amplifier in 1935 in several patent applications.

107. These observations on the deficiencies of the image amplifier are due to Albert Rose in personal communication.

108. Everson, *Story of Television*, p. 216; "CBS-Farnsworth Deal," *Business Week*, 17 April 1937, p. 16.

109. Everson, *Story of Television*, p. 158; "AT & T, Farnsworth, Television," *Business Week*, 14 August 1937, pp. 18–20.

110. Everson, *Story of Television*, pp. 186–87.

111. Maclaurin, *Invention and Innovation*, p. 209; "Banker Backing," *Time*, 20 February 1939, pp. 62–65. After the war Capehart, Farnsworth, and Panamuse televisions were also manufactured. In 1949 Farnsworth Television and Radio Corporation became a subsidiary of IT & T. *International Telephone and Telegraph Corporation Annual Report*, 1949, p. 10; personal communication from Mrs. Philo T. Farnsworth.

112. See McGee, "Distant Electric Vision," pp. 598–602; James D. McGee and Hans G. Lubszynski, "EMI Cathode-Ray Television Transmission Tubes," *Journal of the Institution of Electrical Engineers* 84, no. 508 (April 1939): 468–75; Noel Ashbridge, "Television in Great Britain," in *Technical Development of Television*, ed. Shiers; and *Annual Report of the Radio Corporation of America*, 1933, p. 4. A rate of 25 frames per second was determined by Britain's 50-cycle power system.

113. Ashbridge, "Television in Great Britain," p. 704; Abramson, *Electronic Motion Pictures*, pp. 76–77.

114. Ashbridge, "Television in Great Britain," p. 705.

115. Everson, *Story of Television*, p. 147; "British Get Television," *New York Times*, 20 June 1935, p. 21.

116. Everson, *Story of Television*, p. 149; Abramson, *Electronic Motion Pictures*, p. 77; Ashbridge, "Television in Great Britain," p. 707.

117. McGee, "Distant Electric Vision," p. 602; and McGee and Lubszynski, "EMI Tubes," p. 472. Both claim this device was based on a 1934 British patent of Hans G. Lubszynski and S. Rodda, of Marconi-EMI, although the latter article concedes that Albert Rose and Harley Iams of RCA were working along similar lines. Soviet historians claim P. V. Shmakov and P. V. Timofeyev developed the image iconoscope in 1933; see V. K. Samoylov and B. P. Khromoy, *Television* (Moscow: Mir Publishers, 1977), p. 19.

118. This account of early German telecasting follows Goebel, "Des Fernsehen in Deutschland," pp. 282–83, 291, 384. See also Eckhardt, *Electronic Television*, p. 17.

119. "The Status of Television in Europe," *Electrical Engineering* 54, no. 9 (September 1935): 968.

120. The 1940 summer Olympics in Tokyo were, of course, not held, ruining Japan's plans to display its own television equipment in coverage of the games.

121. This account of German television follows Goebel, "Das Fernsehen in Duetschland," pp. 294, 348–50, 384–85. Fernseh A. G. subsequently became part of the Bosch Group.

122. This account of the Farnsworth-Zworykin patent interference case follows Stephen F. Hofer, "Philo Farnsworth: The Quiet Contributor to Television" (Ph.D. diss., Bowling Green State University, 1977), pp. 73–81.

123. Everson, *Story of Television*, pp. 201–2; Maclaurin, *Invention and Innovation*, p. 212. Eventually Farnsworth won his claim to prior disclosure of the synchronization technique, and RCA won its claim in the case of interlaced scanning.

124. Everson, *Story of Television*, pp. 244–46; Hofer, "Philo Farnsworth," pp. 82–83, appendix H; "Agreement on Patents," *New York Times*, 3 October 1939, p. 32.

125. Harley Iams, George A. Morton, Vladimir K. Zworykin, "The Image Iconoscope," *Proceedings of the IRE* 27, no. 9 (September 1939): 541–47.

126. Ibid. Also McGee and Lubszynski, "EMI Tubes," pp. 472–74; Rose, *Vision*, p. 60; Rose, "Television Pickup Tubes," p. 153; Vladimir K. Zworykin and George A. Morton, *Television: The Electronics of Image Transmission* (New York: John Wiley and Sons, 1940), p. 301.

127. This concept first appears in a 1938 patent disclosure by one of the orthicon's developers, Albert Rose, in U.S. patent no. 2,213,174, issued 27 August 1940 (filed 30 July 1938).

128. Albert Rose and Harley Iams, "Television Pickup Tubes Using Low-Velocity Electron-Beam Scanning," *Proceedings of the IRE* 27, no. 9 (September 1939): 547–66; Albert Rose and Harley Iams, "The Orthicon: A Television Pick-up Tube," *RCA Review* 4, no. 2 (October 1939): 186–99; Rose, *Vision*, pp. 60–62; "The Orthicon," *Electronics* 12, no. 7 (July 1939): 11–14, 58–59; personal communication from Albert Rose.

129. Philo T. Farnsworth, in fact, drew up a list of his patents necessary to the operation of the image orthicon in order to indicate its combination of RCA's engineering achievement with his own (from personal communication from Mrs. Philo T. Farnsworth).

130. Ray D. Kell and George C. Sziklai, "Image Orthicon Camera," *RCA Review* 7, no. 1 (March 1946): 67–76; Albert Rose, Paul K. Weimer, and Harold B. Law, "The Image Orthicon: A Sensitive Television Pickup Tube," *Proceedings of the IRE* 34, no. 7 (July 1946): 424–32; Rose, *Vision*, pp. 62–63; Rose, "Television Pickup Tubes," p. 155; Weimer, "Television Camera Tubes," pp. 393–95.

131. Personal communication from Albert Rose.

132. U.S., Senate, Committee on Interstate Commerce, *Development of Television*, 76th Cong., 3rd sess., 10–11 April 1940, p. 38.

CHAPTER 5

1. W. Rupert Maclaurin, *Invention and Innovation in the Radio Industry* (New York: Macmillan Co., 1949), p. 137; personal communication from David B. Smith, former Philco executive.

2. Maclaurin, *Invention and Innovation*, pp. 137–38; personal communication from David B. Smith.

3. U.S., Federal Communications Commission, Deleted Television License File; "Philadelphia to Look-In," *New York Times*, 20 December 1931, p. ix, 10; personal communication from David B. Smith and James A. Allen, Ford Aerospace and Communication Corporation.

4. "Commercial Television Unlikely in '36, Says Gubb," *New York Times*, 26 January 1936, p. ix, 13.

5. "Ring Fight Shown in Television Test," *New York Times*, 12 August 1936, p. 21. See also "Philco Discloses Its Television Progress," *Broadcasting* 11, no. 4 (15 August 1936): 10–11, 55; "Philco's Television," *Business Week*, 15 August 1936, p. 16; "Television Field Test Shows Progress but Still Not Perfect," *Newsweek*, 22 August 1936, p. 35; "More Television," *Scientific American* 155, no. 4 (October 1936): 240; "Television as Good as Home Movies," *Radio News* 18, no. 5 (November 1936): 265–66, 308; and "Television System of Advanced Design," *Popular Mechanics* 67, no. 1 (January 1937): 97.

6. "Television Shows Big Gain in Clarity," *New York Times*, 12 February 1937, p. 25; "Philco Shows 441-Line Television," *Electronics* 10, no. 3 (March 1937): 8–9.

7. "Philco vs. RCA," *Literary Digest* 122, no. 7 (15 August 1936), p. 8.

8. Frank C. Waldrop and Joseph Borkin, *Television: A Struggle for Power* (New York: William Morrow and Co., 1938), p. 219.

9. Maclaurin, *Invention and Innovation*, pp. 215–16.

10. Peter C. Goldmark, *Maverick Inventor: My Turbulent Years at CBS* (New York: Saturday Review Press/E. P. Dutton and Co., 1973), pp. 40, 49.

11. "Columbia Moves In on Television," *Business Week*, 10 April 1937, pp. 20–21; "Grand Central Is Site of Television Studio," *New York Times*, 22 August 1937, p. x, 10.

12. Goldmark, *Maverick Inventor*, p. 50.

13. Ibid., p. 47.

14. See Chapter 6 for the history of this struggle.

15. Personal communication from Harry R. Lubcke.

16. The technique is described in Harry R. Lubcke, "Television Synchronization

Method and Apparatus," U.S. patent no. 2,037,035, issued 14 April 1936. Lubcke's patent rights, assigned to the Don Lee System, were eventually sold to RCA; see "1939: Television Year," *Business Week*, 31 December 1939, p. 24.

17. Harry R. Lubcke, "Television on the West Coast," in *We Present Television*, ed. John Porterfield and Kay Reynolds (New York: W. W. Norton and Co., 1940), p. 276. Also personal communication from Harry R. Lubcke.

18. Lubcke, "Television on the West Coast," pp. 227–28, 236–38; "Public Television by Don Lee," *Broadcasting* 10, no. 12 (15 June 1936): 18; "Daytime Television Test Is Expanded by Don Lee," *Broadcasting* 11, no. 10 (15 November 1936): 72.

19. Lubcke, "Television on the West Coast," pp. 234–36.

20. Ibid., pp. 230–31; personal communication from Harry R. Lubcke.

21. Harry R. Lubcke, "With the West Coast Televisors," *Radio News* 21, no. 5 (May 1939): 53.

22. Lubcke, "Television on the West Coast," pp. 239–40; "Notes on Television," *New York Times*, 16 April 1939, p. x, 10; personal communication from Harry R. Lubcke.

23. In October 1951 the station's new transmitter on Mount Wilson went into operation.

24. Sid Noel, "How Shall We Teach Television?" *Television News* 2, no. 1 (March–April 1932): 17; FCC, Deleted Television License File.

25. U.S., Federal Communications Commission, *Reports* 6: 867; FCC, Deleted Television License File; personal communication from John J. Smith, chairman, Sparton Corporation.

26. FCC, Deleted Television License File; personal communication from Hollis S. Baird.

27. "Television Committee," *Broadcasting* 5, no. 7 (1 October 1933): 15.

28. Donald G. Fink, "Perspectives on Television: The Role Played by the Two NTSC's in Preparing Television Service for the American Public," *Proceedings of the IRE* 64, no. 9 (September 1976): 1325.

29. Ibid., pp. 1325–26; "Report by the Technical Committee on Television and Facsimile: Radio Progress during 1936," *Proceedings of the IRE* 25, no. 2 (February 1937): 203.

30. "FCC New Rules Issued," *Broadcasting* 10, no. 11 (1 June 1936): 7, 48.

31. "1939: Television Year," *Business Week*, 31 December 1938, p. 23.

32. Fink, "Perspectives on Television," p. 1326.

33. U.S., Federal Communications Commission, *Fourth Annual Report*, 1938, p. 65.

34. FCC, *Reports* 6: 867; U.S., Federal Communications Commission, *Rules and Regulations*, 1939, 4:4.73, p. 15; personal communications from Fred J. Goldsmith, chief, Internal Review and Security Division, FCC; and Jack Krueger, manager of public affairs, WTMJ.

35. U.S., Federal Communications Commission, *Fifth Annual Report*, 1939, pp. 45–46.

36. Ibid.

37. "FCC Goes Exploring," *New York Times*, 23 April 1939, p. x, 12; Fink, "Perspectives on Television," p. 1326.

38. "FCC Stops Gold Rush," *New York Times*, 9 April 1939, p. x, 12.

39. "Public Verdict Awaited," *New York Times*, 28 May 1939, p. x, 10.

40. RCA's position in FCC hearings was that television had achieved such technical perfection. However, without the commission's authorization of industry standards, the danger of obsolescence was present. In fact, all sets retailed between 1938 and 1940 did become obsolete when standards were adopted by the FCC in 1941. See Chapter 6 for a detailed discussion.

41. "Table Television," *Business Week*, 21 May 1938, p. 16; "Television Sets Ready," *New York Times*, 2 June 1938, p. 39; "Early Birds," *Time*, 13 June 1938, pp. 68–69; "Television on Air," *Business Week*, 27 August 1938, pp. 18, 20.

42. "1939: Television Year," *Business Week*, 31 December 1938, p. 25; "Television Receivers in Production," *Electronics* 12, no. 3 (March 1939): 22–25, 78; "Curtain Goes Up on Television," *Business Week*, 6 May 1939, p. 15; "Television an Actuality," *Newsweek*, 8 May 1939, p. 31; "Television: Three Varieties," *Popular Mechanics* 72, no. 4 (October 1939): 615.

43. Oscar B. Hanson, "Here Comes Television," *Scientific American* 160, no. 4 (April 1939): 251–52.

44. "1939: Television Year," *Business Week*, 29 October 1938, p. 31; "New Era for Radio Seen Here," *New York Times*, 3 January 1939, p. 31.

45. "Ceremony Is Carried by Television As Industry Makes Its Formal Bow," *New York Times*, 1 May 1939, p. 8.

46. Ibid.

47. Ibid.

CHAPTER 6

1. "Television II: 'Fade In Camera One!'," *Fortune* 19, no. 5 (May 1939), p. 162.

2. W2XAX's call letters were changed to those of CBS's original television station in May 1939. U.S., Federal Communications Commission, Deleted Television License File.

3. The direction of DuMont's television activity is reminiscent of the activity of Jenkins Television Corporation during the first boom. At that time, Allen B. DuMont was chief engineer for Jenkins's sister corporation, De Forest Radio Company.

4. *Broadcast Yearbook*, 1941, p. 388.

5. Ibid., 1940, p. 336.

6. U.S., Federal Communications Commission, Broadcast License File.

7. Ibid; *Broadcast Yearbook*, 1941, p. 388.

8. Ibid.

9. Personal communication from Mrs. Philo T. Farnsworth.

10. FCC, Deleted Television License File; *The Zenith Story* (Chicago: Zenith Radio Corporation, 1955), p. 15.

11. FCC, Deleted Television License File.

12. "Television for Milwaukee," *New York Times*, 24 November 1940, p. ix, 10; personal communication from Jack Krueger, manager of public relations, WTMJ.

13. "Cincinnati to Look In," *New York Times*, 8 September 1940, p. ix, 10.

14. *Broadcast Yearbook*, 1942, p. 451.

15. *Broadcast Yearbook*, 1941, 1942, 1980; FCC, Deleted Television License File.

16. Samuel Kaufman, "The Video Reporter," *Radio News* 25, no. 4 (April 1941): 59.

17. *Annual Report of the Radio Corporation of America*, 1939, p. 17.

18. "Telecasts," *New York Times*, 29 October 1939, p. ix, 10.

19. "Telecasts," *New York Times*, 3 March 1940, p. x, 10.

20. "Television Takes Three Strides," *Business Week*, 25 November 1939, p. 21.

21. Samuel Kaufman, "The Video Reporter," *Radio News* 23, no. 2 (February 1940): 31; Noran E. Korsta, "The Business Side of Television," *Electronics* 13, no. 2 (March 1940): 13; "A Year of Television," *New York Times*, 28 April 1940, p. ix, 12; and Alva Johnston, "Trouble in Television," *Saturday Evening Post*, 28 September 1940, p. 37.

22. See Chapter 5 for details.

23. "First Television of Baseball Seen," *New York Times*, 18 May 1939, p. 29.

24. Orrin E. Dunlap, Jr., "A Kick-Off on the Air," *New York Times*, 15 October 1939, p. ix, 12.

25. Ibid.

26. Ibid.

27. Orrin E. Dunlap, Jr., "Outside Looking In," *New York Times*, 29 October 1939, p. ix, 12.

28. "Notes on Television," *New York Times*, 17 March 1940, p. x, 10.

29. Samuel Kaufman, "The Video Reporter," *Radio News* 24, no. 4 (October 1940): 58.

30. Oscar B. Hanson, "RCA-NBC Television Presents a Political Convention as First Long Distance Pick-Up," *RCA Review* 5, no. 3 (January 1941): 267–82.

31. Orrin E. Dunlap, Jr., "Seeing Democracy at Work," *New York Times*, 30 June 1940, p. ix, 10.

32. David Sarnoff, *Looking Ahead* (New York: McGraw-Hill Book Co., 1968), pp. 104–5.

33. *A Brief Sketch on the History of KYW-TV* (Philadelphia: KYW-TV, 1979), pp. 1–2.

34. FCC, Broadcast License File.

35. *Zenith Story*, pp. 14–15.

36. T. A. Smith, "RCA Television Field Pickup Equipment," *RCA Review* 4, no. 3 (January 1940): 292.

37. Personal communication from Harry R. Lubcke.

38. "Television an Actuality," *Newsweek*, 8 May 1939, p. 31.

39. "What's Television Doing Now?" *Business Week*, 12 August 1939, p. 24.

40. "Television Takes Three Strides," *Business Week*, 25 November 1939, p. 20; "Price Cuts Sharply on Television Sets," *New York Times*, 13 March 1940, p. 34.

41. "Cuts Spur Television," *New York Times*, 24 March 1940, p. iii, 7.

42. "Inadequate Telecasting Blamed for Slow Sales," *New York Times*, 27 August 1939, p. ix, 10; George R. Town, "Television," *Electrical Engineering* 59, no. 8 (August 1940): 315.

43. "Notes on Television," *New York Times*, 31 December 1939, p. ix, 10.

44. U.S., Federal Communications Commission, *Sixth Annual Report*, 1940, p.

65; "F-M Gets Go Sign," *Business Week*, 25 May 1940, pp. 21–22. For some discussion of the problems involved in frequency allocations, see Edwin G. Krasnow and Lawrence D. Longley, *The Politics of Broadcast Regulation*, 2nd ed. (New York: St. Martin's Press, 1978), and Dallas W. Smythe, *The Structure and Policy of Electronic Communications*, University of Illinois Bulletin Series no. 82, 1957.

45. "Television to Shut-Down," *New York Times*, 21 July 1940, p. ix, 10.

46. Ray D. Kell, Alda V. Bedford, and G. L. Fredendall, "A Determination of Optimum Number of Lines in a Television System," *RCA Review* 5, no. 1 (July 1940): 9–30.

47. "Television in Los Angeles," *New York Times*, 25 August 1940, p. ix, 10.

48. "Better Television," *Business Week*, 24 February 1940, p. 46; Donald G. Fink, ed. *Television Standards and Practices* (New York: McGraw-Hill Book Co., 1943), p. 10. The reduction in frame rate is a result of the need to accommodate the increase in lines within a 6-MHz. frequency bandwidth.

49. W. Rupert Maclaurin, *Invention and Innovation in the Radio Industry* (New York: Macmillan Co., 1949), pp. 215–16. Philco and Hazeltine, although cooperating, proposed two separate synchronizing techniques.

50. Personal communication from David B. Smith, former Philco television executive.

51. Ibid. Britain still maintains its 405-line VHF service, along with its 605-line UHF service.

52. Maclaurin, *Invention and Innovation*, p. 234.

53. Gary N. Hess, "An Historical Study of the Du Mont Television Network" (Ph.D. diss., Northwestern University, 1960), pp. 43–46, 91–94.

54. "The DuMont Proposals," *Electronics* 13, no. 2 (19 February 1940): 22–23, 63–64; Fink, *Television Standards*, p. 10.

55. "The DuMont Proposals," p. 23.

56. U.S., Senate, Committee on Interstate Commerce, *Development of Television*, 76th Cong., 3rd sess. 10–11 April 1940, pp. 59–61.

57. Ibid., pp. 26–27, 39; personal communication from David B. Smith. The action of the RMA board of directors was apparently not clear to the Philco management on this important issue.

58. *Development of Television*, pp. 29, 39–43, 62–64.

59. Ibid., pp. 64–65.

60. *Milwaukee Journal*, 6 November 1938, p. 1.

61. Ibid.

62. Ibid., 10 November 1938, p. 4.

63. See Chapter 5 for details.

64. U.S., Federal Communications Commission, *Fifth Annual Report*, 1939, pp. 45–46.

65. Ibid.

66. "Notes on Television," *New York Times*, 10 December 1939, p. ix, 12.

67. Fink, *Television Standards*, p. 10; "FCC Moves to Widen Use of Television," *New York Times*, 1 March 1940, p. 13; "Television: A Business," *Business Week*, 9 March 1940, p. 29.

68. "FCC Moves," *New York Times*, 1 March 1940, p. 13. (See also Fink, *Television Standards*, p. 11.)

69. Ibid.

70. Ibid.

71. "Television: A Business," *Business Week,* 9 March 1940, p. 29.

72. New York Times, 20 March 1940, pp. 20–22.

73. Quoted in "FCC Stays Start in Television," *New York Times,* 24 March 1940, pp. i, 1, 34.

74. Raymond Moley, "War on Merchandising," *Newsweek,* 13 May 1940, p. 64.

75. Eugene Lyons, *David Sarnoff* (New York: Harper and Row, 1966), p. 219. Lyons notes that Sarnoff claimed that he had shown the RCA ad to Fly before it was run and that Fly had not objected to it. However, Sarnoff made this remark several years later; nothing was said by either man at the time about such an incident.

76. "Television Escaping Lab Again," *Business Week,* 20 April 1940, pp. 22, 24.

77. Sarnoff, *Looking Ahead,* pp. 102–4.

78. *Development of Television,* pp. 1–2.

79. Ibid., p. 17.

80. Ibid., p. 18. Although he refused to withdraw this statement, Fly later did apologize for the word "blitzkrieg."

81. Ibid., p. 31.

82. Ibid., pp. 35, 38.

83. FCC, *Sixth Annual Report,* 1940, pp. 70–73.

84. Ibid.

85. This account of the NTSC follows Fink, *Television Standards,* pp. 3, 13–16.

86. This account of the field sequential color system follows Peter C. Goldmark, *Maverick Inventor: My Turbulent Years at CBS* (New York: Saturday Review Press/ E. P. Dutton, and Co., 1973), pp. 54–57; and "Color Television Demonstrated by CBS Engineers," *Electronics* 13, no. 10 (October 1940): 32–34, 73–74.

87. Goldmark, *Maverick Inventor,* pp. 62–63.

88. Ibid., p. 62. It should be noted that RCA had also developed a color system at this time, although it employed simultaneous transmission on three adjacent channels, reminiscent of the mechanical television experiments of Herbert E. Ives; see Edward W. Herold, "A History of Color Television Displays," *Proceedings of the IEEE* 64, no. 9 (September 1976): 1331–32.

89. "Television Stalled?" *Business Week,* 29 March 1941, p. 43.

90. Hess, "DuMont Television Network," p. 72. This assertion is questionable, however; a survey of CBS's policy on acquiring television licenses during the period when it promoted the field sequential color method suggests that the policy actually put CBS at a competitive disadvantage once it became evident that VHF monochrome television would succeed.

91. Fink, *Television Standards,* p. 42.

92. Ibid., pp. 43–44.

93. Ibid., p. 44.

94. Ibid., p. 27.

95. Donald G. Fink, "Perspectives on Television: The Role Played by the Two NTSC's in Preparing Television Service for the American Public," *Proceedings of the IEEE* 64, no. 9 (September 1976): 1325. There were also some alterations in the original RMA proposals (for example, FM would now be used for the sound signal modulation).

96. Fink, *Television Standards*, pp. 21–24. DuMont briefly used its own method, while the Philco-Hazeltine technique was never commercialized. Eventually a much improved version of RCA's method became accepted as the FCC standard (see Maclaurin, *Invention and Innovation*, p. 238).

97. Millard W. Baldwin, Jr., "The Subjective Sharpness of Simulated Television Images," *Bell System Technical Journal* 19, no. 4 (October 1940): 563–86.

98. Stress in the original; personal communication from Donald G. Fink.

99. Fink would later come to believe that the most serious failure of the NTSC was to accept the existing 6-MHz. bandwidth, the constraint which limited picture definition (personal communication).

100. Personal communication from David B. Smith.

101. "Groundwork Laid for Commercial Television," *Electronics* 14, no. 4 (April 1941): 18–19, 70–80.

102. Ibid.

103. Reproduced in Fink, *Television Standards*, pp. 378–86.

104. Ibid., section 4.261.

105. Ibid., section 4.226. This decision, no doubt, reflected the concern over possible network monopolization of the medium that had earlier prompted the FCC study, *Report on Chain Broadcasting*.

106. "Television Rights Sought by NBC," *New York Times*, 17 June 1941, p. 23; T. R. Kennedy, Jr., "An Auspicious Beginning," *New York Times*, 3 August 1941, p. ix, 10.

107. "Television Rate Card Out," *New York Times*, 1 July 1941, p. 40; "Regular Television On," *New York Times*, 2 July 1941, p. 17; "Imagery for Profit," *New York Times*, 6 July 1941, p. ix, 10.

108. Henry W. Sova, "A Descriptive and Historical Survey of American Television 1937–1946" (Ph.D. diss., Ohio University, 1977), pp. 224–28.

Bibliographical Essay

This study is an exploratory effort to fill the startling lacuna which exists in the history of the American television industry between the two world wars. Although this period largely determined the direction television followed in its meteoric ascent as a medium of communication after 1947, it has hitherto been largely ignored.

Only a very few works survey the entire period. An excellent collection of primary and secondary articles covering the history of television from its nineteenth-century origins to the introduction of compatible color has been assembled by George Shiers in *Technical Development of Television* (New York: Arno Press, 1977). *Electronic Motion Pictures*, by Albert Abramson (1955; reprint ed., New York: Arno Press, 1974), is a useful general history of some of the engineering achievements during the same period. The complicated history of corporate relations and patent disputes in the radio industry by W. Rupert Maclaurin, *Invention and Innovation in the Radio Industry* (1949; reprint ed., New York: Arno Press, 1971), touches on some of the conflicts in the nascent electronic television industry, although the work is unsatisfactorily documented. Erik Barnouw's *A History of Broadcasting in the United States*, 2 vols. (New York: Oxford University Press, 1966–68), with the material relevant to television reprinted in *Tube of Plenty* (New York: Oxford University Press, 1975), provides only an anecdotal account of events in this period. Sydney W. Head, *Broadcasting in America*, 3rd ed. (Boston: Houghton Mifflin Co., 1976), and Christopher H. Sterling and John M. Kittross, *Stay Tuned* (Belmont: Wadsworth Publishing Co., 1978), are standard textbook treatments of the communication industry.

The paucity of scholarly works on the achievements of this period is rather surprising, given its importance for the history of the television system's three components and also given the abundance of primary sources available. This is particularly remarkable since the period before the First World War has attracted considerable attention. Of particular use here are Gerald R. M. Garratt and Albert H. Mumford, "The History of Television," *Proceedings of the Institution of Electrical Engineers* 99, part IIIA, pp. 25–42 (reprinted in Shiers, ed., *Technical Development of Television*); John V. L. Hogan, "The Early Days of Television," in Raymond Fielding, ed., *A Technological History of Motion Pictures and Television* (Berkeley: University of California Press, 1967), pp. 230–34; and two articles by George Shiers, "Early Schemes for Television," *IEEE Spectrum* 17, no. 5 (May 1970): 24–34; and "Historical Notes on Television before 1900," *SMPTE Journal* 86, no. 3 (March 1977): 129–37. Primary sources for this earliest period are found mainly in various issues of *Scientific American* and the British publications, *English Mechanic and World of Science* and *Nature*.

American low-definition mechanical telecasting has been virtually ignored by historians. There is a general tendency to disregard the accomplishments of these efforts, despite their important determinant influence on all three of television's component systems, as demonstrated in the present study. In secondary works only the engineering component has been treated at all, but here discussion has been limited to only some of the achievements along the Eastern Seaboard. Acknowledging these severe restrictions, particularly useful are Axel G. Jensen, "The Evolution of Modern Television," *Journal of the SMPTE* 63 (November 1954): 174–88 (reprinted in Fielding, ed., *A Technological History,* pp. 235–49, and Shiers, ed., *Technical Development of Television,* n.p.); and J. George Knapp and Julian D. Tebo, "The History of Television," *IEEE Communications Society Magazine,* May 1978, pp. 8–22.

However, several books published during the era itself are extremely useful. Essential is Alfred Dinsdale, *First Principles of Television* (1932; reprint ed., New York: Arno Press, 1971); Dinsdale provides an excellent technical survey of contemporary television developments in the U.S. and western Europe. Providing less comprehensive treatment of technical matters, but broader discussions of American television, are Edgar Felix, *Television* (New York: McGraw-Hill Co., 1931); Edgar T. Larner, *Practical Television* (New York: D. Van Nostrand Co., 1928), with an introduction by John L. Baird; and H. Horton Sheldon and Edgar N. Grisewood, *Television* (New York: D. Van Nostrand Co., 1929).

The accomplishments of the television pioneers provide some of the richest sources of knowledge of this period. Unfortunately, while the British have conducted extensive research on the efforts of John L. Baird, American inventors have been almost entirely forgotten. No satisfactory scholarly studies of C. Francis Jenkins exist, despite his obvious importance for television. However, his papers can be found in three repositories in Pennsylvania. In addition, his two books, *Radiomovies, Radiovision, Television* (Washington: Jenkins Laboratories, 1929), and *Vision by Radio, Radio Photographs, Radio Photograms* (Washington: Jenkins Laboratories, 1925), are helpful, as are his articles, "The Drum Scanner in Radiomovies Receivers," *Proceedings of the IRE* 17, no. 9 (September 1929): 1576–83, and "Radio Vision," *Proceedings of the IRE* 15, no. 11 (November 1927): 958–64 (this last reprinted in Shiers, ed., *Technical Development of Television*).

Herbert E. Ives has documented his television contributions briefly in "Television: Twentieth Anniversary," *Bell Laboratories Record* 15, no. 5 (May 1947): 190–93; even more useful are his contemporary articles "Television," *Bell System Technical Journal* 6 (October 1927): 551–59, and "Television in Colors," *Bell Laboratories Record* 7, no. 11 (July 1929): 439–44 (both of these latter articles reprinted in Shiers, ed., *Technical Development* of Television).

No accounts exist of the important contributions of Hollis S. Baird in Boston, of Ulises A. Sanabria in Chicago, or of Western Television's Clement F. Wade. However, Mr. Baird has retained an extensive personal file on his own efforts, as well as those of his contemporaries. Besides materials in Baird's papers, Sanabria's television equipment is detailed in Edwin B. Kurtz, *Pioneering in Educational Television 1932–1939* (Iowa City: State University of Iowa, 1959); this book is also a valuable documentary survey of Kurtz's own efforts in Iowa. The pioneering television research at Purdue University is thoroughly described in C. F. Harding, B. H. George, and Howard J. Heim, "The Purdue University Experimental Television Station," (Purdue University Engineering Bulletin, Research Series no. 65, March 1939). No information on the experiments at Kansas State College of Agriculture has yet been located.

Extremely useful to the researcher are the FRC records on experimental visual broadcast stations found in the National Archives. Although sadly incomplete, they do provide detailed information on the design and operation of many of these pioneering stations, as well as insight into the functions and problems of the commission in attempting to regulate the new medium. In addition, the FRC *Annual Reports* all provide important information, as do the U.S. Department of Commerce's *Radio Service Bulletins*, 1929–32.

NBC is quite helpful in making available materials related to its low-definition television endeavors. CBS, on the other hand, is consistently unhelpful; even in his autobiography, *As It Happened* (New York: Doubleday and Co., 1979), William S. Paley ignores the topic completely, as does Robert Metz, *CBS Reflection in a Bloodshot Eye* (Chicago: Playboy Books, 1975).

Essential to any study of this era is the material to be found in technical journals and the popular press. For American mechanical telecasting, articles in the *Proceedings of the IRE, Popular Mechanics, Popular Science Monthly, Radio Broadcasting, Radio News, Scientific American,* and *Television News* are invaluable. Of great use, too, are the television reports to be found in several daily newspapers, especially the *New York Times* and the *Chicago Daily News,* and to a lesser estent in the trade publication *Broadcasting*.

The successful development of electronic television techniques remains a subject of intense controversy, and all accounts of it must therefore be treated critically. Good secondary discussions of the engineering achievements can be found in Abramson, *Electronic Motion Pictures;* Garratt and Mumford, "The History of Television"; Jensen, "The Evolution of Modern Television"; Albert Rose, "Television Pickup Tubes and the Problem of Vision," in *Advances in Electronics,* vol. 1, Ladislaus Marton, ed. (New York: Academic Press, 1948), pp. 131–66; and Paul K. Weimer, "Television Camera Tubes: A Research Review," in *Advances in Electronics and Electron Physics,* vol. 13, Ladislaus Marton, ed. (New York: Academic Press, 1960), pp. 387–437. Harry W. Sova, "A Descriptive and Historical Survey of American Television, 1937–1946," (Ph.D. dissertation, Ohio University, 1977), provides some discussion of corporate and programming developments during this era, but is limited by too great a reliance on a very limited range of trade sources. Extremely useful are the extensive discussions of the history of international engineering and corporate cooperation found in Gerhart Goebel, "Das Fernsehen in Deutschland bis zum Jahre 1945," *Archiv für das Post-und Fernmeldewesen* 5, no. 5 (August 1953): 259–393.

However, beyond these secondary works, the researcher will find an immense array of original source material available. For instance, the achievements of Vladimir K. Zworykin are detailed in several important contemporary articles. Of particular importance are Zworykin's articles "Description of an Experimental Television System and the Kinescope," *Proceedings of the IRE* 21, no. 12 (December 1933): 1655–73; "The Iconoscope: A Modern Version of the Electric Eye," *Proceedings of the IRE* 12, no. 1 (January 1934): 16–32; "Iconoscopes and Kinescopes in Television,"

RCA Review 1, no. 1 (July 1936): 60–84; "Television," *Journal of The Franklin Institute* 215, no. 5 (May 1933): 535–55, and "Television with Cathode Ray for Receiver," *Radio Engineering* 9, no. 12 (December 1929): 38–41 (the last two articles reprinted in Shiers, ed., *Technical Development of Television*). Zworykin also composed a brief memoir, "The Early Days: Some Recollections," in Lawrence W. Lichty and Malachi C. Topping, eds., *American Broadcasting* (New York: Hastings House, 1975), p. 69–72.

RCA's employment of Zworykin's design in building its television system is documented in a series of articles found in *Television*, vol. 1 (New York: RCA Institutes Press, 1936); and in Lewis M. Clement and Elmer W. Engstrom, "RCA Television Field Tests," *RCA Review* 1, no. 1 (July 1936): 32–40. Further embellishments of the system are described in Alfred N. Goldsmith, "The Progress of Television, 1938–1941," in *Television*, vol. 3 (Princeton: RCA, 1946), pp. 441–47; Oscar B. Hanson, "Experimental Studio Facilities for Television," *RCA Review* 1, no. 4 (April 1937): 3–17; Harley Iams, George A. Morton, and Vladimir K. Zworykin, "The Image Iconoscope," *Proceedings of the IRE* 27, no. 9 (September 1939): 541–47; and Albert Rose and Harley Iams, "Television Pickup Tubes Using Low-Velocity Electron-Beam Scanning," *Proceedings of the IRE* 27, no. 9 (September 1939): 547–66.

Discussion of the nonengineering components of the RCA system can be found in Noran E. Kersta, "The Business Side of Television," *Electronics* 13, no. 2 (March 1940): 10–13, 90–91; and in articles by David Sarnoff: "The Future of Television," *Popular Mechanics* 72, no. 3 (September 1939): 321–25 and 142A; and "Probable Influence of Television on Society," *Journal of Applied Physics* 10, no. 7 (July 1939): 426–31; and in his collected speeches, *Looking Ahead* (New York: McGraw-Hill Book Co., 1968). Eugene Lyons, *David Sarnoff* (New York: Harper and Row, 1966), adds further details to these views in a generally balanced biography of this commanding figure in communications history. However, none of these works on the RCA system provides any information on its rival.

Important collections of the papers of Philo T. Farnsworth are possessed by his widow, Elma E. Farnsworth, and by his close friend and business associate, George Everson. Everson's sympathetic memoir of Farnsworth, *The Story of Television* (1949; reprint ed., New York: Arno Press, 1974) provides useful insights, although it must be used cautiously. This is also true for Stephen F. Hofer, "Philo Farnsworth: The Quiet Contributor to Television," (Ph.D. dissertation, Bowling Green State University, 1977), and "Philo Farnsworth: TV's Pioneer," *Journal of Broadcasting* 3, no. 2 (Spring 1979): 153–65. Both works discuss the patent conflict between Farnsworth and Zworykin from a view clearly sympathetic to the former; although this particular dispute is otherwise handled well, Hofer simplifies the full range of patent conflict between RCA and Farnsworth; for instance, he never mentions the key cases over the Purdue University patents. Farnsworth's engineering accomplishments are most adequately described by his chief engineer, Archibald H. Brolly, in "Television by Electric Means," *Electrical Engineering* 53, no. 8 (August 1934): 1153–60; and by Philo T. Farnsworth, "Television by Electron Image Scanning," *Journal of The Franklin Institute* 218, no. 4 (October 1934): 411–44 (reprinted in Shiers, ed., *Technical Development of Television*).

Contemporary discussion of the rival electronic techniques can be found in Knox McIlwain, "Survey of Television Pick-up Devices," *Journal of Applied Physics* 10, no. 7 (July 1939): 432–42; Lee De Forest, *Television Today and Tomorrow* (New York: Dial Press, 1942); and George H. Eckhardt, *Electronic Television* (1936; reprint ed., New York: Arno Press, 1974). Because all three authors attempt to adopt a neutral position in the dispute, their discussions are remarkably sanguine about the future of the image dissector despite its clear limitations. Eckhardt is notable, in particular, for his extensive treatment of the RCA facsimile radio relay system and also for rather emphasizing Farnsworth's connection with the German firm, Fernseh A. G.

Material on the other contenders in the race to perfect electronic television is much more sparse. No satisfactory treatment of Philco exists, and the original firm is now defunct. Oral testimony and materials in the contemporary technical and popular press, therefore, are the only available sources. Information about CBS's operation is similarly limited, although this is the result of deliberate corporate policy. However, Peter C. Goldmark's memoir, *Maverick Inventor* (New York: Saturday Review Press/E. P. Dutton and Co., 1973), does provide much valuable information on CBS television efforts between 1936 and 1941, although the book is a defense of Goldmark's controversial color system. The papers of Allen B. DuMont are in the Library of Congress, and a sympathetic, well-documented study of his efforts exists in Gary N. Hess, "An Historical Study of the Du Mont Television Network," (Ph.D. dissertation, Northwestern University, 1960). Hess's work unfortunately concentrates mainly on the post–Second World War period. The only useful account of the activities of the Don Lee System in Los Angeles is by Harry R. Lubcke, "Television on the West Coast," in John Porterfield and Kay Reynolds, eds., *We Present Television* (New York: W. W. Norton and Co., 1940), pp. 224–41, although Mr. Lubcke retains a useful collection of relevant materials. Lawrence Lessing, *Man of High Fidelity* (Philadelphia: J. B. Lippincott Co., 1956), traces the creation and struggle of television's rival, FM radio, in this sympathetic biography of its inventor, Edwin H. Armstrong. Finally, Frank C. Waldrop and Joseph Borkin, *Television: A Struggle for Power* (New York: William Morrow and Co., 1938), provides a contemporary, ideologically motivated discussion of the contending forces in the emerging medium.

The most valuable contemporary technical discussions can be found in the RCA-dominated *Proceedings of the IRE* and in the more independent *Electronics*. The trade publication, *Broadcasting*, is quite useful after 1935; *Radio News*, while impatient for the inauguration of public telecasting and suspicious of the reasons offered for its delay, is also helpful. The publication most active in discussing television, exclusive of communications journals, was *Business Week*. Quite helpful, although tending to partisanship for the new medium, are the *New York Times* articles of Orrin E. Dunlap, Jr., and also his *The Future of Television* (New York: Harper and Brothers, 1942).

For the crucial work of the FCC during this important period and for its relations with specific telecasters, the FCC *Annual Reports* are helpful. For some of the legal disputes, the FCC *Reports* are also informative. The commission's files on television licenses and deleted licenses are also useful. However, many of the materials for this period have been misfiled in storage; retrieval is difficult, but not impossible. But since much of the conflict between the industry and the commission was fought publicly, the relevant, and conflicting, reports in the popular press are essential. To help evaluate the nature of this conflict three general studies provide some assistance: Edwin G. Krasnow and Lawrence D. Longley, *The Politics of Broadcast Regulation*, 2nd ed. (New York: St. Martin's Press, 1978); Dallas W. Smythe, *The Structure and Policy of Electronic Communications*, University of Illinois Bulletin Series no. 82 (Urbana, 1957); and Thomas E. Will, *Telecommunications Structure and Management in the Executive Branch of Government, 1900–1970* (Boulder, Colo.: Westview Press, 1978). However, the details of the dramatic confrontation between David Sarnoff and James L. Fly have not been sufficiently researched, and all accounts of it are rather general or are mired in partisanship.

Still the most inclusive account of the work of the NTSC is Donald G. Fink, *Television Standards and Practice* (New York: McGraw-Hill Book Co., 1943; partially reprinted in Shiers, ed., *Technical Development of Television*). Fink has added a further interpretation in his "Perspectives on Television: The Role Played by the Two NTSC's in Preparing Television Service for the American Public," *Proceedings of the IEEE* 64, no. 9 (September 1976): 1322–31. So far all other published accounts of the NTSC are derivative from Fink.

Finally, research on all phases of the interwar creation of the American television industry must actively pursue the contributions available from the numerous participants still active. Much in the discussions in the printed materials glosses over important details, even to the point of distortion. Of course, such testimony from these sources must be subjected to the same evaluative criteria as any other evidential data.

Index

DATE DUE

OCT 2 9 1996	

BRODART, INC.

Cat. No. 23-221